THE LANGUAGE LIBRARY

English Dialects

THE LANGUAGE LIBRARY

ED-TED BY ERIC PARTRIDGE AND SIMEON POTTER

G. L. BROOK

English Dialects

ANDRE DEUTSCH

FIRST PUBLISHED OCTOBER 1963 BY
ANDRE DEUTSCH LIMITED
105 GREAT RUSSELL STREET
LONDON WC1

SECOND EDITION FEBRUARY 1965
REPRINTED JULY 1972

PRINTED IN GREAT BRITAIN BY
REDWOOD PRESS LIMITED
TROWBRIDGE, WILTSHIRE

ISBN 0 233 95641 7

To

SIR HAROLD PARKINSON, K.B.E.

President
of the
Lancashire Dialect Society

Contents

Maps

Table of Abbreviations

AE	American English
AN	Anglo-Norman
Ang	Anglian
BE	British English
CUP	Cambridge University Press
EDD	Joseph Wright's *English Dialect Dictionary*
EDS	English Dialect Society
EETS	Early English Text Society
EM	East Midland
Fr	French
Gmc	Germanic
JLDS	*Journal of the Lancashire Dialect Society*
LSE	*Leeds Studies in English and Kindred Languages*
M	Midland
ME	Middle English
MnE	Modern English
MUP	Manchester University Press
N	Northern
Nhb	The Northumbrian dialect of Old English
OE	Old English
OED	*Oxford English Dictionary*
OF	Old French
ON	Old Norse
OUP	Oxford University Press
PADS	*Publications of the American Dialect Society*
PMLA	*Publications of the Modern Language Association of America*
RES	*Review of English Studies*

TABLE OF ABBREVIATIONS

RSE	Received Standard English
S	Southern
Sc	Scottish
SE	South-Eastern
SPE	Society for Pure English
SW	South-Western
TPS	*Transactions of the Philological Society*
TYDS	*Transactions of the Yorkshire Dialect Society*
VP	*Vespasian Psalter*
WGmc	West Germanic
WM	West Midland
WS	West Saxon

Preface to the First Edition

IT HAS BEEN my principal aim in writing this book to suggest some of the ways in which the study of English dialects can be of interest and how far their continued use is to be encouraged. It has been no part of my aim to make a survey of English dialects; that task has already been undertaken by hands more competent than mine. I have preferred where possible to write of dialects of which I have first-hand knowledge, and that is the reason why so many of my examples are chosen from the dialects of northern England. I have, however, tried not to confine my attention to these dialects, and readers who are more familiar with the dialects of other parts of the country will have no difficulty in providing their own illustrative examples.

One of my aims has been to make a plea for a wider application of the word 'dialect' than the one, often passing current today, which restricts the word to the regional dialects spoken in Great Britain. I have preferred to regard a dialect as any subdivision of a language that can be associated with a particular group of speakers smaller than the group who share the common language. Since groups of speakers can often be subdivided, the dialects that they speak can also be subdivided. Hence, I regard British and American English as major dialects of the language which it is convenient to call English, and I regard each of these major dialects as having a number of sub-dialects. I need hardly say that such a view does not involve disparagement of either of these major varieties of English nor does it involve the subordination of one variety to the other. If this wider view of the word 'dialect' is accepted, it is possible to take a much less gloomy view of the survival of English dialects than that which claims that they are dying and that it will soon be too late to study them at all.

PREFACE

The reader that I have had in mind is the general reader with no specialized knowledge of linguistics or the history of the English language, though I hope that students in universities and training colleges will find something to interest them. Chapters II and III will have more meaning for readers with some knowledge of Old and Middle English and in these chapters I have included short illustrative extracts. Each chapter in the book is largely self-contained, and Chapters II and III can be omitted by readers who are interested only in present-day English.

The list of those to whom I am indebted is a long one. The passage on p. 181 is reprinted, by permission, from *The Times* and the passage from *The Mayor of Casterbridge* on p. 200 is reproduced by permission of the Trustees of the Hardy Estate and Messrs. Macmillan & Co. Ltd. Mr Eric Partridge, the General Editor of The Language Library, has encouraged me by his interest and helped me by his advice. Miss E. A. Lowcock, Cartographer to the Department of Geography of the University of Manchester, has prepared the maps and advised me on their presentation. Miss Bernadette Griffith has typed successive versions of the book with the utmost patience and accuracy. I owe a heavy debt to colleagues at Manchester and elsewhere who have allowed me to profit by their comments. Chapter v in particular has gained from the advice of scholars with special knowledge. Mr Emrys Evans has advised me on English as spoken in Ireland, Professor Marcus Cunliffe and Mr Arnold Goldman on American English, and Professor and Mrs A. C. Cawley, Mr G. R. Cochrane and Miss Coral Readdy of the University of Queensland, Mr G. W. Turner of the University of Canterbury and Professor D. P. Costello on the English of Australia and New Zealand. I am deeply indebted to Miss Joyce Bazire, Mr Eric Colledge, Mr J. D. Jump, Professor R. E. Keller, Dr R. F. Leslie and my wife, who have read the typescript, reducing the number of my errors and providing me with valuable material. I am indebted to Professor Angus McIntosh for information about the Linguistic Survey of Scotland and the work in progress at Edinburgh on Middle English dialects.

Greatest of all is my debt to Professor Harold Orton of Leeds, who has read my typescript and allowed me to profit from his unrivalled knowledge of English dialects. He has added to my indebtedness by allowing me to reproduce Maps 1, 4 and 5, which are based upon maps prepared by him in connexion with the Linguistic Survey of England.

G. L. B.

Manchester, January, 1963.

Preface to the Second Edition

The chief innovation in this edition is the replacement of the map of the Dialects of the Eastern United States on p. 124 by a reproduction of the map of the Speech Areas of the Eastern United States from Hans Kurath's *A Word Geography of the Eastern United States* (University of Michigan Press, 1949). I am very much indebted to the publishers for their courtesy in allowing me to reproduce this copyright map.

G. L. B.

Manchester, January, 1965.

CHAPTER I

Dialect and Language

DIALECT IS A subject on which many people have strong views. We have all met dialect enthusiasts who repeat a few dialect words which seem to them to be wonderfully expressive and who seem disappointed or incredulous when their friends do not share their enthusiasm. At the other extreme there is the man who hates dialect and who thinks that anyone who advocates its deliberate use is an amiable or mischievous eccentric whose energies should be redirected into more profitable channels. Between these extremes there is the man who announces in a rich regional accent that he used to speak a dialect himself before he abandoned it for Standard English.

Some of this diversity of opinion arises from lack of clear knowledge about the nature of dialect. The dialect enthusiast very often loves dialects in general or one particular dialect not for any linguistic reason but because of the accident of early associations; he loves to hear dialect words or pronunciations because they remind him of his childhood and of friends and relatives who were in the habit of using such expressions. On the other hand, hatred of dialect often springs from the mistaken idea that dialect is simply Standard English badly pronounced. At the outset, therefore, it is necessary to arrive at a definition of the word.

The word *dialect* is first recorded in English in the sixteenth century. It is of Greek origin and was borrowed into English through Latin and French. The Greek word from which the word is derived meant 'discourse, way of speaking', and the primary meaning of the English word given in *OED* is 'manner of speaking, language, speech, especially a manner of speech characteristic of a particular group of people'. In this sense *OED* equates the word with *phraseology* and *idiom*. The secondary meaning of the word given in *OED* is 'one of the subordinate forms or varieties of language arising from local peculiarities of vocabulary, pronunciation and idiom'.

It is convenient to keep the word *dialect* to refer to the speech of a group of people smaller than the group who share a common language, and to remember that the basis of subdivision of a language into dialects need not necessarily be geographical; it may be social or occupational. The quotations given by *OED* include one, dated 1740, referring to 'the lawyer's dialect' and another, dated 1805, referring to 'the theological dialect'. This use of the word suggests a distinction that is important from the point of view of the development of language. If a group is based merely on occupation or shared interests it may develop its own technical vocabulary but not a dialect that is ever likely to develop into a separate language; if the group forms a real community consisting of people with common interests who are in frequent touch with one another, it will tend to develop a dialect of its own with a distinctive phonology as well as a distinctive vocabulary, and if the group is cut off from other speakers of the same language, the dialectal characteristics will become more and more marked and in course of time the dialect may develop into a separate language. The distinction between a dialect and a language is not clear-cut, and in philological works related languages are sometimes referred to as dialects, especially if they are not very well-known. The word *dialect* is sometimes used as a pejorative substitute for *language*. This distinction between the two words is found in Gibbon:

> Such was the general division of the Roman empire into the Latin and Greek languages. To these we may add a third distinction for the body of the natives in Syria, and especially in Egypt. The use of their ancient dialects, by secluding them from the commerce of mankind, checked the improvements of those barbarians.[1]

[1] *The Decline and Fall of the Roman Empire*, Ch. 2.

This pejorative use of the word still survives today, and the last sentence sums up the attitude of many speakers of Standard English to the English regional dialects.

An attempt is sometimes made to distinguish between a language and a dialect on the basis of the culture which the speakers share. Thus W. J. Entwistle says:

> A language is the expression of a community which enjoys a culture with some pretension to permanence. Even a dialect is wont to show a geographical centre of radiation and to be associated with some social organism; but a dialect is, at the same time, in evident dependence on some greater linguistic centre. The characteristic mark of a language is its equipoise with reference to a cultural centre.[1]

This distinction does not seem to be entirely satisfactory. It would be difficult to say what is the cultural centre to which the speakers of both British and American English look, and yet these two varieties of English cannot yet be regarded as constituting different languages. Association with a cultural centre may have the effect of raising the prestige of a dialect without making it into a separate language. Scottish and Irish dialects enjoy greater prestige in England than do the dialects of the North of England, and it may be that the reason for this is that they are national, and not merely regional, dialects. This difference in prestige has often been commented upon. An Irish peer once said that, although he preferred to live in England, he returned to Ireland once or twice a year just to freshen up his accent, and a barrister is reported to have said that his Irish brogue was worth a thousand a year to him.

One test that can be used, along with others, in making a distinction between a dialect and a language is the degree of mutual intelligibility: if the differences between two dialects are so great that speakers of one are unable to understand those who speak the other, the two dialects are well on the way to developing into separate languages. The test is only approximate because mutual intelligibility cannot be measured with precision. Although it is sometimes said that speakers of two

[1] W. J. Entwistle, *The Spanish Language, together with Portuguese, Catalan and Basque* (Faber and Faber, 1936), p. 82.

different English dialects cannot understand each other, it is doubtful whether such a statement is ever really true, given intelligence, patience and co-operation in both speaker and hearer. Similarly, the differences between the English language as used in America and as used in Great Britain are heavily outnumbered by the resemblances, and it is only occasionally that a speaker of the one form of English completely fails to understand a speaker of the other. It is therefore reasonable to describe British and American English as different dialects of the same language. On the other hand, the various Romance languages, although at one time they were different dialects of the same language, have diverged so considerably that French, Italian, Spanish and Portuguese can now reasonably be regarded as distinct languages.

Divergent linguistic development is always likely to take place when there is any interruption in the freedom with which the speakers of a language can communicate with one another. It is natural, therefore, that the spread of the English language to distant parts of the world should have been accompanied by linguistic changes resulting in the development of new dialects. American English, the varieties of English spoken in different parts of the Commonwealth, and British English can all be regarded as dialects of the language which it is convenient to call English, without any attempt to subordinate any one of these dialects to another or to claim special prestige for any dialect. Each of these national dialects may have a number of sub-dialects. It is reasonable to take a special interest in the variety of English that is current in one's native land without thereby assuming that it is a norm from which speakers in other countries diverge only by reason of ignorance or perversity. What Professor A. G. Mitchell says of Australian English is true of the sub-dialects of English spoken in every part of the world: 'we should speak of difference rather than of corruption, of characteristics rather than of faults'.[1] The study of the differences between the dialects of two English-speaking countries

[1] A. G. Mitchell, *The Pronunciation of English in Australia* (Angus and Robertson, 1946), p. 2.

enables us to see languages in process of evolution. The linguistic developments that are now taking place in different parts of the English-speaking world are similar to the divergent developments which led to the differences that now exist between English and German and between French and Italian. Whether the divergences between one variety of English and another will ever proceed so far as to produce two languages as dissimilar as English and German is a matter for conjecture. On the whole, it is unlikely that they will. Improved communications, widespread education, broadcasting and printed books and newspapers are all influences that are likely to retard the rate of change and to resist the centrifugal tendencies resulting from geographical separation.

Although the group of speakers using the same dialect may have its basis in regional, social or occupational homogeneity, there must be a link of some kind to join the speakers together. A way of speaking that is peculiar to one person is known as an idiolect, and if the human ear were sufficiently sensitive to record all the differences, we should probably find that every speaker had his own idiolect. Most of these idiosyncrasies of speech, however, differ from the norm so slightly that even a trained phonetician does not notice them, and the average man will tolerate very considerable differences in pronunciation without noticing them. For example, experiment has shown that many educated northerners have difficulty in saying which of their friends use a short vowel [æ] and which of them use a long vowel [ɑː] in words like *laugh* and *pass*, in spite of the very considerable differences between the two sounds. There are individual eccentricities in the pronunciation of particular words, especially of rather bookish words which are not often met with in conversation. Words like *gaseous* and *hegemony* are notorious for the wide variety of their pronunciations, but we have probably all noticed other examples which we associate with particular speakers. Variations are particularly liable to result from the substitution of a long vowel (or its development) for a short one or *vice versa*. For example, some speakers pronounce *hostile* with the diphthong heard in *host*, and others pronounce *thesis* with the first vowel short. Such variations result from the varying importance which different speakers attach to etymology and to the analogy of other words similar in form. They are liable to occur anywhere in the region where a language is spoken, but, since the speakers who share these eccentricities do not constitute a group, the variations cannot be regarded as dialectal, and they may cut across dialectal divisions.

Lovers of dialect are fond of making a distinction between genuine dialect and slovenly mispronunciation. One is entitled to ask what is the difference between the two, and why certain pronunciations should be stigmatised as slovenly while others are tolerated or lauded as dialectal. One difference is in the history of the pronunciations in question; dialectal pronunciations which appeal to the philologist or the lover of dialect are generally survivals of older variations whereas pronunciations which have few defenders are generally of recent development. It may be doubted, however, whether this archaistic approach to dialect is completely adequate. A more objective distinction is provided if we regard variant pronunciations which are shared by a group as dialectal, whether they are old or new, and individual eccentricities which may occur sporadically in any place or among any social class as non-dialectal. Whether they are slovenly or not is another matter. In so far as 'slovenly' is more than a mere snarl-word, it can properly be applied to any pronunciation which sacrifices intelligibility to the speaker's ease in articulation, and such developments are liable to take place in the speech of individuals, in dialect, and in Standard English, though common sense will call a halt to the process of change if the interference with intelligibility becomes too great. The study of dialect has hitherto been in the main archaistic and has therefore concentrated on country speakers, who preserve old words and pronunciations best, but there is no reason why it should continue to do so. The new dialects that have developed in towns can be studied, though the nature of their appeal is rather different from that of country dialects.

Town and city dialects have been less studied than country dialects and in general they have aroused less enthusiasm, but

22

the dialects of London occupy a special position, and the best-known of these London dialects, Cockney, has attracted a good deal of attention. Cockney is a class, as well as a regional, dialect, and it has consequently often been disparaged. This disparagement has led to a compensatory enthusiasm on the part of some speakers of Cockney, who have put forward claims that may well be excessive. As far as the sentimental appeal of dialects goes, Cockneys have as much right as the speakers of country dialects to feel a fondness for forms of speech which owe their attraction to early associations, but when lovers of Cockney claim that their dialect has an ancestry comparable with that of country dialects, it is well to enquire what is the meaning of the metaphor. Since all English dialects, including Cockney and Standard English, have developed from Old English, there is a sense in which they may all be said to be equally old. When we speak of the long ancestry of English country dialects, however, we generally mean more than that: we mean that their distinctive characteristics have had dialectal significance for a long period of time, and it is doubtful whether Cockney can claim a long ancestry in this sense; not many of the characteristics of Cockney speech of today can be traced back as features of the dialect of London even as far as the seventeenth century. There is no difficulty in finding early spellings which seem to represent pronunciations similar to those of modern Cockney; the difficulty lies in showing that they were Cockney characteristics at the time when they were used. Most of these early spellings seem to be either individual eccentricities or characteristics shared by Cockneys and by many writers who were not Cockneys.

Dialect has something in common with slang, but the differences are more marked than the resemblances. One thing that they have in common is that they are both generally colloquial. Although slang can be used in writing as well as in speech and although there are dialects in the written language, both slang and dialect are more at home in the spoken language than in writing. Another point of resemblance is that both slang and dialect are regarded by many people as being below the level of

23

normal educated speech, though such a view would not be accepted without opposition. The differences between slang and dialect are great. In the first place, dialect is a wider term: it is concerned with pronunciation as well as vocabulary, whereas slang is concerned only with vocabulary. A further difference is that slang words generally have a very short life in the language; most slang words are of recent invention whereas most dialect words have a long ancestry. A third difference is that slang is generally used deliberately, whereas dialect as a rule is not. In general, slang is used especially by young people. This does not mean that older speakers never use it, but slang changes so quickly that its use by the middle-aged, who are liable to use the slang current when they were young, is not free from danger. A middle-aged man who uses slang in the hope of getting on good terms with his juniors is likely to evoke a smile that is not one of sympathy. It is possible to regard slang as a class dialect, though its use is now so widespread that to define the class who use it is a task of some difficulty. Certain types of slang can be associated with particular groups: stockbrokers and actors have their own slang expressions, and rhyming slang, Cockney in origin, is used especially by criminals and their admirers. Some justification for the view that slang is a class dialect used by a group within the group of speakers of a language is provided by the difficulty which it causes to foreigners. An example of the misunderstanding of slang that has been attributed to foreigners of many different nationalities is the angry reply of a victim of teasing: 'You think I know damn nothing, but I know damn all'.

It is easy to make out a case against the use of dialect. The primary purpose of language is to express meaning, and it may seem rather perverse to encourage dialectal differences which have the effect of interfering with intelligibility. Even if they do not seriously interfere with intelligibility, they can very easily have the effect of distracting a hearer's attention from what the speaker is saying to his manner of saying it.

A further objection to the use of dialect is that it adds to the difficulty of learning a language and consequently lessens the usefulness of the language as a means of international communication. Much has been written about the difficulty caused to children and foreigners by our complicated and inconsistent system of spelling, but it is well to remember that regional differences of pronunciation add to the difficulty. Incidentally, these differences constitute one of the minor obstacles in the way of spelling reform. Inconsistent as English spelling is, it is at least uniform over the whole of the British Isles; if any serious attempt were to be made to link spelling with pronunciation, there are many everyday words like *laugh, off, go, poor,* and *lord* which would be transcribed differently in different parts of the country.

Moreover, it is necessary to face the fact that many speakers of Standard English feel a distaste for the regional dialects and for those who speak them. This attitude towards dialect may be completely mistaken or it may be merely superficial, but the existence of the attitude is a fact that dialect speakers have to reckon with, and their reactions to it will vary according to their character and personality. Some will accept it and will do all that they can to remove traces of dialect from their speech; others will react against it and will deliberately preserve their own dialect and regard speakers of Standard English with a contempt that cannot easily be justified. The problem is complicated by the fact that most people move in many different circles in each of which a different attitude towards dialect prevails. Many university students living away from home have to perform at least six acts of linguistic re-adjustment each year, one at the beginning and one at the end of each term. Those who live at home often have to make this re-adjustment twice a day. Such problems arise in the use of both regional and class dialects, and the attitudes adopted towards anyone who tries to change his dialect are not always friendly. Such a man has to encounter hostility from two groups: those who speak the dialect that he is trying to drop and those who speak the dialect that he is trying to adopt. One group will accuse him of 'putting it on' or 'trying to talk lah-de-dah'; the other may be less actively hostile but cannot always be counted upon to welcome the newcomer with open arms. The problem is not one that admits of an easy solution, but the remedy would seem to be that those who are not prepared to adopt Standard English as their manner of speech on all occasions should be prepared to be bilingual: they should continue to understand and to use their native dialect, but in the world of today it is well for a dialect speaker to be able to speak and understand Standard English, or something near it, when the occasion requires it. It is not uncommon to find that people who have been brought up as dialect speakers learn to speak a modified form of Standard English, but revert to their native dialect when tired or excited or in old age.

A further contribution to a solution of the same problem would be increased tolerance towards linguistic variations. It is well to remember that even Standard English is a dialect, although it is one that has attained a special status. One could hope for more of the equanimity shown by a London schoolmaster when asked whether the evacuation of his pupils to the country during the Second World War had had much effect on their speech. His reply was: 'Not particularly. They went away saying "We was" and they came back saying "Us be"'.

The best general argument in favour of tolerating variations from Standard English is that speech is an aspect of personality. Most people agree that variety of personality is desirable, and such variety finds its expression in variety of speech, which is more common than is generally realized. Much has been said about the influence of the BBC in imposing uniformity of speech, but the influence is not all in one direction. One can hear a great variety of accents on sound radio and television, and not merely on the programmes, such as *The Northcountryman*, which deliberately set out to cater for regional interests. The very individual speech-habits of Sir Winston Churchill are well-known and frequently imitated, and they illustrate the way in which speech is a reflection of personality. Such individual characteristics may be regarded as idiolects rather than dialects, but quite a number of statesmen of the nineteenth and twentieth centuries spoke local dialects all their lives. There has been much discussion about the exact nature of the 'northern burr' in Gladstone's speech and Lord Curzon is said to have habitually pronounced *answer* and *example* with a short *a*. Sir Robert Peel, and the two Earls of Derby who were statesmen in Queen Victoria's reign spoke with Lancashire accents,[1] and so too, in the twentieth century, did George Tomlinson, at one time Minister of Education.

The most common reason for using dialect is the accident of early associations. The children of dialect-speakers may grow up to speak modified Standard English, but they will often keep a fondness for a particular dialect because it reminds them of their childhood. There is something friendly about the use of dialect, and that is one reason why it is used so freely by music-hall comedians who wish to get on good terms with their audience. Many a north-country employer has found in dialect a useful way of taking the sting out of a reprimand or an insult. One northerner said that he would resent being called stupid but that he would have no objection to being called gaumless, because the use of the dialectal word would make him feel that the speaker was still well-disposed towards him. Similarly, a northern bank manager said of a former colleague, whom he very much admired, that sometimes he was 'as nowty as sin'. In a dialect dictionary *nowty* would be glossed as 'ill-tempered', but the dictionary definition does not express the affectionate overtones of the word.

Dialect often reflects the characteristics of people living in different parts of the country. The grim, laconic quality of many of the dialect stories coming from Lancashire and Yorkshire reflects the characteristics of the Scandinavians from whom many of its speakers are descended, and it is easy to find in the Icelandic sagas parallels to the north-country speech of today.

The question is sometimes asked: Are stories more effective when told in dialect than when told in Standard English? The truth probably is that if the hearer has no knowledge of people who speak the dialect in question, its use makes the story not

[1] See G. N. Clark, *The Bull's Bellow and the Ratton's Squeak* (SPE No. 33, OUP, 1929).

more but less effective. If, however, the hearer is familiar with speakers of the dialect, the use of dialect enables him to fit the story into its context of human character and behaviour. He is able to think of people that he knows who would have made just such a reply and he is able to derive satisfaction from thinking how well it fits in with some aspect of their character.

It is necessary to distinguish between tolerating dialect in others and using it oneself. It is doubtful whether it is worth while for anyone to try to acquire a regional dialect, but the large number of people who speak a regional dialect as well as some form of modified Standard English have a lot to gain by keeping alive the power to use both forms of speech. There are certain ways in which the regional dialects differ from Standard English where it may be claimed that the dialects have something to contribute to English speech. This is true of the quality of the voice, of the pronunciation of particular sounds, and of vocabulary.

The attitude of many northcountrymen to Southern speech, including that variety of it known as Standard English, is that expressed by Mr Yorke in Charlotte Bronte's *Shirley*:

> if he usually expressed himself in the Yorkshire dialect, it was because he chose to do so, preferring his native Doric to a more refined vocabulary. 'A Yorkshire burr', he affirmed, 'was as much better than a Cockney's lisp, as a bull's bellow than a ratton's squeak'. (Ch. 4).

Many speakers of Southern English might accept Mr Yorke's description of a northerner's speech without necessarily accepting his view on its superiority; probably most people would prefer something between the bull's bellow and the ratton's squeak. Fortunately there are many intermediate varieties of speech, one of which is Standard English. Belief in the value of dialect need involve no disparagement of Standard English, but there are varieties of Southern English, some of them regional dialects, some class dialects and some idiolects, which diverge considerably from Standard English and deserve all Mr Yorke's strictures, though 'bleat' would perhaps be a better description of them than 'squeak'.

28

In the pronunciation of particular sounds we find that dialects preserve distinctions between sounds which have fallen together in Standard English, often with a loss of intelligibility. Thus, many speakers in Cumberland and Northumberland agree with Scotsmen and Irishmen in making a distinction between *which* and *witch* and between *while* and *wile*, whereas southerners as a rule do not. In the South the context is the only guide to tell the hearer which word is meant.

Diphthongs and triphthongs are often badly treated by southerners. There are two triphthongs in English, which occur in the words *our fire*. In Southern English both triphthongs tend to be replaced by a long *a* sound: *ah fah*. Northerners generally make a distinction in pronunciation between *poor* and *pour* and between *moor* and *more*, but most Southern speakers get along without the [ʊə] diphthong altogether, and it is common in the South to find the sound undergoing the further change to [ɔː] as in *paw little chap*. To take one more diphthong: the vowel sound in *go* is in the North pronounced with an *o* as the first element of the diphthong, whereas in the South the diphthong shows an increasing tendency to begin with a central vowel *er* [ɜː].

There is in Southern English a tendency for many vowels and diphthongs to be replaced by this [ɜː] sound. For example, a common pronunciation of the word *cheerful* is [tʃɜːful], and the first syllable of the word *railway* is often pronounced with a similar vowel. The advantage from the point of view of the speaker is that the *er-* sound [ɜː] is the easiest of vowels to pronounce. It is the noise made when the tongue is lying at rest in the middle of the mouth; that is why some of us make the sound unconsciously when we are thinking what to say next. But just as easy writing makes hard reading, so lazy speech shifts the burden on to the hearer. It should be added that there are so many different pronunciations in the various English dialects that there is always a danger of oversimplifying the picture. There are some Northern English dialects in which the [ɜː] sound is even more common than it is among speakers of Southern English; the use of [ɜː] for [ɛə] in words like *there*, for example, is one of the most easily recognizable features of the dialects of Liverpool and South-West Lancashire. It is nevertheless true that broadly speaking the English diphthongs are distinguished from each other more clearly in the North than in the South.

When we consider the contribution which dialects can make to the vocabulary of Standard English, it is well to remember that they have already made some contribution. *Hale* and *raid* are well-known Standard English words which have been borrowed from Northern dialects. There are many more words habitually used by northerners which might profitably be borrowed into Standard English. The best test of whether such a borrowing is desirable is: can the dialect word be adequately translated into Standard English? There are very many north-country words which cannot be so translated without losing valuable shades of meaning. As an example one may take the word *thoil*, common in Lancashire and the West Riding of Yorkshire and found also in Scots in the form *thole* 'to endure'. It is derived from OE *polian* 'to suffer, undergo'. The expression in which the word is most often used is 'I couldn't thoil t'brass', and when a northerner says this he means more than he would if he said he could not afford the money. The word, with its associations with suffering, describes the pain which a good northcountryman feels on seeing money wasted. Other dialectal words which cannot easily be translated by single Standard English words are: *meaverly* 'apprehensively, with caution', *witchert* (i.e. wet-shod) 'with wet feet', and *slaht*. The last word does not quite mean 'to sprinkle with water'; there is more force behind *slahting* than behind sprinkling but not as much as in splashing. In dialects the word is often applied to slight rain. Another common north-country word is *jannock* 'fair, honest, genuine'. It is a sign of the rather grim view which northerners take of human nature that this word is generally used with a negative. Two more northern words which are untranslatable are *gaumless* and *feckless*. Both describe unsatisfactory varieties of character or conduct, but they are not synonyms, and it is very difficult to find satisfactory Standard English equivalents of either word. The nearest Standard English equivalent of *gaumless* is perhaps 'stupid', but *gaumless* is at once stronger and more friendly than *stupid*. If one had to find a Standard English equivalent of *feckless*, one would have to use twice as many syllables and say 'ineffective', but even then the meaning is not quite the same. Consequently both *gaumless* and *feckless* are showing signs of being adopted into Standard English; *feckless* has gained the stronger foothold but the meaning of *gaumless* is understood by many people who would not use the word themselves. The verbs *to frame*, *to shape* and *to oss* are used in dialects to express an idea for which a word is needed. They mean 'to set about doing something in an efficient or workmanlike way'. Like most words involving praise, they tend to be used in the North chiefly in the negative, as in *Tha doesn't frame a bit*. Other expressive words are *moither*, with its variant *moider* 'to confuse, perplex, bewilder', and *thrutch* (OE *pryccan*) 'to crowd, huddle together'. The meaning of the latter word is illustrated by the well-known dialect story of Noah's refusal to accept as a passenger on the Ark a man who was swimming about looking for land. Noah explained his refusal by saying 'We're thrutched up wi' elephants'. *Nesh* (OE *hnesce* 'soft') is a north-country word to describe anyone who is too fond of sitting in front of the fire and who is consequently unduly sensitive to cold. *Chuff* means 'pleased with oneself and anxious to make a good impression on others'; the word denotes a combination of fussy self-satisfaction with a lack of restraint which arouses the contempt of northerners. *To chunner*, with its variant *to chunter*, means to keep up a running fire of muttered complaint. Vivid imagery is found in some dialect words, such as *cat-lick* 'a hasty wash'.

The use of dialectal pronunciations or words by speakers who at other times use Standard English presents practical problems but they are not insuperable. When both speaker and hearer are familiar with a dialect there is, of course, no problem. The dialectal pronunciations that can most profitably be used when speaking to people who have no knowledge of dialect are generally of a kind to increase rather than to lessen intelligibility, since they make distinctions between sounds which are tending to fall together in Standard English. So far as vocabulary is concerned, it would seem to be as proper to introduce loan-words into Standard English from English dialects as from foreign languages. Those which satisfy a need in the language may secure general acceptance, as many dialectal words have done already; if they do not, no great harm is done by their occasional use.

The case for the study of dialects is one which appeals to many people who feel no strong urge to speak a dialect themselves. A note that is frequently struck in newspaper comments on dialect research is one of surprise, even though it is usually gratified surprise, that philologists should take an interest in dialects. This surprise reveals misconceptions about the nature of both dialects and philologists. It shows that dialects are in some quarters thought of as not quite respectable, or at any rate as not quite fit subjects of serious study. It suggests too that philologists should be pre-occupied with the supposedly 'correct' standard language rather than with local varieties of English. But local English dialects are not simply Standard English badly pronounced; they are varieties of speech with a pedigree as good as that of Standard English, which is simply one of the English dialects which, for various non-linguistic reasons, has acquired greater prestige than the other dialects. Philologists are not concerned with prescribing what is correct but with describing, and as far as possible explaining, what exists and what they believe to have existed in the past. Because dialects are more free than Standard English from the stereotyping influence of the prescriptive grammarian, they offer better material for linguistic study.

The study of a language can be undertaken in two ways, sometimes called synchronic and diachronic respectively. The synchronic study of a language aims at describing it as it is at any one time; diachronic study aims at tracing the historical development of a language. During the nineteenth century and the earlier part of the present century very remarkable progress was made in the diachronic study of languages, but at the present time there are signs of growing interest in synchronic study. The study of dialects is important whether the approach is synchronic or diachronic.

It is clear that the student of English as it is at the present time has enormous advantages over the student of English of any earlier period. He can obtain first-hand knowledge of the spoken language, with which the philologist is chiefly concerned, whereas the student of an earlier period in the history of a language has to rely on various kinds of indirect evidence, all of them more or less unsatisfactory, such as spelling or the evidence of contemporary grammarians. The importance of dialects to the student of contemporary English arises from the fact that contemporary English is really a group of dialects, and it is only when the range and characteristics of those dialects have been investigated that it is possible to say whether there is such a thing as Standard English at all.

General statements about a language are based upon thousands of millions of utterances of individuals. The speech activity of individuals can be investigated scientifically, and from such an investigation it is possible to draw conclusions about the language as a whole. Philologists will differ about the value of the generalizations that can be made about the language as a whole and about the number of speakers whose utterances must be investigated, but without the preliminary descriptive study of the speech of individuals no general statements about a language can claim to have any scientific value. The field-worker who investigates a dialect is investigating the speech of individuals and so providing the basis for a description of language as it is rather than as it is supposed to be.

It is essential for the investigator who wishes to describe speech in this way to free himself from the idea that one form of speech is more 'correct' than another. It may or may not be, but the question is one which should be discussed, if at all, only when we have gained the factual information about the way in which people actually do speak. The dialect speaker is thus just as important to the student of speech as is the speaker of Standard English; indeed, he may be more important, since

33

among the speakers of Standard English there are some who have deliberately tried to acquire a standard speech and who are therefore likely to speak less naturally than dialect speakers.

One of the first things to become clear when the speech of individuals is studied is the very considerable variety that exists in the speech-habits of those who speak the same language. It is not only true to say that no two people speak in exactly the same way, but one can go further and say that no one speaker speaks in the same way at all times. In view of this variety, it may seem that human speech is so complex that it is not possible to study it at all. Fortunately, this is not so. Although no speaker attains complete accuracy in his attempts to imitate the speech of others or to repeat his own speech-sounds, the in- accuracy of the speaker is matched by a corresponding inefficiency on the part of his hearers. Most of a speaker's variations of pronunciation will be so slight as to be imperceptible to any but a trained listener, and, even if they are perceived, not all of them will be felt as distinctive. Sometimes, of course, the difference between one man's pronunciation and another's is so great as to be distinctive, and when this happens the speaker's meaning is liable to be misunderstood. Americans have been known to confuse the British pronunciation of *clerk* with their own pro- nunciation of *clock*, and a man from the South of England who asked for a double room at a north-country hotel was surprised to receive a large Jamaica rum.

The study of local dialects has placed at the disposal of the investigator a vastly greater amount of material than he had when he confined his attention to the standard language, and it has encouraged the substitution of precise observation for hasty generalization. The methods of dialect research have been used in the past chiefly by investigators with an avowedly historical bias who were anxious to study the older forms of speech before they disappeared, but the same methods can be followed in the study of all kinds of contemporary speech.

One way in which dialect research has helped in the study of the historical development of language is to be seen in the theories that have been put forward to explain how languages have split up. The survival of little pockets preserving older forms all over a dialect area has done a good deal to modify our views about the way in which related languages like English, Dutch and German came to diverge from each other. The older view was that languages split up like a family tree, but the complicated picture presented by the investigations of dialect geographers accords better with the wave theory which suggests that linguistic changes may spread like waves over a speech-area, and each change may be carried out over a part of the area that does not coincide with the part covered by an earlier change.[1]

Another reason why local dialects are of value to the student of the history of a language is that they often preserve features which have not been preserved in the standard language. Of course, it does not follow that whenever a local dialect differs from the standard language, it is the local dialect that preserves the older form, but country dialects enjoy an advantage over the standard language in that they have remained more free from outside interference. Nothing encourages linguistic change so readily as a mixture of peoples speaking different languages or different varieties of the same language. The small village communities which have lived their own lives for centuries are just the places where a language is likely to remain with little change. For much the same reason, Iceland, cut off by the sea from the rest of the Scandinavian world, has preserved the linguistic characteristics of Old Norse much better than have the other Scandinavian languages. Down to the end of the fourteenth century any English author would write in the dialect of the district in which he happened to live. From the fifteenth century onwards one dialect, that of the East Midlands, began to be regarded as a standard, largely because of the accident that the two universities and the capital of the country were in that area. Hence those who lived in other parts of the country learnt how to speak and write Standard English, and the other dialects fell into comparative disuse.

English dialects have had a good deal of influence on Standard English. There are certain everyday words whose pronunciation

[1] L. Bloomfield, *Language* (George Allen and Unwin, 1935), p. 317.

today is irregular. They are dialectal forms which have been borrowed into the standard language. For example, historically *among* ought to rhyme with *hang* or *long*, as it does in some dialects; the Standard English form rhyming with *hung* is from West Midland dialects, especially those of South Lancashire. The regular development of OE *ān* 'one' would have been *own*, as in *only* (OE *ānlic*); the development of initial *w* in the pronunciation of RSE *one* is the result of dialectal influence. Similarly, the initial *v* of *vat*, *vane* and *vixen* is the result of a tendency to voice initial voiceless fricatives in Southern dialects. *Bruise* (OE *brȳsan*) and *cudgel* (OE *cycgel*) are South-Western forms; in the East Midland dialect, which forms the the basis of Standard English, OE *y*, whether long or short, would regularly have become *i*, as in the North, and the forms *brize* and *kidgel* survive in Northern dialects. The common dialectal pronunciation *bile* for *boil* sb. (OE *bȳl*) is the regular development of the Old English word; the Standard English *boil* is irregular.

One of the attractions of the study of dialect is that it links up with a remarkably large number of other subjects which throw light on dialect and which in their turn have something to gain from dialect studies. There are close links between dialect and literature, folk-lore, history, geography and sociology. Professor A. H. Smith has pointed out[1] that one point of importance for dialect study is the direction in which the inhabitants of a particular village look when they want to visit their market town, and such questions have much more than linguistic interest. The links between dialect study and both history and geography are clearly to be seen when we try to discover the reasons for the position of dialect boundaries. Historical causes, such as the boundaries of parishes and dioceses or the ownership of land, have probably been less important than the geographical setting, and the historical factors themselves have often been dependent on topographical causes. In general any natural feature that interferes with communication is liable to cause a dialect boundary. High hills form a very effective barrier;

---

[1] In 'English Dialects' in *TPS* 1936, pp. 76–84.

THE WEAKEST PIG OF THE LITTER

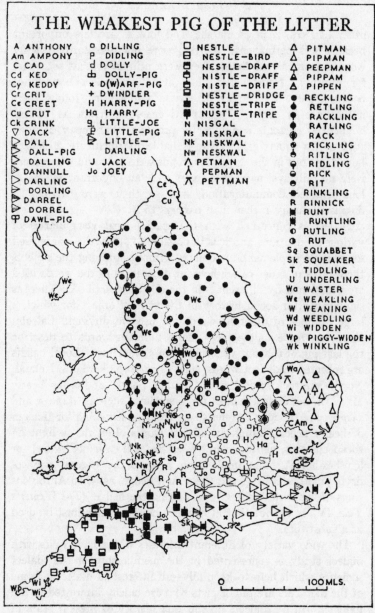

Map 1.   The Weakest Pig of the Litter

other barriers, such as marshes and forests, are less important because less permanent. Forests were not necessarily thickly wooded in medieval times; they were primarily areas set apart for hunting. Nevertheless they acted as dialect boundaries because they were areas of sparse population; today their importance is slight. The effectiveness of rivers as dialect boundaries presents a number of problems that repay detailed study. An unnavigable river is liable to constitute a dialect boundary, but in the days when roads were poor and when there were no railways, navigable rivers were an important means of long-distance communication, and so they were carriers of linguistic change rather than barriers to it.

Dialect is concerned with the special local vocabularies of various occupations and it is impossible to study the words used for various implements or objects without studying the objects themselves in order to see how far differences in the words used are occasioned by differences in the objects described. There is significance for social history in the type of object for which a large number of different words are used in different dialects; there are, for example, very many different words to describe the last pig of a litter, which is often a weakling. Local beliefs are reflected in dialect words, such as *attercop* (Scotland, Ireland, North Country) 'spider', from OE *attor* 'poison' and *coppe* 'head'. Many of the dialect names for a starling, such as *shepster* and *sheppy*, are thought to refer to its habit of searching for ticks in a sheep's fleece. Similarly, dialect words often throw light on social customs, as, for example *wintredge* (i.e., *winter hedge*) for 'clothes-horse'. The implication is that the normal way of drying clothes is to spread them on a hedge, as when Autolycus sings of 'The white sheet bleaching on the hedge' (*The Winter's Tale*, IV, iii, 5), but that in winter a clothes-horse must be used as a substitute.

The wide variety of different interests which have links with dialect study is represented in the membership of the dialect societies which help to keep alive an interest in dialect. Some of the members are philologists who are chiefly interested in the light thrown by dialects on the past history or present state of the English language; others study dialects in order to make a permanent record of forms that time will submerge; others study them because they think that they reveal the character of the people who speak them; others are chiefly interested in writing, reading or reciting dialect literature; others are primarily interested in natural history and are fascinated by the variety of names given to animals and plants in different parts of the country; and finally there are the exiles who can rarely hope to attend meetings but who value some link with their native county.

CHAPTER II

Old English

THE STUDY OF the dialects spoken in England during the Old English period, that is before the end of the eleventh century, is rendered difficult by the scarcity of surviving texts. Enough manuscripts have survived to enable us to say what were the chief dialects and what were the characteristic features of each dialect, but the boundaries of the various dialects cannot be precisely indicated. Four main Old English dialects can be distinguished: Northumbrian, Mercian, West Saxon and Kentish. Very approximately we may say that Northumbrian included the dialects spoken North of the River Humber; Mercian was spoken in the Midlands between the Humber and the Thames; West Saxon was spoken South of the Thames in the ancient kingdom of Wessex; and Kentish was spoken in the South-East over an area rather larger than that covered by the modern county of Kent. Northumbrian and Mercian had some features in common, and the term Anglian is sometimes used to describe the dialect of which they can be regarded as subdivisions. We cannot tell whether the boundaries between these dialects remained the same throughout the Old English period; in view of the unsettled political conditions of Anglo-Saxon England it is probable that they did not. One thing that we can say with confidence is that it is most unlikely that any of the four areas mentioned had a completely homogeneous dialect at any time during the Old English period. Even the scanty texts that are available enable us to distinguish two subdivisions within the dialect of Northumbria, and it is probable that in Anglo-Saxon

England there were many dialects of which we have no knowledge because of the accident that no manuscripts have been preserved containing texts written in those dialects. At the end of the Old English period Wessex enjoyed political supremacy, and that is no doubt the reason why most of the surviving texts are written in the West Saxon dialect. The non-West-Saxon texts are so few that in speaking of non-West-Saxon dialects it is safer to speak of the dialect of a particular text rather than that of a particular geographical region. A further advantage of this practice is that it serves as a reminder that the Old English period extended in time over several centuries, and the linguistic differences between two texts may be the result of a difference of date as well as one of dialect.

Since most of the extant Old English manuscripts are written in the West Saxon dialect, West Saxon forms are those with which students of Old English are most familiar. It is, however, important to remember that the Standard English of today is derived not from the West Saxon dialect but from a variety of Mercian, although a few isolated words have been borrowed from other dialects. For example, MnE *hear* cannot be derived from WS *hīeran*; it is from the Anglian *hēran*. *Cheese* is not from WS *cȳse* but from an Anglian form in which the *ā* of Latin *cāseum*, from which the word was borrowed, was fronted to *ǣ* and later raised to *ē*. *Old* and *cold* are from Anglian *ald* and *cald*; the West Saxon forms *eald* and *ceald* would have given MnE *eald* [iːld] and *cheald* [tʃiːld]. Similarly the preterite *sold* is from Anglian *salde*; WS *sealde* would have given *seald* [siːld]. Exceptionally, *chalk* is derived from the West Saxon form *cealc*, as is shown by the initial consonant *ch* [tʃ]; the Anglian form would have given *c* [k], just as Ang *calf* has given MnE *calf*.

Old English dialectal variations are preserved more thoroughly in place-names than in ordinary words, because in place-names the levelling influence of Standard English is less active. Corresponding to the difference between *chalk* and *calf*, we have place-names like *Chalford* (O) and *Chawton* (Ha), side by side with *Calverley* (WRYks), *Caldecote* (Nf) and *Coldwell* (Nb). The distinction between Ang *ald* and WS *eald* is reflected in place-names. OE Ang *wald*, WS *weald* originally meant 'forest, especially on high ground'. When forests were cleared, the name often came to mean 'open uplands, waste ground'. The West Saxon form has survived in *The Weald* of Kent, while the Anglian form is preserved in *The Cotswolds* and in the Yorkshire and Lincolnshire *Wolds*. Another group of place-names shows the developments of three different dialectal forms of the noun meaning 'well' or 'spring'. The usual West Saxon form was *wiella*; Mercian had *wælla*; most other Anglian dialects and Kentish had *wella*. WS *wiella* became ME *wille* or *wulle*, and these forms survive in *Wilton* (So) and *Woolcombe* (Do); Mercian *wælla* became ME *walle*, which is hard to distinguish from *wall*, but it is probably found in *Aspinwall* (La) and *Heswall* (Ches); the form *wella* is found in *Well* (NRYks) and *Wells* (Nfk). As a result of the influence of Standard English, forms with *e* are liable to occur in any part of the country. Sometimes a sound-change that seems to be dialectal is abundantly illustrated by place-name evidence although literary forms are not very common. Of such a kind is the shift of stress from the first to the second element of the initial diphthong *ĕa*, which had the result that the first element of the new rising diphthong became the semi-vowel [j], spelt *y*. This sound-change is especially common in Devonshire, although occasional examples are found elsewhere. Examples are *Yalland*, the first syllable of which is derived from OE *eald* 'old', and *Yeo* (OE *ēa* 'river'), a name which is used to describe more than twenty different places in Devonshire.

CHARACTERISTICS OF THE OLD ENGLISH DIALECTS

There were very few linguistic features of Old English that were to be found exclusively in any one dialect, since dialectal forms were freely borrowed from one dialect into another. The differences between one Old English dialect and another depended for the most part upon the relative frequency of occurrence of a particular group of forms. When we speak of a sound-change being characteristic of a particular dialect, we mean that forms

OLD ENGLISH DIALECTS

NORTHUMBRIAN

ANGLIAN

MERCIAN

WEST SAXON

KENTISH

0   100 MLS.

Map 2.   Old English Dialects

reflecting the change are common or normal in that dialect, whereas in other dialects they are found only occasionally. Sometimes the distribution of variant forms is so complicated that no clear picture emerges, but fortunately there are some forms whose distribution does enable us to make general statements about Old English dialects. Brief mention may be made of the chief texts on which our knowledge of Old English dialects is based and of the chief characteristics of the dialects in order to show what is the justification for the generally accepted classification.

ANGLIAN

The chief characteristics of Anglian, which includes both Northumbrian and Mercian, are:

(1) The use of *a* as the development of WGmc *a* before *l* + consonant, whereas West Saxon and Kentish have *ea*. Hence we have Ang *all* 'all', *haldan* 'to hold' beside WS *eall*, *healdan*. The Anglian forms often spread to West Saxon and Kentish, even in early texts, but the spread of *ea*-forms to Anglian is not common.

(2) The monophthongization or 'smoothing' of the diphthongs *ĕa*, *ĕo* and *ĭo* to *ǣ* (later often *ĕ*), *ē* and *ĭ* respectively when they were followed by *c*, *g* or *h*, whether standing alone or preceded by a liquid consonant (*l* or *r*). Thus we have Ang *ǣge*, *ēge* 'eye', beside WS *ēage*, Ang *werc* 'work' beside WS *weorc*.

(3) A tendency to keep the front rounded vowel *ǖ*, which in West Saxon was unrounded to *ĕ*. Hence the digraph *œ* does not normally occur in West Saxon texts at all whereas in Anglian texts both *ǖ* and *ē* are found. Examples are Ang *œle* 'oil,' *œþel* 'home' beside WS *ele*, *ēþel*.

(4) The retention of *-u* or *-o* as the ending of the 1st person singular present indicative of verbs. In West Saxon and Kentish this ending is replaced by *-e* from the optative.

44

Examples are Ang *bindu* 'I bind', *dœmu* 'I judge' beside WS *binde, dēme.*

NORTHUMBRIAN

The great period of Northumbrian history extended from the later part of the seventh to the early part of the ninth century. The best-known writer of this period was Bede, who was born near Wearmouth in Durham in 672 and lived for most of his life at Jarrow, where he died in 735. His *Historia Ecclesiastica Gentis Anglorum* is one of the most important sources of our knowledge of Anglo-Saxon history; several manuscripts of the Latin text have been preserved and there is also a translation into the West Saxon dialect of Old English. A fragment of five lines of verse, generally called *Bede's Death Song*, is preserved in the St Gall MS. No. 254, a manuscript of the ninth century, and this is one of the earliest records that we have of English vernacular writing. Another early Northumbrian text that has been preserved is *Cædmon's Hymn*, a poem of nine lines. In Book IV of the *Historia Ecclesiastica* Bede tells the story of Cædmon, a herdsman and lay brother in the abbey of Whitby in the seventh century, who was endowed with the gift of composing religious verse. *Cædmon's Hymn*, which Bede quotes as a specimen of Cædmon's work, is preserved in its Northumbrian version in some of the manuscripts containing the Latin text of Bede's *Historia*, and a West Saxon version of the *Hymn* is incorporated in the West Saxon translation of that work. A third early Northumbrian poem, consisting of fourteen lines, is known as *The Leiden Riddle* because it is preserved in a manuscript which is now at Leiden, in the Netherlands. There is a later West Saxon version of the same riddle. Another specimen of the early Northumbrian dialect is to be found on the Ruthwell Cross in Dumfriesshire. On this cross are inscribed in runic characters a few lines of an Old English religious poem *The Dream of the Rood*, which is preserved in a later West Saxon version in the Vercelli manuscript. We thus have four short texts to illustrate the Old Northumbrian dialect, and we are fortunate in having West Saxon versions of three of them available for comparison. The task of comparison is, however, made complicated by the fact that the West Saxon versions are a good deal later than the Northumbrian.

Three longer texts are available for the study of Northumbrian of the tenth century: *The Durham Ritual*, *The Lindisfarne Gospels*, and part of *The Rushworth Gospels*. All three manuscripts are in Latin, but they all contain interlinear glosses in Old English.

The manuscript of *The Durham Ritual* is in the Cathedral Library at Durham, and consists of a tenth-century service-book with a Northumbrian gloss.

The Lindisfarne Gospels are preserved in a beautiful manuscript, which is now MS. Cotton Nero D. iv in the British Museum. The Latin text was written on the island of Lindisfarne towards the end of the seventh century. The Northumbrian interlinear gloss is two and a half centuries later, and was made about 950 by a priest called Aldred, at a time when the manuscript had been taken to Chester-le-Street, near Durham, for greater safety. The manuscript was later removed to Durham, where it remained for several centuries.

The Rushworth Gospels are so called because they are preserved in a manuscript which was presented to the Bodleian Library by John Rushworth, who was deputy clerk to the House of Commons during the Long Parliament. The Latin text was written in the eighth century, and the Old English glosses were added about two centuries later. They were the work of two scribes: the glosses to the whole of St Matthew's Gospel and a small part of St Mark were the work of Farmon, a priest 'æt harawuda', which may be Harewood, near Ross-on-Wye; the remaining glosses were the work of a scribe called Owun. The two scribes wrote in different dialects. Farmon's work may be regarded as North Mercian; the remaining glosses seem to be copied, with slight variations, from those in *The Lindisfarne Gospels*, and are therefore in a Northumbrian dialect.

The chief characteristics of Northumbrian dialects are:

(1)   The development of *a* from WGmc *a* before *r* + consonant,

especially when a labial consonant (*p*, *b*, *f*, *m* or *w*) precedes the vowel or follows the *r*. This Northern development spreads to a few Mercian texts, but for the most part the Old English dialects other than Northumbrian have *ea* before *r* + consonant as a result of the sound-change known as fracture. Examples are Nhb *barn* 'child', *ward* 'protector,' beside *bearn*, *weard* in the other dialects.

(2) The tendency of initial *w* to cause rounding of a following vowel or diphthong. Northumbrian often has *o* after *w* in words which, in other dialects, have *eo* as the result of fracture or back mutation, two sound-changes which bring about the diphthongization of front vowels. Thus Northumbrian has *worða* 'to become', *cuoða* 'to say' beside WS *weorðan* and *cweðan*.

(3) The loss of final -*n*. This loss is especially marked in late Northumbrian, although some categories of words, such as the past participles of strong verbs, are not as a rule affected. Examples are Nhb *bigeonda* 'beyond', *wosa* 'to be', beside WS *bigeondan* and *wesan*.

MERCIAN

The Mercian dialects have a special interest since it is from one of these dialects that the Standard English of today is derived. Unfortunately we cannot feel so confident about the provenance of the Old English texts that are generally regarded as Mercian as we can about the Northumbrian texts. The earliest texts that have been assigned to a Mercian dialect are the Corpus and Epinal Glossaries of the eighth century. The names of the Glossaries indicate the present location of the manuscripts: Corpus Christi College Cambridge and Epinal in the department of Vosges in France respectively. These glossaries differ from the Northumbrian glosses that have been mentioned in that they are alphabetically arranged and therefore represent a further stage in the development of the dictionary. They consist of lists of Latin words whose meanings are explained sometimes in Latin and sometimes in English.

The Vespasian Psalter derives its name from the press-mark of the manuscript in the British Museum: Cotton Vespasian A.i. The manuscript contains the Latin text of *Psalms* and a dozen hymns, generally known as the *Vespasian Hymns*, to which has been added an interlinear gloss of the early ninth century. Professor R. M. Wilson has recently pointed out[1] how slight is the evidence for assigning the glosses to a Mercian dialect. The evidence of Middle English dialects which have some features in common with that of *The Vespasian Psalter* shows that there is no absurdity in assigning the glosses to the Mercian area, but there is much to be said for the cautious approach which avoids localization and refers to the dialect of the glosses as 'the dialect of *The Vespasian Psalter*'.

The chief Mercian characteristics are:

(1) The 'second fronting' by which æ was raised to e and a was fronted to æ. These changes are especially characteristic of the dialect of *The Vespasian Psalter*. Examples are *VP deg* 'day', pl. *dægas, feder* 'father' beside *dæg, dagas, fæder* in the other dialects.

(2) The back mutation of æ to ea, caused by a back vowel in the following syllable. The change did not take place when the intervening consonant was c or g. As a result of back mutation we find *VP featu* 'vessels' beside *fatu* in the other dialects.

KENTISH

The Kentish dialect had a number of distinctive features, though the Old English texts written in this dialect are short and not very well-known. There are several Kentish charters: those belonging to the seventh and eighth centuries are short and in Latin, only the proper names being in Old English, but there are ninth-century charters written in Old English. There are also glosses and a Kentish version of the fiftieth Psalm.[2]

---

[1] *The Anglo-Saxons: Studies . . . presented to Bruce Dickins* (Bowes and Bowes, 1959), pp. 292–310.
[2] Psalm 50 in the Vulgate, 51 in A.V.

The chief characteristics of **Kentish** are:

(1) The lowering and unrounding of $\check{y}$ to $\check{e}$. Thus we find Kentish *senn* 'sin' beside *synn* in the other dialects.

(2) The raising to $\bar{e}$ of the $\bar{æ}$ which results from the *i*-mutation of $\bar{a}$, from Gmc *ai*. Thus we find Kentish *ēnig* 'any', *mēst* 'most', beside *ǣnig* and *mǣst* in the other dialects.

WEST SAXON

There are more extant texts written in the West Saxon dialect than in all the other Old English dialects put together. This preponderance is a result of the political supremacy of Wessex during the tenth century, which is the period when most of the extant manuscripts were written. The two great names in West Saxon literature are those of King Alfred and Abbot Ælfric, and they both left works which have been preserved in several manuscripts. Alfred's works, representing the West Saxon dialect of the ninth century, include translations of the *Cura Pastoralis* and the world history of Orosius. Ælfric's works, which belong to the end of the tenth century, include many homilies and a Grammar which shows great ingenuity in the devising of English terms to describe grammatical concepts. Another important late West Saxon text is a translation of the Gospels into West Saxon. The *Anglo-Saxon Chronicle* is in the main in West Saxon, but it is not suitable for the illustration of dialect because it has survived in a number of versions which are not dialectally homogeneous.

The chief characteristics of West Saxon are:

(1) The use of $\bar{æ}$ as a development of WGmc $\bar{a}$ from Gmc $\bar{æ}$, whereas in most other dialects the $\bar{æ}$ was raised to $\bar{e}$. This dialectal feature may date back to a time before the Germanic invasion of Britain, since the raising to $\bar{e}$ is found also in Old Frisian. Examples are WS *dǣd* 'deed', *hǣr* 'hair' beside *dēd*, *hēr* in the other dialects. One poetical word, *mēce* 'sword', has the raised vowel even in the predominantly West Saxon poetical manuscripts. This irregularity is thought to be due to the fact

that *mēce* was an Anglian literary word not normally used by West Saxon speakers.

(2) The diphthongization of vowels by the influence of preceding palatal consonants. Rather surprisingly, in view of the geographical separation, this is a feature which West Saxon shares to some extent with late Northumbrian, although there are differences of detail between the diphthongizations in the two dialects. Characteristic West Saxon forms are *gielp* 'boast' and *forgieldan* 'to pay', beside *gelp* and *forgeldan* in the other dialects. In these words *g* had a palatal pronunciation [j], like that of the *y* in MnE *young*.

(3) The change of *ĕa* and *ĭo* to *ĭe* by *i*-mutation. In the other dialects *ĕa* became *ĕ* and *ĭo* remained unchanged. Examples are WS *hīeran* 'to hear', *þīestru* 'darkness', *hliehhan* 'to laugh', beside *hēran*, *þīostru*, *hlehhan* in the other dialects.

(4) The absence of back mutation in many words which show the change in the other dialects. In West Saxon back mutation took place only when the consonant intervening between the stem-vowel and the back vowel causing the change was a liquid or a labial and the effects of the change were often removed by analogy; in the other dialects it took place before any consonants except *c* and *g* in Anglian. Examples are WS *gebedu* 'prayers', *wita* 'scholar', beside *gebeodu* and *wiota* in the other dialects.

(5) The use of syncopated forms of the 3rd person singular of the present indicative of verbs; in the other dialects we generally find forms with the ending *-eð* and with the effects of *i*-mutation on the stem-vowel removed by analogy. Thus we find WS *cīest* 'chooses', *hielt* 'holds' beside *cēoseð*, *haldeð* in the other dialects.

SPECIMENS OF OLD ENGLISH DIALECTS

Since *Cædmon's Hymn* has been preserved in a Northumbrian as well as a West Saxon version, it is interesting to compare the two. The Northumbrian version is:

Nu scylun hergan   hefænricæs uard,
Metudæs mæcti   end his modgidanc,
uerc uuldurfadur;   sue he uundra gihuæs,
eci Dryctin,   or astelidæ.
He ærist scop   ælda barnum
heben til hrofe,   haleg Scepen;
tha middungeard,   monncynnæs uard,
eci Dryctin,   æfter tiadæ
firum foldu,   Frea allmectig.[1]

The West Saxon version is:

Nu we sculan herian   heofonrices weard,
Metodes mihte   and his modgeþonc,
weorc wuldorfæder;   swa he wundra gehwæs,
ece Dryhten,   ord onstealde.
He ærest gesceop   eorðan bearnum
heofon to hrofe,   halig Scyppend;
ða middangeard,   monncynnes weard,
ece Dryhten,   æfter teode
firum foldan,   Frea ælmihtig.

It is important to remember that the two versions differ in date as well as in dialect. The West Saxon version is more than two centuries later than the Northumbrian, and several of the differences between the two versions are due to this difference of date. Archaisms in the Northumbrian version include the -æs of *hefænricæs* and *monncynnæs* and the -i of *mæcti* and *eci*. There are other differences which are not due to either date or dialect, such as that between the -ll- of *allmectig* and the -l- of *ælmihtig*, and some of the distinctive features of the Northumbrian version are merely differences of spelling, such as the use of *c* for *h* before *t* in *mæcti*, *Dryctin* and *allmectig*, of *u* for *w* in *uard*, *uerc*, *uuldurfadur*, *uundra*, and *gihuæs*, and *th* and *d* for *þ* or *ð* in *tha* and *modgidanc*. There remain, however, several differences that are due to dialect. The *a* in *uard* and *barnum* in the Northumbrian version beside *ea* in the West Saxon, shows the lack of fracture in the neighbourhood of labial consonants.

---

[1] 'Now we ought to praise the Protector of the Kingdom of Heaven, the might of the Lord and the thought of his heart, the work of the Glorious Father, as He, the Eternal Lord, made a beginning of every wonderful thing. He, the Holy Creator, first made Heaven as a roof for the children of men. Then the Protector of Mankind, Eternal Lord, the All-powerful God, afterwards created the world, the earth for men.'

The form *ælda* is also Anglian: it is the genitive of a plural word meaning 'men', which appears in West Saxon as *ielde*. There was earlier an *i* in the ending which caused *i*-mutation of the stem-vowel. The WS *ie* is from earlier *ea*, whereas the Anglian *æ* is from *a*, the difference between the two forms being due to the fact that there was no fronting and fracture of *a* before *l* + consonant in Anglian. Another Anglian form is *uerc*, with smoothing of the diphthong found in the corresponding WS *weorc*. In vocabulary the preposition *til* is a rare Northern form in Old English, although later, reinforced by ON *til*, it became the everyday non-dialectal English word *till*.

NORTHUMBRIAN

An example of later Northumbrian is provided by the Lord's Prayer as it is preserved in the interlinear gloss in *The Lindisfarne Gospels*. Since the purpose of the gloss was to translate each Latin word separately, the following extract does not provide a specimen of Old English syntax but it provides a good illustration of Northumbrian phonology.

> Fæder ure[1], ðu arð in heofnum. Sie gehalgad noma ðin. Tocymeð ric ðin. Sie willo ðin suæ is in heofne and in eorðo. Hlaf usenne oferwistlic sel us to dæg and forgef us scylda usra, suæ uoe forgefon scyldgum usum, and ne inlæd usih in costunge ah gefrig usich from yfle.

The dialectal forms in this passage include some which might occur in any non-West-Saxon text as well as others which are more specifically Northumbrian. The non-West-Saxon forms include the pronouns *ūsih*, *ūsich* (cf. WS *ūs*), the past participle *gehālgad* (cf. WS *gehālgod*) and the forms *forgef* and *forgēfon* without front diphthongization (cf. WS *forgief, forgēafon*). The form *forgēfon* shows also the non-West-Saxon raising of *æ*[1] (from fronting of WGmc *ā*, from Gmc *æ*) to *ē*, since the WS *ēa* is from earlier *æ*[1]. Northumbrian forms include *arð*, (with lack of fracture before *r* + consonant and with final ð corresponding

---

[1] MS. urer.

to WS *t*), and *uoe* (where *u* is a spelling for *w* which has caused rounding of the following *ē*).

MERCIAN

The following is an extract from the *Vespasian Hymns*:

Ic ondettu ðe Dryhten: forðon eorre ðu earð me, gecerred is hatheortnis ðin ond frofrende earð mec. Sehðe, God hælend min· getreowlice ic dom ond ne ondredu, forðon strengu min ond herenis min Dryhten ond geworden is me in haelu. Gehleadað weter in gefian of wellu[m] haelendes ond cweoðað in ðæm dege, 'Ondettað Dryhtne ond gecegað noman his; cyðe doð in folcum gemœtinge his; gemunað forðon heh is noma his. Singað Dryhtne forðon micellice dyde: seggað ðis in alre eorðan. Gefeh ond here eardung Sione forðon micel in midum ðin halig Israel'.[1]

Some of the dialectal characteristics of this extract are shared by all the non-West-Saxon dialects, some are Anglian, while others are characteristic of the dialect of *The Vespasian Psalter*. Non-West-Saxon forms include *eorre* (corresponding to WS *ierre*, where the *eo/io* has undergone *i*-mutation), *gecerred*, *gecēgað* (with non-West-Saxon mutation of *ĕa* to *ĕ*; cf. WS *gecierred*, *gecīegað*), *hēlend* (with *ǣ²* (which arises by *i*-mutation of *ā*, from Gmc *ai*) raised to *ē* by the influence of the following alveolar consonant in Anglian; in Kentish, *ǣ²* was raised to *ē* by an independent change), and *cweoðað* (with back mutation taking place even through a dental consonant; cf. WS *cweðað*). Anglian forms include *ondettu* and *ondrēdu* (with the old ending -*u* in the 1st person singular present indicative; West Saxon had -*e* from the optative), *dōm* 'do' (with the Anglian addition of -*m* in monosyllabic forms on the analogy of *eam* 'am'), *hēh* and *gefeh* (with Anglian smoothing; cf. WS *hēah* and *gefeoh*), and *gemœtinge* (with retention of a front rounded vowel as the *i*-mutation of *ō* (WS *gemēting*). The two changes that are most characteristic of the dialect of *The Vespasian Psalter* are reflected in *weter* and *dege* (with raising of *æ* to *e*), and *gehleadað* (with back mutation of *æ* which in other dialects was retracted to *a*).

[1] For a translation of this Hymn see *Isaiah*, Ch. 12.

KENTISH

The following is an extract from the Kentish Psalm:

Aðweah me of sennum, saule fram wammum,
gasta Sceppend, geltas geclansa,
þa ðe ic on aldre æfre gefremede
ðurh lichaman leðre geðohtas.
For ðan ic unriht min eall oncnawe
and eac synna gehwær selfum æt eagan
firendeda geðrec beforan standeð,
scelda scinað; forgef me, Sceppen min,
lifes liohtfruma ðinre lufan blisse.
Nu ic anum ðe oft syngode
and yfela feola eac gefræmede
gelta gramhegdig, ic ðe, gasta breogo,
helende Crist helpe bidde,
ðæt me forgefene gastes wunde
an forðgesceaft feran mote,
þy ðine wordcwidas weorðan gefelde,
ðæt ðu ne wilnast weora æniges deað.

The clearest indication of the Kentish dialect here is to be seen in the forms with *ĕ* where other dialects would have *ў*. Thus we have *sennum* (WS *synnum*), *geltas*, *gelta* (WS *gyltas*, *gylta*), *lēðre* (WS *lўðre*), *gramhegdig* (WS *gramhygdig*), but it is to be noticed that side by side with these forms there are forms with *y*: *synna, syngode, yfela*. Another Kentish form is *breogo*, with back mutation before a back consonant, whereas *weora*, with back mutation caused by *a*, could occur in any non-West-Saxon dialect. A characteristically Kentish form is *līohtfruma*, with *īo* corresponding to *ēo* in most other dialects. Non-West-Saxon forms are *scelda* and *forgef* (where West Saxon would normally have front diphthongization of *e* to *ie*), *Sceppend* (where West Saxon would have *ie* by *i*-mutation of *ea*), and *firendēda* (where West Saxon would have *ǣ*).

CHAPTER III

Middle English

IN THE STUDY of Old English dialects our chief difficulty is the scarcity of evidence. For the study of Middle English dialects a much larger mass of evidence is available. There are in existence many manuscripts containing Middle English texts which show strongly marked dialectal features, and each of the major regions into which England can be divided is represented by several texts of adequate length. Close examination of these texts, however, shows that, despite the quantity and complexity of the available material, we still have much less than we need to gain an adequate idea of the nature and distribution of Middle English dialects.

There is one major difficulty inherent in the attempt to write of the dialects of any past age: in speaking about dialects we are as a rule primarily concerned with the spoken language, but our knowledge of the spoken language of the past is derived almost wholly from written records. This approach to the study of dialect has not gone unchallenged, and Professors Angus McIntosh and M. L. Samuels have undertaken a large-scale investigation of Middle English dialects which is based on the spellings recorded in Middle English manuscripts irrespective of the sounds which may have been represented by those spellings.[1] It may be that this investigation will reveal dialectal criteria that are purely graphic, but the student of Middle English dialects will never be free from the responsibility of asking

[1] On the general problem see Angus McIntosh, 'The Analysis of Written Middle English,' *TPS* 1956, pp. 26–55.

himself whether the variations that he finds are merely variations of spelling or whether they arise from variations of pronunciation. One possible difference between Middle English written and spoken dialects is that the former were current over fairly large areas whereas the spoken dialects may well have been current over smaller areas. There were probably many variations in the spoken dialects of Middle English that are hardly reflected at all in literary texts. The evidence for the study of Middle English dialects is complex because most of the extant manuscripts have been copied from earlier manuscripts which are now lost, and as a rule a Middle English scribe would no more try to preserve the spelling of his original than a modern copyist would try to imitate the handwriting of his original. At the same time the scribe did not feel any obligation to observe complete consistency in adapting the spelling of his original to make it conform to his own practice. It would, of course, sometimes happen that the dialect of the original was identical with the scribe's own dialect, but in most Middle English manuscripts we have to allow for the possibility of a mixture of forms, some in the dialect of the original and others in the dialect of the scribe. In poetical texts it is sometimes possible to distinguish between the two dialects by an examination of the rhymes. Rhyming words are more likely than the rest of a text to preserve forms from the original dialect because the substitution of a form from another dialect was often avoided when such a substitution would spoil the rhyme. If a scribe showed no such scruples, it may still be possible to draw conclusions about the original dialect from an examination of the imperfect rhyme: it is often possible to tell what the rhyming word must have been in the original.

The best starting-point for the study of Middle English dialects is provided by the few texts which are in the handwriting of their authors. Such are the lyrics by the Franciscan friar William Herebert of Hereford, who died in 1333[1], and

<hr>

[1] Carleton Brown, *Religious Lyrics of the Fourteenth Century*, pp. xiv, 15–29. Other texts of which we have the original or a contemporary copy written in the same locality are listed by Samuel Moore, Sanford B. Meech and Harold Whitehall in *Middle English Dialect Characteristics and Dialect Boundaries* (University of Michigan, 1935).

Michael of Northgate's *Ayenbyte of Inwyt*. The latter text is particularly valuable from the point of view of the study of dialect, since it is not only written in the author's own handwriting but it is exactly dated and localized. It was finished on October 27, 1340 in the 'cloystre of Sauynt Austin of Canterberi'. Legal documents might be expected to provide similarly dated and localized specimens of Middle English dialects, but unfortunately during the Middle English period such documents were usually written in Latin or Anglo-Norman. These documents are of some use for the study of English dialects, since a Latin document often includes place-names in the vernacular and the spellings of such place-names may be dialectal, but this evidence is often misleading since the scribes were usually clerics, the most mobile class in medieval England, and it is always necessary to remember that the dialect of the scribe is not necessarily that of the place mentioned. Even if the original place of composition of a text is unknown, the text may supply evidence of dialect provided that we can localize the manuscript.

The greater wealth of material which is available in Middle English makes it possible for us to say something about the vocabulary of the Middle English dialects, although it is only words of frequent occurrence whose distribution can be profitably discussed. With rare words the accident of preservation has to be taken into account. It is natural that words of Scandinavian origin should be plentiful in the areas covered by the Danelaw, and such words are most common in the North and the East Midlands. They are not very common in Scottish texts but they are very frequently found in Yorkshire and Lincolnshire. A notable point about Scandinavian loan-words is that they include such words as pronouns and particles, which are not often borrowed from one language into another. Thus, in the *Ormulum* we find *occ* 'and', *summ* 'as'. The pronouns *they*, *their*, *them* and the conjunction *though* have passed from Scandinavian into the standard language.

The alliterative tradition, which was characteristic of Old English poetry, survived with vigour in the North and preserved or brought into use many words not known in the East Midlands or the South. The Old English poetic vocabulary survives best in West Midland texts, especially in Layamon's *Brut* and the alliterative poems. It is notable that the poetic word *blonke* 'horse' (OE *blanca*) is used in Northern texts in its West Midland form with a rounded vowel.

Most medieval English writers took their dialect for granted and showed no consciousness of dialectal variations. There is, however, one work belonging to the fourteenth century which gives an outline account of Middle English dialects. This is the Latin *Polychronicon*, a chronicle covering the period from the Creation to the middle of the fourteenth century, by Ranulph Higden. a monk of St Werburgh's at Chester, who died in 1364. The work was translated into English by John of Trevisa, a Cornishman who died in 1402. Trevisa writes:

> Also Englische men, þey þei hadde from the bygynnynge þre manere speche, norþerne, sowþerne, and middel speche in þe myddel of þe lond, as þey come of þre manere peple of Germania, noþeles by comyxtioun and mellynge firste wiþ Danes and afterward wiþ Normans, in meny þe contray longage is apayred, and som vseþ straunge wlafferynge, chiterynge, harrynge, and garrynge grisbayting.[1]

This passage shows that dialectal variations in English are of long standing. The suggestion that some of the distinctive features of the Southern, Midland and Northern dialects of Old English can be traced back to a period before the crossing of the Germanic tribes to England may well be true, though most of them developed after the settlement in Britain. It is interesting to see that, as early as the fourteenth century, there was inter-mixture of dialects as a result of the movement of population, and this process has been carried much further since then. The forceful conclusion of the passage shows that hostility to an unfamiliar dialect is no new thing.

Trevisa, still translating Higden, goes on to speak in greater detail of the three English dialects:

> Also of þe forsaide Saxon tonge þat is i-deled aþre, and is abide scarsliche wiþ fewe vplondisshe men is greet wonder;

[1] Higden's *Polychronicon* (Rolls Series, 1869), vol. II, p. 159.

for men of þe est wiþ men of þe west, as it were vndir þe same
partie of heuene, acordeþ more in sownynge of speche þan men
of þe norþ wiþ men of þe souþ; þerfore it is þat Mercii, þat beeþ
men of myddel Engelond, as it were parteners of þe endes,
vnderstondeþ bettre þe side langages, norþerne and souþerne,
þan norþerne and souþerne vnderstondeþ eiþer oþer. Al þe
longage of þe Norþhumbres, and specialliche at ʒork, is so
scharp, slitting, and frotynge and vnschape, þat we souþerne
men may þat longage vnneþe vnderstonde. I trowe þat þat is
bycause þat þey beeþ nyh to straunge men and naciouns þat
spekeþ strongliche, and also bycause þat þe kynges of Engelond
woneþ alwey fer from þat cuntrey; for þey beeþ more i-torned
to þe souþ contray, and ʒif þey gooþ to þe norþ contray þey
gooþ wiþ greet help and strangþe.[1]

Trevisa's comment that men from the Midlands had an advantage
over northerners and southerners in understanding something of
all the English dialects helps to explain why it was a Midland
dialect which became the basis of the Standard English of today.
There were, of course, other reasons and Trevisa indicates one of
them: the importance of the language of the Court. It is
interesting to note that the distinctive nature of the Northern
dialects, still noticeable today, was already a subject of comment
in the fourteenth century.

We have seen that linguistic differences between two Old
English texts may be the result of differences either of date or
of dialect, and the same is true of Middle English. The Middle
English period lasted from the eleventh to the fifteenth century,
and during that time the English language was constantly
changing. Not only did sounds change but also the boundaries
which separated one dialectal feature from another. For
example, in early Middle English, Southern dialects had *e* as the
development of OE *æ*, but in later Middle English forms with *e*
were gradually replaced by forms with *a* from Midland dialects.

The distinction between Old and Middle English is an arbitrary
one. In all essentials there has been continuity in the development of the English language from the earliest recorded texts in
the eighth century to the present day, and this continuity extends
to dialects. Some of the characteristic features of Middle

[1] *op. cit.*, pp. 161–163.

English dialects are simply the preservation of Old English variations. For example, the South-Eastern dialect of Middle English has *ĕ* as the development of OE *ў*, but this sound-change had already taken place in the Kentish dialect of Old English.

In view of the greater amount of material available, it is possible to distinguish more dialect areas in Middle English than in Old English. The same broad division into major dialect regions can be made, but further subdivision is possible in Middle English. The main Middle English dialect areas are Northern, East Midland, West Midland, South-Eastern and South-Western. The Northern dialect can be regarded as descended from the Northumbrian dialect of Old English. It extends northward from the Ribble and the Aire and it can be subdivided into Scottish and the dialect of the North of England. East and West Midland together correspond to the Mercian dialect of Old English, South-Eastern to Kentish and South-Western to West Saxon.

Just as place-names often preserve Old English dialectal variations, they also preserve some of the variations that developed in Middle English. The threefold development of OE *ў* is illustrated by many place-names, since it happens that the vowel *y* occurs in a large number of place-name elements, such as *cnyll* 'hillock', *brycg* 'bridge', *hyll* 'hill', *hyrst* 'copse', *pytt* 'pit', *rysc* 'rush', and *hȳð* 'port'. Western development is found in *Hulton* (La) and *Solihull* (Wa); the Northern *i* is found in *Hilton* (NRYks), *Hirst* (Nb, WRYks) and *Windhill* (WRYks); and the South-Eastern *e* is found in *Helsted* (K), *Knell* (Sx) and *Petworth* (Sx).

Perhaps the most noticeable characteristic of Northern dialects in Middle English was the retention of *ā*, which became open *ō* in the South and Midlands. This distinction is reflected in many place-names. OE *rā* 'roe' has given *ae* in *Rae Burn* (Cu) and *ay* in *Rayhead* (WRYks) but it is *o* in *Rodden* (So) and *oe* in *Roecombe* (Do). OE *āc* 'oak-tree' and its dative plural *ācum* have given *Skyrack* (WRYks) and *Acomb* (NRYks), but *Oake* (So) and *Broadoak* (Gl). In many Northern dialects OE *ā* has survived as *ya*, as in *yan* 'one' (OE *ān*) and this pronunciation is found in the Northern place-names, since *Acomb* is pronounced locally as *Yeckam* and *Yackam*.

The voicing of Middle English initial *f* and *s* in Southern dialects is reflected in place-names such as *Varracombe* (D) 'fair valley', *Zeaston* (D) 'at the seven stones', and *Venn* (He) and *Venton* (Co), both from OE *fenn* 'marsh'.

CHARACTERISTICS OF THE MIDDLE ENGLISH DIALECTS

NORTHERN

The Northern dialects are the most distinctive of the Middle English dialects, since they have many characteristics not found in any of the other dialect groups. The boundary between this group of dialects and the other dialect areas is more sharply defined than any of the other dialect boundaries. The linguistic boundary between North and Midlands is rather more northerly than one might expect. For example, Yorkshire is generally thought of as a Northern county, but in Middle English, as in Modern English, a good deal of the county falls within the North Midland dialect area.

There are very few Northern texts belonging to the early Middle English period but a large number belonging to the fourteenth and fifteenth centuries. One of the earliest Middle English texts in a Northern dialect is a metrical version of the Psalms, belonging to the late thirteenth century, which is sometimes called the *Surtees Psalter* because it was first printed for the Surtees Society in 1843–47. Another text written about the end of the thirteenth century is the *Cursor Mundi*, a long poem preserved in several manuscripts. The *Songs* of Lawrence Minot belong to the first half of the fourteenth century. A number of alliterative poems in Northern dialects were written about the end of the fourteenth century: *The Awntyrs of Arthur*, *The Wars of Alexander*, remarkable for the large Scandinavian element in its vocabulary, and *The Destruction of Troy*, a text which may

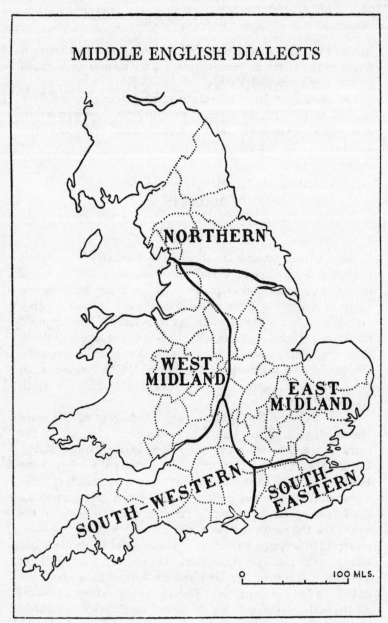

MIDDLE ENGLISH DIALECTS

NORTHERN

WEST MIDLAND

EAST MIDLAND

SOUTH-WESTERN

SOUTH-EASTERN

0   100 MLS.

Map 3.   Middle English Dialects

have been written in North Lancashire but which has some West Midland characteristics. As an example of a fifteenth-century Northern text we may mention one of the cycles of medieval plays, *The York Plays.*

The scarcity of early texts is even more marked when we come to Scottish texts. The earliest Scottish text is Barbour's *Bruce,* which was completed in 1387, though the manuscript is about a century later. Wyntoun's *Chronicle,* Blind Harry's *Schir William Wallace,* and the anonymous *Rauf Coilʒear* belong to the fifteenth century. From the end of the fifteenth and the beginning of the sixteenth centuries we have the poems of Henryson and Dunbar.

Some of the most easily recognizable characteristics of Northern dialects may be enumerated:

1. OE *ā* was not rounded, as it was in the other dialects, but remained until the fifteenth century, when it was fronted and raised to [ɛː] in pronunciation, although *a* generally remained in spelling. Hence we have N *stane* (OE *stān* 'stone') beside S and M *stone,* N *hale* (OE *hāl* 'whole') beside S and M *hool.* The Northern form *hale* was later adopted into Standard English.

2. In the second half of the fourteenth century the diphthongs *ai, ei, oi, ui* were often simplified by the loss of their second elements to *ā, ē, ō, ū* respectively. The simplified sounds sometimes continued to be spelt *ai, ei, oi, ui,* and consequently the *i* came to be regarded as a sign of length which could be added to any long vowel whether originally a diphthong or not. This use of *i* as a mark of length was regular in Scottish; in Northern English it was frequent but not so common as in Scottish. MeE *raid* (OE *rād*) has been adopted from the Northern dialects: the *ai* is a spelling for *ā* which, as we have seen, remained unrounded in the North. The rounded vowel is seen in MnE *road,* which is from the same Old English source.

3. In the Northern and East Midland dialects OE *ȳ* was unrounded to *ī.* The old spelling *y* often remained after the sound-change had taken place, and consequently the spelling *y* is often used to represent long and short *i* of other origins.

4. In open syllables of dissyllabic words ME *a, e, o* were lengthened in all dialects. In Northern dialects this lengthening extended to *i* and *u*, which were lengthened and lowered to close *ē* and close *ō* respectively. In a few words the forms with lengthened vowels spread to other dialects. Hence MnE *week* is from ME *wēke* (OE *wicu*).

5. Before nasal consonants early OE *a* had become a sound intermediate between *a* and *o*, which was sometimes spelt *a*, sometimes *o*. In Northern dialects of Middle English we have *a*, even before consonant groups which caused lengthening of a preceding vowel. Hence we have *lang* in *Auld lang syne*.

6. OE and ON *ō* was raised to [y:] in the early fourteenth century, as in *sune* (OE *sōna* 'immediately'), *buik* (OE *bōc* 'book'). The vowel resulting from this change rhymes with *u* in French loan-words; thus we find *sune* (OE *sōna*) rhyming with *fortune* (OF *fortune*).

7. In most Middle English dialects the vowels *a, e, o* were diphthongized when followed by the voiceless velar fricative which is usually spelt *gh* or *ch*. In Northern dialects *a* was diphthongized but *o* and *e* were generally unchanged. Hence we have N *taught* 'taught', *aught* 'eight' beside *soght, socht* 'sought'.

8. In all English dialects final lightly-stressed *-e* was lost in pronunciation by the fifteenth century, although final *-e* has often remained in spelling until the present day. In Northern dialects the loss of final *-e* took place much earlier than in the rest of the country. It probably occurred in the thirteenth century, and the loss of *-e* is generally reflected in spelling in fourteenth-century texts. Thus, we have N *luf* (OE *lufian* 'to love') beside M *love(n)*.

9. Before a consonant in the lightly-stressed final syllable of a dissyllabic word, *e* became *i* in Northern dialects during the

thirteenth century. Hence we have *wallis* 'walls', *wondir* 'wonder'.

10. The Northern dialects have the plosive consonants *g*, *gg* and *k* in many words which in the Midlands and South have [j] (spelt *y* or *ȝ*), [dȝ] (spelt *dg*), and [tʃ] (spelt *ch*) respectively. The Northern preference for plosive consonants is due in part to Scandinavian influence, but it is found in some words, such as N *spek* 'speech' beside M and S *spech*, where there is no Scandinavian cognate. A contributory cause of the variation is to be found in analogy. In Old English many words had front *g* or *c* in some grammatical forms of the word and back *g* and *c* in others, according to the quality of the vowel of the ending. Thus OE *swilc* had the genitive *swilces*, with front *c*, and the dative *swilcum*, with back *c*; the front *c* later became an affricate. One consonant or the other was generally levelled throughout the paradigm. Southern and Midland dialects tended to level the developments of the front consonants; Northern dialects tended to level the back consonants, perhaps because Scandinavian settlers in the North were more familiar with these consonants.

11. In the Northumbrian dialect of Old English the initial consonant in the group *hw-* was articulated with greater force than in the other dialects, with the result that in *The Lindisfarne Gospels* we find such spellings as *chwa* to represent *hwā* 'who.' In the Northern dialects of Middle English this strongly articulated consonant group remained, spelt *qu(h)*, *qw(h)*, whereas in the other dialects OE *hw-* became first of all voiceless *w* and afterwards voiced *w*, though the spelling *wh* has remained to the present day. We thus find N *quat*, *quhat* (OE *hwæt* 'what') beside M and S *what*, *wat*. The quality of initial *hw-* in the North can be inferred not only from the spelling but also from alliteration: the developments of OE *hw-*, OE *cw-* and OF *qu-* alliterate with one another in the North, and they are all spelt *qu-*.

12. ME *sh* (from OE *sc*) became *s* in the North when it occurred finally or in lightly-stressed words. Hence we find

fless (OE *flǣsc* 'flesh'), *fiss* (OE *fisc* 'fish'), *Inglis* (OE *Englisc* 'English'), *sal* (OE *sceal* 'shall').

13. In verbal inflexions the most characteristic Northern features are the 3rd singular present indicative in -(*e*)*s*, the plural of the present indicative in -(*e*)*s*, and the present participle in -*and*. In the conjugation of strong verbs Northern dialects generally show the levelling of the vowel of the preterite singular into the plural, and preterite indicative forms replace the subjunctive. For example, we find *band* as the preterite singular and plural of *bind*, whereas Old English had *band* in the 1, 3 singular and *bundon* in the plural.

The differences between Northern English and Scottish were not very great during the Middle English period, but there were enough minor differences to make subdivision possible. The unvoicing of final *d* to *t* in lightly-stressed syllables was common in Scottish and the North-Western counties of England but not in the North-Eastern counties. Confusion in spelling between *w* and *v* and the metathesis of *r* were especially common in Scottish, as in *gers* 'grass', *tharl* 'thrall'. For certain common words there are variant forms that occur in Scottish texts more often than in Northern English: Scottish prefers the native forms *is* 'is' and *ar* 'are', while Northern English prefers the Scandinavian forms *es* and *er*; Scottish prefers *gif* to *if*; as auxiliaries to help to represent the past tense *bigouth* and *couth* are more common in Scottish than in Northern English, which generally prefers *gan* or *can*.

EAST MIDLAND

One of the earliest East Midland texts is *The Ormulum*, which was written about the end of the twelfth century. This is a text of first importance for dialect study because the author, Orm, was a spelling reformer who attached far more importance to details of spelling than did most medieval scribes. We can therefore feel confident that, when we have mastered the rules that govern his rather eccentric spelling, we are in a position to draw from it conclusions about pronunciation. *The Ormulum* belongs to the northern part of the East Midland area, as do *Havelok the Dane*, written about a century later, and Robert Mannyng of Bourne's *Handlyng Synne* (begun in 1303). Many texts were written in the southern part of the East Midland area, including the twelfth-century *Peterborough Chronicle*, the thirteenth-century texts *Genesis and Exodus*, and *The Bestiary* and, in the fourteenth century, the works of Chaucer. Gower's *Confessio Amantis* was written near the end of the fourteenth century, in the main in the dialect of London but with an admixture of South-Eastern forms.

Since the Standard English of today is based upon the East Midland dialect of Middle English, the characteristics of the East Midland dialect do not seem to a reader of today to be strongly marked. Some East Midland features are found also in West Midland.

1. OE *a* or *o* before nasal consonants generally appears as *o* in West Midland, but in East Midland it was unrounded to *a* except when it had been lengthened before *nd*, *ng* or *mb*. Thus we have EM *name* beside *hond* and *lond*.

2. OE *ĕo* became a front half-close rounded vowel [ø] in all dialects in early Middle English. In the East Midland dialects this vowel was unrounded in the twelfth century, but in West Midland and South-Western dialects a rounded vowel remained much later. Hence we find EM *herte*, WM *heorte*, *huerte* (OE *heorte* 'heart'), EM *dep*, WM *deop* (OE *dēop* 'deep').

3. East Midland shared the Northern unrounding of OE *ȳ* to *ī*.

4. The diphthongization of *a* to *au* and of *o* to *ou* before *h* (often spelt *gh*) was less common in the East Midlands than in the South and West. For example, manuscripts of Chaucer normally have *broght* 'brought' and *wroght* 'wrought'.

5. In both East and West Midland the plural of the present indicative of verbs normally ends in -*e*(*n*).

WEST MIDLAND

The West Midland group stands midway between East Midland and South-Western; the southern part of the area, understandably, resembles the South-Western group most closely. There are historical causes of the relationship. At first in the Old English period the dialect of the West Midland area was Mercian, but after the Danish wars the West Midlands became part of the West Saxon kingdom, and even after all England was united under one king the West Midlands remained more closely associated with Wessex than with the East Midlands. Hence in dialectal characteristics of early origin, such as the varying mutations, West Midland resembles East Midland, but in those characteristics which are of later origin West Midland agrees with South-Western.

The West Midland area extends from Herefordshire to Lancashire and is remarkable for its productiveness in lyric poetry and alliterative texts. Some of the more important texts are Layamon's *Brut*, written in Worcestershire, and the 'Katherine Group', consisting of a number of religious texts, including the *Life of St Katherine* and *Ancrene Wisse*, written in Herefordshire. All these texts were written near the beginning of the thirteenth century. From the end of that century we have the lyrics of MS Harley 2253, a manuscript which was probably written in Herefordshire, although several of the lyrics were originally written in other dialects.[1] From the last quarter of the fourteenth century we have *Sir Gawain and the Green Knight*, *Pearl*, *Patience* and *Purity* all in the same manuscript and probably in the dialect of South Lancashire.

West Midland characteristics are:

1. As in the South-West, OE $\bar{y}$ remained as a front close rounded vowel, generally spelt *u* as a result of French influence, as in *hude* (OE *hȳdan* 'to hide'), *kusse* (OE *cyssan* 'to kiss').

2. Before nasal consonants *o* is preferred to *a* even in open syllables, as in WM *nome* (OE *nama* 'name'). The only words

---

[1] See G. L. Brook, 'The Original Dialects of the Harley Lyrics', *LSE*, ii (1933), pp. 38–61.

in which *a* was regularly used before nasal consonants in the West Midlands were lightly-stressed words, such as *man* 'one' and the conjunction *and*. The use of *o*-forms in open syllables provides a way of distinguishing between West Midland and South-Western dialects, since in the South-West the *o* was generally unrounded to *a* by the fourteenth century, except when the vowel was lengthened before consonant groups.

3. In the northern part of the West Midland area *o* was raised to *u* before *ng*. We find examples of *long* (OE *lang*) rhyming with *tonge* (OE *tunge*). This is the origin of the Standard English pronunciation of *among* [əmʌŋ]: it is one of several dialectal forms which have passed into Standard English.

4. The West Midland dialects, like the South-Western, kept a rounded vowel [ø], spelt *eo, oe, u, ue*, as the development of OE *ĕo* until well into the fourteenth century. A special West Midland development was the raising of this front half-close rounded vowel to a close rounded vowel [y], generally spelt *u*. This raising is found especially before *r* but occasionally in other positions also. Examples are *burn* (OE *beorn* 'man'), *lude*, *leude* beside *lede* (OE *lēod* 'people').

5. Final *b*, *d* and *g* were often unvoiced to *p*, *t* and *k* when preceded by a liquid or nasal, as in *ʒonke* (OE *iung* 'young'), *þynke* (OE *þing* 'thing'), *ant* (OE *and*). Final *d* was also often unvoiced in lightly-stressed syllables, as in *hadet* 'beheaded'.

SOUTH-EASTERN

The region where South-Eastern dialects were spoken included Kent and the eastern part of Surrey. The dialect of Essex had some distinctive features, and it may best be regarded as a sub-division of South-Eastern. Texts in the Kentish dialect include sermons from the twelfth and thirteenth centuries, the religious poems of William of Shoreham, written in the first quarter of the fourteenth century, and, most important of all, Michael of Northgate's *Ayenbyte of Inwyt*, completed in 1340. The Essex dialect is represented by *Vices and Virtues*, written about the beginning of the thirteenth century.

Some of the characteristics of the South-Eastern dialects are shared by South-Western. The most distinctive South-Eastern characteristics are:

1. OE *ȳ* was lowered and unrounded to *ĕ*, as in *kesse* (OE *cyssan* 'to kiss'), *helle* (OE *hyll* 'hill'). This change had taken place in Kentish in Old English; during the Middle English period it was extended to neighbouring counties, and a few forms with *e* are found in the East Midland area. We sometimes find *e* as the development of OE short *y* in dialects far away from the South-East; an example that has survived in Standard English is *evil* (OE *yfel*). The probable explanation of these forms is that the *e* represents long close *e*, which is the development of *i* in open syllables of dissyllabic words in those dialects in which *i* was lengthened. Such forms can be recognized by the fact that the manuscripts in which they occur often have *e* as the development of OE *i* as well as of OE *y*.

2. OE *æ* had become *e* in Kentish in the ninth century. In early Middle English it became *e* also in South-Western texts, but in the Midlands and North it became *a*. Midland forms with *a* spread South during the Middle English period. They became usual in the South-West by the end of the thirteenth century. In Kentish, forms with *e* survived longer, and fourteenth-century Kentish texts show a preponderance of *e*- forms. The development of OE *æ* thus provides a good illustration of the importance of the date of a text when one is determining its dialect. As a result of lack of stress, *e* is found in words like *wes* 'was' (OE *wæs*) in some dialects, such as the West Midland dialect of *The Harley Lyrics*, in which *æ* has normally become *a*.

3. The South-Eastern dialects have distinctive developments of the Old English diphthongs. OE *ĕa* became [ɛ] and [ɛː] in most Middle English dialects, but in South-Eastern dialects the spellings *ya* and *yea* are common, as in *dyaf* (OE *dēaf* 'deaf'), *dyead* (OE *dēad* 'dead'). OE *ĕo* is often written *ie, ye io* beside *e*, in South-Eastern, as in *hierte* (OE *heorte* 'heart'), *þiode* (OE

þēod 'people'), *þyef* (OE *þēof*) 'thief'). It is not certain what
sounds these spellings represent; they may represent rising
diphthongs, but *ie* is used elsewhere as a spelling for [eː], and it
is possible that *ye* is so used in Kentish.

4. Initial voiceless fricative consonants are often voiced in
South-Eastern and South-Western. Thus we find SE *zenne*
(OE *synn* 'sin'), *vlesshe* (OE *flæsc* 'flesh').

5. OE *h* disappeared initially before *l* in most Middle English
dialects, but in Kentish we often find *lh-* as the development of
OE *hl-*, as in *lhord* (OE *hlāford* 'lord'). The spelling *lh* may
represent voiceless *l*.

6. The most noticeable feature of the dialect of Essex is the
development of OE *æ*[1] and *æ*[2] to *ā* from the beginning of the
thirteenth century. Thus we find *strāte* (OE *stræt* 'street'),
clāne (OE *clæne* 'clean').

7. In South-Eastern texts *ō* is often spelt *uo*.

SOUTH-WESTERN

This group is descended from the West Saxon dialect of Old
English. That dialect was by far the most important of the
Old English dialects, if we measure importance by the extent
to which it was used in texts that have been preserved, and the
South-Western dialects are represented by several texts in early
Middle English, but in the course of the Middle English period
distinctive South-Western features were replaced by those of
Midland dialects. Not many features are peculiar to the South-
Western dialects; some are shared by South-Eastern and some
are shared by South-West Midland.

Among the best-known South-Western texts are the *Poema
Morale* or *Moral Ode*, belonging to the beginning of the thirteenth
century, and *The Proverbs of Alfred* and *The Owl and the
Nightingale*, belonging to the middle of that century.

The chief features of the South-Western dialects are:

1. As in the West Midlands, OE $\acute{y}$ remained as a front close rounded vowel, generally spelt *u*.

2. We have seen that in Old English the diphthong *īe* was characteristic of West Saxon. In late West Saxon this *īe* was monophthongized to $\acute{y}$ or, in some texts, to *ī*. In Middle English the sound [y] remained unchanged but, like OE $\acute{y}$ of other origins, as a result of French influence it was spelt *u*; when long it was also spelt *ui* or *uy*. These forms are characteristically South-Western, since other dialects were descended from Old English dialects in which *īe* did not normally occur. Examples are *hurde* (WS *hierde*, Ang *hiorde, heorde* 'shepherd'), *huiren* (WS *hīeran*, Ang *hēran* 'to hear'). In late Middle English the South-Western forms are replaced by forms with *e*.

3. As in South-Eastern dialects, OE *æ* becomes *e* in early Middle English texts.

4. As in South-Eastern dialects, initial *f* and *s* are often voiced to *v* and *z*.

5. In general the Southern dialects are the most conservative of Middle English dialects. We find, for example, that the Old English prefix *ge-* is preserved as *y-* longer than in the Midlands.

6. In strong verbs there is a tendency in the South-West and the southern part of the West Midlands for the vowel of the preterite plural or the past participle to spread by analogy to the preterite singular. This is to be contrasted with the practice in Northern dialects, where analogy operates in the other direction. South-Western forms are *gun* 'began' (OE *-gann* sg. *-gunnon* pl.), *bounde* 'bound' (OE *band* sg. *bundon* pl.).

7. As in South-Eastern dialects, the 3rd person singular and all persons of the plural of the present indicative of verbs end in *-eth*, and, in early Middle English, the present participle ends in *-inde*. In the course of the Middle English period the Southern plural ending *-eth* was gradually replaced by the Midland *-e(n)*, and the participial ending *-inde* gave way to *-ing*.

SPECIMENS OF MIDDLE ENGLISH DIALECTS

The numbers in brackets in the comments which follow these illustrative extracts refer to the dialectal features enumerated in the paragraphs dealing with the corresponding dialects on pp. 61 to 72.

NORTHERN

As a specimen of a Northern Middle English dialect we may take the opening lines of *Cursor Mundi* as they appear in the British Museum MS. Cotton Vespasian A.iii, belonging to the first half of the fourteenth century.

> Man yhernes rimes for to here,
> And romans red on maneres sere,
> Of Alisaundur þe conquerour;
> Of Iuly Cesar þe emparour;
> O Grece and Troy the strang strijf,
> þere many thosand lesis þer lijf;
> O Brut þat bern bald of hand,
> þe first conquerour of Ingland;
> O Kyng Arthour þat was so rike,
> Quam non in hys tim was like,
> O ferlys þat hys knythes fel,
> þat aunters sere I here of tell,
> Als Wawan, Cai and oþer stabell,
> For to were þe ronde tabell.

Not all the dialectal forms in this extract are Northern; for example, *non* (OE *nān*) shows the Midland and Southern open *ō* (1), although *a* occurs in *bald*, where *a* had probably been lengthened before *ld*. There are, however, enough Northern forms to enable us to assign the text to the Northern area. The use of *a* before the groups *nd* and *ng* is found in *strang* and *hand* (5). The loss of final *-e* occurs in *red*, *tim*, and *tell* (8). The raising of lightly-stressed *e* to *i* is found in *lesis* (9). The Northern preference for the plosive *k* (10) is seen in *rike* (OE *rīce* or OF *riche*); in the rhyming word *like* the form with *k* has ceased to be dialectal. The strongly aspirated Northern development of OE initial *hw* is seen in *quam* (11). The Northern -*s* ending of the 3rd singular present indicative of verbs (13) is seen in *yhernes*, and the plural verbal ending in -*s* (13) is seen in *lesis*.

As a specimen of Scottish dialect we may take the opening lines of Barbour's *Bruce*:

> Storys to rede ar delitabill,
> Suppos that thai be nocht bot fabill;
> Than suld storys that suthfast wer,
> And thai war said on gud maner,
> Hawe doubill plesance in heryng.
> The fyrst plesance is the carpyng,
> And the tothir the suthfastnes
> That schawys the thing rycht as it wes;
> And suth thyngis that ar likand
> Tyll mannys heryng, ar plesand,
> Tharfor I wald fayne set my will,
> Giff my wyt mycht suffice thartill,
> To put in wryt a suthfast story.

Northern features in this extract include the raising of long close *o* to a sound represented by *u* (6) in *gud*, *suth*, *suthfast* and *suthfastnes*, the present participle in -*and* (13) in *likand* and *plesand*, the initial plosive consonant (10) in *giff*, the lack of diphthongization in *nocht* (7), the use of *s* for OE *sc* in the lightly-stressed *suld* (12), and in vocabulary the forms *tyll* and *thartill*.

EAST MIDLAND

The following extract from *Havelok the Dane* will serve as a specimen of an East Midland dialect:

> Auelok it saw and þider drof,
> And þe barre sone vt-drow,
> þat was unride and gret ynow,
> And caste þe dore open wide
> And seide, 'Her shal Y now abide:

Comes swiþe vn-to me;
Daþeyt hwo you henne fle!'
'No,' quodh on, 'þat shaltou coupe,
And bigan til him to loupe,
In his hond his swerd ut-drawe;
Hauelok he wende þore haue slawe
And with [him] comen oþer two,
þat him wolde of liue haue do.
Hauelok lifte up þe dore-tre,
And at a dint he slow hem þre.

Taken in isolation, the dialectal forms in this extract are characteristic of fairly extensive areas, but, taken together, they enable
us to localize the passage fairly closely. Thus, the development
of OE or ON $ÿ$ as i (3) in *unride* (cf. OE *ungerÿde*), *dint* (OE
dynt) and *lifte* (ON *lypta*) points to the North or East Midlands,
whereas the development of OE $ā$ as open o in *drof* (OE *drāf*),
þore (OE *þār*), *on* (OE *ān*) excludes most of the Northern area.
The imperative plural *comes* and the preposition *til* are Northern
forms, and the only area that satisfies all these conditions is the
North-East Midlands. Confirmation of the conclusion that the
dialect is East Midland rather than West Midland is provided
by the unrounding of OE a/o before nasal consonants to a except
when the nasal belongs to a group like *nd* or *mb*, which causes
lengthening of a preceding vowel (1). We thus have *bigan*
beside *hond*. Further confirmation is provided by the development of $ĕo$ as e (2) in *henne* (OE *heonane*), *fle* (OE *flēon*), *swerd*
(OE *sweord*), *dore-tre* (OE *duru* + *trēo*), and *þre* (OE *þrēo*).

WEST MIDLAND

A specimen of a West Midland dialect is provided by the
opening stanza of a poem about the man in the moon in MS.
Harley 2253.

Mon in þe mone stond ant strit,
On is bot-forke is burþen he bereþ;
Hit is muche wonder þat he nadoun slyt,

For doute leste he valle, he shoddreþ ant shereþ.
When þe forst freseþ, muche chele he byd;
þe þornes beþ kene, is hattren to-tereþ.
Nis no wyþt in þe world þat wot wen he syt,
Ne, bote hit bue þe hegge, whet wedes he wereþ.

The most obvious feature of the dialect of this extract is its close resemblance to South-Western dialects, a resemblance which has to be reconciled with the likelihood that the manuscript was written in Herefordshire. One reason for the South-Western features is that many dialectal features are shared by South-Western and West Midland dialects, but there is another reason: the poem was probably written in a dialect more southerly than that of the manuscript in which it has been preserved. There is evidence for this view in the fact that of the five syncopated verbal forms in the extract (*stond, strit, slyt, byd, syt*), four are fixed by rhyme, and these forms are among the most marked southerly features of the passage (cf. p. 50). Another Southern form is *valle*, with voicing of initial *f*. Forms that might be either West Midland or South-Western are *burþen* (OE *byrþen*) and *muche* (OE *mycel*), with a rounded vowel as the development of OE *y* (1), but *chele* is developed from a non-WS *cele*. Here, as always, it is necessary to remember the date of the manuscript, since West Saxon forms tended to give way to non-West-Saxon in the course of the Middle English period. As the development of OE *ēo* (4) we have a rounded vowel in *bue*, but an unrounded one in *freseþ* and *beþ*. Whereas in the East Midland extract we saw a distinction between the development of *a* before single nasals and before *nd* or *mb*, here we find *o* in both positions (2): *mon* (OE *mann*) beside *stond* (OE *standeþ*). This is a West Midland characteristic.

SOUTH-EASTERN

The following is an extract from the most famous of South-Eastern texts, Michael of Northgate's *Ayenbyte of Inwyt*.

Efterward þer wes a poure man, ase me zayþ, þet hedde ane cou; and yhyerde zigge of his preste ine his preching þet God

zede ine his spelle þet God wolde yelde an hondreduald al þet
me yeaue uor him. Þe guode man, mid þe rede of his wyue,
yeaf his cou to his preste, þet wes riche. Þe prest his nom
bleþeliche, and hise zente to þe oþren þet he hedde, þo hit com
to euen, þe guode mannes cou com hom to his house ase hi wes
ywoned, and ledde mid hare alle þe prestes ken, al to an
hondred.

This extract shows unmistakeable South-Eastern features: the
lowering and unrounding of $\bar{y}$ to $\bar{e}$ (1) in *ken* (OE *cȳ*, pl. of *cū*),
the raising (2) of *æ* to *e* (a South-Eastern characteristic by 1340,
the date of this manuscript) in *efterward, wes, hedde, þet,* the
use of the digraph *ye* in *yhyerde* (3), the voicing of initial voiceless
fricatives (4) in *zayþ, zigge, zede, zente, uor,* the use of the spelling
uo to represent OE $\bar{o}$ in *guode* (7), and the pronominal forms *his*
and *hise,* meaning 'them' (see *OED* sv. HIS, HISE, *pers. pron.*).

SOUTH-WESTERN

The following specimen of a South-Western dialect is from
the Jesus College manuscript of *The Owl and the Nightingale*:

> þe wrenne wes wel wis iholde,
> Vor þeih heo nere i-bred a wolde,
> Heo wes itowen among mankunne,
> & hire wisdom brouhte þenne:
> Heo myhte speke hwar heo wolde,
> To-fore þe kinge þah heo scholde.
> 'Lusteþ,' heo queþ, 'leteþ me speke.
> Hwat! wille ye þis pays to-breke,
> & do þanne kinge such schome?
> Yet nys heo nouþer ded ne lome.
> Hunke schal i-tyde harm & schonde,
> If we doþ gryþbruche on his londe.
> Leteþ beo, & beoþ i-some,
> & fareþ riht to eure dome,
> & leteþ dom þis playd to-breke,
> Al so hit wes erure bi-speke.'

The most clearly marked Western feature, which is shared by
South-Western and West Midland dialects, is the preservation

of a rounded vowel as the development of OE *y* (1) in *mankunne* (OE *manncynn*), *lusteþ* (OE *hlystan*) and *grypbruche* (OE *grip-bryce*). The faulty rhyme of *mankunne* with *penne* is one of several examples which suggest that the poem was originally written in a South-Eastern dialect, since the South-Eastern form *mankenne* would provide a good rhyme. As in the West Midland extract quoted above, OE *a/o* before a nasal generally appears as *o* whether the nasal is single or followed by another consonant, as in *schome* (OE *scamu*), *lome* (OE *lama*), *among* (OE *onmang*), *schonde* (OE *scand*), *londe* (OE *land*). On the other hand *a* is found in *mankunne* and *panne* (OE *pone*). As the development of OE *æ* (3) we have *e* in *wes* (OE *wæs*) and *queþ* (OE *cwæþ*) beside *a* in *hwat* (OE *hwæt*). The form *wes* is found in many dialects, perhaps because of its lack of stress, but *queþ* is a distinctively Southern form. Another mainly Southern feature is the conservatism shown by the preservation of the Old English dual pronoun *hunke* (OE *unc*) (5).

CHAPTER IV

Modern English

THE MODERN ENGLISH period may be said to have begun during the fifteenth century, and one of its characteristics was the rise of Standard English as a medium of spoken and written communication in all parts of the country, although many regional dialects have continued to the present day to exist side by side with Standard English.

The difficulties presented by dialect are of two kinds. The first is the difficulty presented by unfamiliar vocabulary, and it is surprising how much difference a single unknown word can make to the intelligibility of a conversation. The dialect speaker is not always very helpful if asked for an explanation, sometimes because the word which causes the difficulty is so familiar to him that he cannot believe that anyone really needs a gloss, sometimes because it is the only word he knows to describe the object in question, and sometimes, one suspects, because he enjoys the sense of superiority given to him by his knowledge of the meaning of a word which is unknown to his questioner. The following instance is one of many that could be quoted.

In the course of the trial of an action at Worcester Assizes, a witness kept referring to a field full of 'oonty-toomps'. The judge, a townsman, was puzzled by this word and the following exchanges took place:

Judge: 'What are these oonty-toomps you keep mentioning?'

Witness: 'What be oonty-toomps? They be the toomps the oonts make'.

Judge: 'But what are oonts?'

Witness: 'Why, them as makes the toomps'[1].

It should perhaps be added that *oonty-toomps* are molehills.

The second kind of difficulty presented by dialect is the difficulty of identifying words which may be perfectly familiar. The difficulty here is increased by the fact that a word is a logical, not a phonetic, unit, and a hearer who is unfamiliar with a particular dialect often has some difficulty in knowing where one word ends and the next word begins. There is one sentence which is frequently used as an appeal for tobacco. It is pronounced without any pauses between the separate words, and many of those who use it enjoy the difficulty that it causes to strangers. It may be transcribed *Azonyonyeonyonye?* A phonetic transcription makes it slightly easier, though not very much: [æzɒniɒnjəɒniɒnjə]. The correct translation is: 'Have any of you any (tobacco) on you?' Part of the difficulty is that a certain group of sounds may represent one word in a dialect and another quite different word in Standard English. The fault is not only with the village dialects. A clergyman asked the children in a Sunday-school class if they had heard of Moses and received the reply: 'Yes, cats kill 'em'. The analogical plural was the child's contribution to the misunderstanding; the clergyman's contribution was the use of a centralized vowel as the first element of the diphthong [ou], a pronunciation which is becoming increasingly common among speakers who are convinced that they speak Standard English.

VOCABULARY

The wide extent of English dialect vocabulary may be inferred from the existence of 100,000 entries in Joseph Wright's *English Dialect Dictionary*. The outspoken nature of much of this vocabulary can be gathered from the ideas that are most productive of synonyms. There are 1300 ways of telling someone that he is a fool and 1050 words for a slattern. There are 1350 words meaning to give someone a thrashing. It is often possible to divide the different words for the same object into groups.

[1] David Gunston, *Lawnswood Chronicles* (Dent, 1953), p. 121.

For example, among the many different dialectal words for 'newt' it is possible to distinguish one group derived from OE *āðexe*, often with the addition of a suffix, and another derived from OE *efete*. The first group is found especially in the North and West Midlands; the second group is found in the South (see Map 4).

It is natural that men living in the country should draw their vocabulary and imagery from activities with which they are familiar. There are in dialects many words to describe different kinds of sheep and cattle. The horse has had a good deal of influence on dialect vocabulary, not all of it obvious.[1] When Viola in *Twelfth Night* (II, ii, 34) says 'How will this fadge?' she is using a dialect word in a figurative sense. *To fadge* is to ride at the slowest pace at which a horse can trot; Viola uses the word in the sense 'to turn out'. *Meat for work* is a phrase used to describe the practice of allowing a horse to graze in exchange for the work that it does, without payment on either side. Two expressions commonly used in the now fast-disappearing tailors' workshops of the West Riding of Yorkshire are *dead horse* and *live horse*. The first of these refers to a backlog of work left over from the previous day which has to be finished before the day's work is begun; the second describes work done in excess of a day's stint which lightens the burden on the following day. Two words originally applied to an animal which has had too much to eat and therefore refuses its food are *overfaced* and *stalled*. The first of these is often applied to children confronted by too big a meal. The second, which is used in the original sense in the biblical reference to 'a stalled ox' (*Proverbs*, xv, 17), is today used in a wider sense more or less equivalent to the slang *fed up*. The expressions *stalled* and *fed up* are semantically parallel. Both originally referred to excess of food; both have come to be used in a wider sense to describe weariness arising from many different causes.

A few Scottish dialectal words, such as *canny*, *dour*, *pawky* and *bairn*, have passed into Standard English as a result of their

[1] See J. Fairfax-Blakeborough, 'A Note on Equine Terms in Yorkshire', *TYDS*, lix (1959), 21-4.

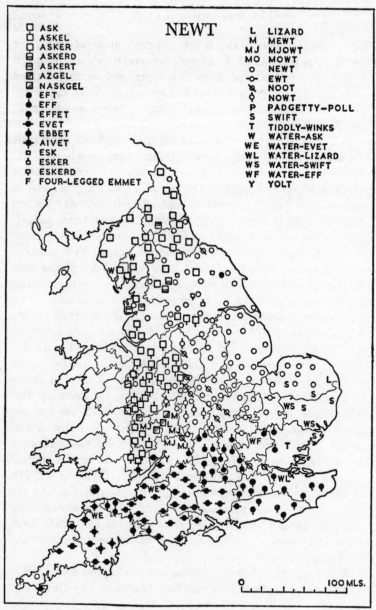

Map 4. Words for 'Newt'

use by educated Scotsmen. Although such words are now recognized as Standard English, they have not lost their north-country associations, and the first three of the examples quoted are generally used to describe Scotsmen.

Modern English dialects owe their preservation to their comparative freedom from outside influences, yet the number of words of foreign origin in English dialects is surprisingly large, even if we exclude loan-words like *tea* and *sugar*, which describe everyday objects and which occur in both dialects and Standard English.

The number of Celtic loan-words in Standard English is very small, but there are some occurring in dialects which are not well-established in the standard language. Two of the oldest loan-words of this kind, which are recorded in Old English, are *brat* 'pinafore' (OE *bratt*) and *bannock* 'cake of oatmeal or barley' (OE *bannuc*). There is often some uncertainty about the history of Celtic loan-words. In order to establish that a word is borrowed from Celtic, it is not enough to show that it occurs in both English and a Celtic language; we have always to allow for the possibilities that the word was borrowed from English into Celtic or that the two words are derived from a common source. We can, however, include among dialect words that are certainly or probably of Celtic origin *airt* (Scottish) 'a direction of the wind', *banshee* (Irish) 'ghost', *boggart* (North and Midlands) 'supernatural monster', *brock* 'badger', *crowd* 'fiddle', *gob* 'mouth' and *tocher* 'dowry'.

The two most prolific sources of loan-words in English dialects are Scandinavian and French. Scandinavian words are naturally most common in the dialects of the Danelaw. One result of Scandinavian influence is the existence in dialects of many words beginning with the group *sc-* or *sk-*. Not all of these words are Scandinavian loan-words, but the presence in dialects of large numbers of Scandinavian words with initial *sc-* has probably led to the use of *sc-* instead of *sh-* in native words. Similarly northern dialects often have [k] where Standard English has [tʃ], and [g] where Standard English has [dʒ], as in *thack* 'thatch, roof', *kirk* 'church', and *brig* 'bridge'. Some of these forms may be Scandinavian loan-words (cf. ON *þak* 'roof', *kirkja* 'church', *bryggja* 'gangway'), but others are probably examples of sound-substitution due in part to Scandinavian influence. In the question *Wheer are ta bahn?* 'Where are you going?' the last word is from the Old Norse past participle *búinn* 'prepared'; the Standard English form, *bound*, is less close to the original in that it has acquired an excrescent *d*, like the noun *sound* (OF *son*). *Drucken*, for *drunken*, is. from the Old Norse past participle *drukkinn*, in which the group *nk* has become *kk* by assimilation. The comparative adjective *war* 'worse' (pronounced with an unrounded vowel) is from ON *verr* adv. or *verri* adj. It is common in dialects and is used in a phrase which shows that dialect is just as capable as Standard English of using oxymoron: *Tha mends war* 'You get worse instead of getting better'. Other Scandinavian loan-words include *addle* 'to earn' (cf. ON *ødlast* 'to acquire property'), *big* 'to build' (ON *byggja*), *birr* 'impetus' (ON *byrr* 'favourable wind'), *dag* 'dew' (ON *dögg*), *intake* 'new enclosure' (*in* + ON *taka* 'to take'), *ettle* 'to intend' (ON *ætla*), *force* 'waterfall' (ON *fors*), *frosk* 'frog' (ON *froskr*), *lake* 'to play' (ON *leika*), *mense* 'good manners, hospitality' (ON *mennska* 'humanity'). The auxiliary verb *mun* 'must' is from ON *munu*. It is unusual for words so common as auxiliary verbs to be borrowed from one language into another, and the borrowing of *mun*, like the borrowing of the pronouns *they* and *them* into Standard English, is evidence of the closeness of the contacts between Scandinavians and English in the Danelaw. *Nowt* 'cattle' (ON *naut*) and *loup* 'to leap' (ON *hlaupa*) are borrowed from Scandinavian words which have cognates in English. ON *au* corresponded to OE *ēa*, and so we have in Standard English *neat* sb. (as in *neatherd*; OE *nēat*) and *leap* (OE *hlēapan*).

There are several French loan-words in English dialects. *Agist* 'to receive cattle to graze' is from Old French *agister* 'to lodge'; the derivative *agistment* is frequently used in advertisements in north-country newspapers. *Bastile* 'workhouse' is from the French prison La Bastille. Its use in the dialect sense has no doubt puzzled many readers of the early chapters of Arnold Bennett's *Clayhanger*. *Ratten* is from Old French *raton* and occurs in Middle English in the account of the 'raton of renon' who suggested belling the cat (*Piers Plowman*, B Text, Prologue v. 157); RSE *rat* is from OE *ræt*. *Mort* 'quantity' is used in such expressions as *It did me a mort o' good*, and is from the Norman dialect of French, where *à mort* means 'to a large extent'. Other examples are *arain* 'spider' (OF *araigne*), *dole* 'sorrow' (OF *dol, duel*), *guiser* 'masquerader' (from Fr. *guise*), *frumenty* (OF *frumentée*), *hogo* 'disagreeable smell' (Fr. *haut goût*), *stravaig* to wander about aimlessly' (OF *estravaguer*), and *dis(h)abil* 'disorder, working dress' (Fr. *déshabillé*), used in the phrase *in my disabils*. The influence of French on Lowland Scots has often been mentioned. The number of French loan-words that are especially common in Scotland includes *ashet* 'dish' (Fr. *assiette*), *gigot* 'leg of mutton' (Fr. *gigot*), *fash* 'to trouble' (usually reflexive; Fr. *fâcher*), *vivers* 'food' (Fr. *vivres*). In *Rob Roy* (Ch. 5) Scott uses the word *jeistiecor* 'jacket', and adds a footnote suggesting that it may be from the French *justaucorps*.

In Standard English there are many doublets, or pairs of words, usually loan-words, which can be traced back to a common source but which have diverged in form, and sometimes in meaning, as a result of having been borrowed at different times or from different dialects. There are several such pairs of words one of which is dialectal and the other Standard English. Examples are *aunter* (AN *aventure*) beside *adventure*, Scots *descrive* (OF *descrivre*) beside *describe*, and *kiver* (from OF *cuev-*, the stressed stem-form of OF *covrir*) beside *cover*. *Liver* for *deliver* is from Fr *livrer* beside *delivrer*. *Noy* for *annoy* is an aphetic form which was common in Middle English. *Causey* 'pavement' is from AN *caucé* beside Central French *chausée*; RSE *causeway* is a blend of *causey* and *way*. French *rendezvous* has given rise to two words in English dialects: *rumsey-voosey* (Wilts) 'to make a date', and *randyvoo* (Dev, Cor) 'uproar'. A few dialect words are of surprisingly learned origin. For example, the Greek loan-word *nous* 'good sense' is in general dialect use.

There are some Latin loan-words that were borrowed into English so early that they have had time to become assimilated into the language and are not thought of as being of learned origin. Such are *sicker* 'safe' (OE *sicor*, from Latin *securus*) and *taffel* (Sc) 'a small table' (OE *tæfl* 'chessboard', from Latin *tabula*). Some have obviously been corrupted, like *oilins-boilins* (Cumb) 'whether you want to or not' (Latin *nolens volens*), *momenty-morries* (Nb) 'skeletons' (Latin *memento mori*), and *non-plush* 'dilemma, surprise' (Latin *non plus*). The north-country *nominy* is from the invocation used by a preacher before the sermon: *In nomine Patris*, etc. It has two meanings: a folk rhyme and a wordy, tiresome speech. *Jommetry* (Glos) means 'magic'; *all of a jommetry* means 'in pieces or tatters'. *Lattiprack* (Wilts) 'paralytic' shows the same kind of distortion of sounds that we find in the slang *trick cyclist* for *psychiatrist*.

One aspect of dialect vocabulary which has recently been surveyed[1] is the language of schoolchildren. Some words used in children's games are surprisingly widespread; others are confined to a very small area. There are more than sixty names in use in different parts of the country to describe the practice of knocking at doors and running away. They include such fascinating and mysterious terms as *knocking down ginger*, *chicky-doory*, *bing bang skoosh*, *black and white rabbit*, *chickie mellie*, *nanny*, *napper*, and *rosy apple*. There is an interesting contrast between the uniformity of the practice and the variety of the names used to describe it.

There is very wide variety in the ways of demanding a truce, and the various ways illustrate several different aspects of language. Gesture language is used, for the usual way in which a child indicates that he wants to drop out of a game is by crossing the first and second fingers of one hand. There is also class dialect, since *pax* is used especially in private schools. There are, besides, innumerable regional variants, of which perhaps the most widespread is *barley*. The importance in dialect research of consulting more than one informant from each place is illustrated by the fact that several quite different truce terms are often current in the same school and it is not

---

[1] By Iona and Peter Opie in *The Lore and Language of Schoolchildren* (OUP, 1959), from which book most of the examples quoted here are taken.

always easy to say which word is the prevailing one. For example, the children at Kirkcaldy High School produced the following terms: *barleys, barrels, bees, tibs, tubs, dubs, dubbies, thumbs, checks, peas, pearls,* and *parleys*.[1]

Schoolchildren are fond of replacing words by other words or phrases which somewhat resemble them in sound. A very familiar example of this sort of distortion is Lewis Carroll's 'Drawling, Stretching and Fainting in Coils' (*Alice's Adventures in Wonderland*, Ch. 9). Children will say *eggs, ham and bacon* for *examination* and *stiff cat* for *certificate*. Such forms are not as a rule regional, but they have a parallel in such dialectal pronunciations as *viadock* for *viaduct*. This distortion of words is not quite the same thing as popular etymology, since the speakers probably feel that the resemblances are merely accidental.

Dialect is rich not only in expressive single words but also in pungent phrases. For example, *He thinks 'at we're hung up at t'back o't'door* is an expressive way of describing anyone who assumes that the person that he wants is always at his disposal. Other expressive phrases are *Fain would be but can't*, used to describe someone who tries to appear better than he is, *a lick and a promise* 'a hasty wash or any work done perfunctorily' *to cut smoke with a leather hatchet* 'to attempt the impossible', and *words cost nowt, but they dooan't want wasting for all that.* Sometimes the meaning of a phrase is clear from the context in which it occurs, but it is not always clear how the meaning arose. For example, a common phrase used in the West Riding of Yorkshire to describe someone who tells a story with too much circumstantial detail is *He tells you t'tale from t'thread to t'needle.* A frequent form of humour appears in comparisons. Some of these are concise; some are of the more circumstantial kind that we generally associate with Sam Weller. To the first class belong such comparisons as *as busy as a cat in a tripe-shop.* The longer similes are generally allusive, and there are degrees of initiation in the understanding of such

---

[1] Opie, *op. cit.*, p. 143.

phrases. To the fully initiated it is enough to say *Th'art same as Mark Dawson's dog*. The less fully initiated need the amplification *Tha thowt a lie*, i.e., 'You were mistaken'. The mistake made by Mark Dawson's dog was that it thought that its master was bringing it its dinner when he was really coming to have it destroyed. The grim note is one that often recurs in dialect phrases. Another such phrase is *As lazy as Ludlam's dog*, with the amplification added when necessary *'at leeaned 'is 'eead agen t'wall to bark*. Another comparison is *Th'art same as Silly Sidney*. If the person addressed seems puzzled, the speaker may vouchsafe the explanation *allus uneim*. The word *uneim* (OE *un-* + *efen* 'even') means 'not evenly balanced', and the allusion is to a tramp with a robust appetite and an undeserved reputation for stupidity. When given a meal consisting of meat and vegetables, he would first eat the meat in order to ask for more to go with his vegetables; he would then eat the vegetables and point out that he was 'uneim' because he still had some meat left. This could go on for a long time.

Dialect speakers often show a fondness for alliteration and rhyme, and the choice of a particular word often seems to be determined by neighbouring words. *Christian* is used in dialects to describe a human being, as distinct from an animal, but its use in the expression *careful Christian* probably owes something to the attractions of alliteration. Other alliterative phrases in use in dialects include *to glunch and gloom* 'to look sulky, grumble', *to tug and tew* 'to work hard', *to meddle or make* 'to interfere', *I've neither brass nor benediction* 'I am completely destitute', *it neither means nor matters* 'that is neither here nor there', and the form of farewell, *I'll love you and leave you*. As examples of rhyme there are *to swap and cop* 'to give and take' and *to toil and moil* 'to work hard', an expression in such widespread use that it may perhaps be regarded as Standard English.

There are in the dialects many euphemistic phrases to describe half-wittedness, such as *to have a slate loose, nobbut ninepence to't shilling*, and *a bit of a toby-trot*. On the other hand there are phrases used to denote shrewdness, like *He's got all his chairs at home*.

Some dialect phrases show a fondness for grim imagery. *To marry t'midden for t'muck* means to marry for money. *My belly thinks my throit's cut* means 'I'm hungry'. They are often concise and semi-proverbial scraps of homely wisdom or scathing comment, such as *Them as 'as gets, It's easy to bury other folks' bairns,* and *He talks and says nowt.*

One proverb that is not thought of as dialectal is the result of the misunderstanding of a dialect word. The proverb *Don't spoil the ship for a ha'porth of tar* is recorded as early as 1636 in the form: 'Hee that will loose a sheepe (or a hogge) for a penny-worth of tarre cannot deserve the name of a good husband'. Here *hogge* is used to denote a kind of sheep and *husband* means 'husbandman'. The modern proverb is due to a misunderstanding of the dialect form *ship* 'sheep' followed by the alteration of *lose* to *spoil* in an attempt to make sense of the proverb. Tar was used for marking the initials of the owner on the sheep's back.

Many everyday words are used in dialects in senses different from those current in Standard English. Words like *soft* and *simple* can be used in Standard English without pejorative implications, but in northern dialects they suggest feeble-mindedness. *Cake* in Yorkshire is often used in the sense 'bread' and conversely *bread* is sometimes used for *cake,* as in *Christmas bread;* in the same county *spice* is the word commonly used by children for 'sweets'. A *pig* or *piggy* is used in Scotland and Northumberland as a term for a hot-water bottle. A traveller is said to have reported with horror that in northern England people slept with pigs for warmth. Another traveller, unfamiliar with the north-country use of *maiden* in the sense 'clothes-horse', was startled when he saw an advertisement *Maiden For Sale. Clever* often means 'in good health, active' and *comical* means 'unwell, out of sorts'. *Funny* means 'awkward, liable to make unnecessary difficulties', whereas *false* or *fause* does not always imply blame; it often means 'shrewd, clever, precocious', and an animal may be described admiringly as being 'as fause as a Christian'. *Suited* often means 'pleased' or 'pleased with oneself'. In Standard English *frightful* means 'liable to cause fright in others', but in dialects it has the equally logical meaning 'timid'. *Sad* means 'solid, firm' and is applied to bread that has failed to rise properly. Among verbs mention may be made of *to call* meaning 'to scold' and *to own* meaning 'to recognize'.

Sometimes the difference in meaning is the result of the preservation of an older meaning in dialect. The adjective *quick* once meant 'alive' (OE *cwic*) and it has this sense in the Authorized Version of the Bible and in the Book of Common Prayer. This sense is preserved in the dialectal variant *wick* and in the compound word *quickset*; a quickset hedge is a living one as contrasted with a dead fence. Similarly *proper* has in dialects the meaning 'handsome', a sense which it had in Shakespeare: 'as proper a man as ever went on four legs' (*The Tempest*, II, ii, 66). The dialectal sense of *admire* 'to wonder at, notice with astonishment' is very similar to that of the Latin word from which the word is derived. Another example is *anatomy* 'a skeleton, a very thin person'; the word is used in this sense by Shakespeare in 'They brought one Pinch, a hungry lean-faced villain, a mere anatomy' (*Comedy of Errors*, V, i, 238). *Meat* is used in dialects, like the OE *mete* from which it is derived, in a wider sense than in Standard English. The dialectal sense is 'food of any kind', whereas in Standard English the meaning has been restricted to the flesh of animals. As often, the older sense is preserved in a proverb, *One man's meat is another man's poison*, and in a compound noun *sweetmeat*. Other examples of proverbs preserving older senses which are found too in dialects are the use of *tide* (OE *tīd* 'time') in *Time and tide wait for no man*, and of *speed* (OE *spēd* 'success') in *More haste, less speed*. The biblical use of *tell* in the sense of 'count' in 'Our years pass away as a tale that is told' is sometimes misunderstood by speakers of Standard English, but this use of *tell* survives in dialects; the older sense is preserved in Standard English in set phrases, such as *to tell one's beads*. The use of *learn* in the sense of 'teach' may be due in part to confusion between Old English *lǣran* 'to teach' and *leornian* 'to learn'. The sense 'teach' is common in Middle English and is common today in dialects.

90

In dialects the word has acquired an ironical use, with the result that *I'll larn him* does not mean the same as *I'll teach him*, and the word can be added to the large number of examples of the power of dialect to express a shade of meaning which cannot be expressed in Standard English. In dialects, as in Early English, *painful* has the meaning 'painstaking, active'; a speaker of dialect would not misunderstand the inscription on a seventeenth-century memorial brass which begins 'The body of Henry Rogers, a painful preacher in this church two and thirty years'.

The word *while* was originally a noun meaning 'time', as in the expression 'worth one's while'. In Shakespeare it means 'until', as when Macbeth says 'we will keep ourself Till supper-time alone: while then, God be with you' (*Macbeth*, III, i, 42 f.). This meaning is still very common in northern dialects but not in Standard English. A northern schoolmaster, teaching in the South of England, was puzzled by the amusement of his class when he said 'You'll never make any progress while you listen to me'.

Some dialect words are common in literature but are not in colloquial use in Standard English. Thus, a blackbird is known as a *merle* or an *ousel*. *Mead* is commonly used for a field or a meadow. A *cabal* is 'a group of people' or 'noise'. The verb *to rue* is generally thought of as a literary word but it is common in dialects. The word *fain* 'glad' is now an archaism even in literature, but it is commonly used in dialects, as in *fain to be wick* 'glad to be alive' and the pleonastic *I'm fain and glad*. *Cower*, when used as a literary word, has pejorative associations suggesting cowardice, and perhaps the meaning of the word has been influenced by the similarity in sound to *coward*, but *cower* is commonly used in dialects without these associations. A child may be told *to cahr quiet*, i.e. 'to remain quiet'. Sometimes a dialectal word is familiar to readers with no knowledge of dialect from a particular literary occurrence, as, for example, *point-vice* 'exact, perfect', which recalls Malvolio's 'I will be point-devise the very man' (*Twelfth Night*, II, v, 167).

Dialect words have a range of meanings as wide as those of most words in Standard English. The word *suant*, from Old

91

French *suant*, present participle of *sivre* 'to follow', is a common dialect word. *EDD* records many examples, all of them from Southern and South-Western counties; the word is found also in the North, and it may be the origin of WRYks *sooin* (an adjective identical in pronunciation with the adverb *soon*). The meanings recorded in *EDD* are:

> Smooth, even, regular; all alike or of one piece; sharp (of an edge); (of rain) gentle, continuous; pleasant, agreeable, pliable, equable, kindly, especially in looks; (of a voice) well-modulated; grave, meek, demure; 'proper', sly; smoothly, easily, without friction; evenly, regularly; also used figuratively.

The sense in which the word is used in Yorkshire adds another to the wide variety of meanings recorded in *EDD*; it is (applied to a face) 'with an indeterminate expression as of a child who has not made up his mind whether to laugh or cry'.

We have seen that certain objects and concepts are remarkably productive of synonyms to describe them. On the other hand, there are some everyday Standard English words which do not normally occur in certain dialects. For example, in many dialects such words as *boy* and *girl*, *yes* and *no* are hardly ever used; they are replaced by *lad* and *lass* (or, in some dialects, *maid* or *wench*), *aye* and *nay*. The word *son* has passed out of use in many dialects, being replaced by *lad*. This disappearance is sometimes said to be due to a clash with the homophone *sun*. Such a clash may have helped to bring about the obsolescence of the word, but it is clear that common words can pass out of use in dialects without any such assistance.

PRONUNCIATION

The phonology of the Modern English dialects is an extremely complicated subject, but one that is very important for the scientific study of dialect. Since sounds are less easily borrowed from one dialect into another than words, phonology forms the most useful basis for the demarcation of the boundaries of the various dialects. Much new information about the phonology of dialects is to be expected after the completion of the detailed investigations now in progress at the Universities of Leeds and Edinburgh. Phonology does not lend itself to summary treatment, and all that is practicable here is a brief mention of some of the sound-changes which have taken place in the modern dialects, especially those which are characteristics of the major regions.

In Scots, *a* before a nasal has become a sound intermediate between *a* and *o*, usually spelt *o*, as in *con, mon*. Most Scottish speakers make a distinction in pronunciation between initial *wh* (from OE *hw*) and *w*, and in some Scottish dialects the *h* in OE *hw* has remained as a velar fricative [x]. In some North-Eastern Scottish dialects the group *hw-* has become [f] in such words as *what, wheel*, and *which*. Other changes that are often found reflected in Scottish speech are the disappearance of *l* after a back vowel in such words as *all* and *full* and the pronunciation of *r* as a trilled consonant in all positions, whereas in Standard English it has generally become a fricative or a single-tap consonant before vowels and has disappeared before consonants.

Perhaps the most noticeable feature of Northern English is the use of a short vowel [æ] before voiceless fricatives in words like *laugh, fast* and *path*, where Standard English has a long vowel [ɑː]. In Standard English [u] has been centralized and lowered to [ʌ] except sometimes in the neighbourhood of certain consonants such as labials and *l*, but many Northern speakers fail to make any distinction between the vowel of *run* and that of *pull*. Many dialects have [u] in both words, while some have [ʌ]. The use of [ʌ] in words like *pull, cushion* and *butcher* may sometimes be the result of an unskilful attempt to avoid the well-known Northern pronunciation of [u] in words like *run* and *mutton*. A short vowel is often used in the North before *nd* in words like *find* and *pound*, where Standard English has diphthongs descended from Middle English long vowels. Long vowels are not diphthongized so readily in the North as in Standard English and words like *go* and *home* often have [oː] in the North whereas in the South they are pronounced with various diphthongs of which [u] is the second element.

93

In some Midland dialects ME *a* or *o* has become [u] or [ʌ] before *ng*. This pronunciation has been taken over from these dialects into Standard English in such words as *among*, *mongrel* and *ironmonger*. OE *o*, when lengthened in open syllables, and *ā* have fallen together in Standard English, as in *throat* and *stone*, but in some North Midland dialects they are kept apart; for example, in one dialect of this region these two words are pronounced [ərɔit] and [stuən]. Similarly in some North Midland dialects OE *e*, when lengthened in open syllables, *ǣ*[1] (from WGmc *ā* by fronting) and *ǣ*[2] (from earlier OE *ā* by *i*-mutation) are kept apart, whereas in Standard English they have fallen together. Examples are *steal* (OE *stelan*), *sleep* (OE *slǣpan*) and *heal* (OE *hǣlan*). A common North-West Midland characteristic, found especially in South Lancashire and Sheffield, is the use of [ŋg] in words which in Standard English have [ŋ] (see Map 5). Speakers of these dialects often give to both *ng*'s in *singing* the [ŋg] pronunciation found in RSE *finger*. South Midland changes include the development of the initial group *shr-* to *sr-*, as in *srimp* and *srub*.

In South-Eastern dialects initial *th* has sometimes become *d* before *r* as in *dri* 'three'. Another South-Eastern change is that of initial and medial *v* to *w*.

In South-Western dialects initial *f* and *s* are often voiced, and a few words with the voiced initial consonant, such as *vat* (OE *fæt*) and *vixen* (OE *fyxen*), have passed into Standard English. This voicing represents the preservation of a Middle English change, which has normally affected only native English words, because it took place before the influx of French loan-words in Middle English. Another change common in this region is the development of *d* between such phonetically closely related consonants as *l-r*, *r-l*, and *n-r*. Thus we find *parlder* 'parlour' and *carnder* 'corner'.

The most easily recognizable features of Cockney pronunciation are in the development of long vowels (which have become diphthongs) and diphthongs (which have become long vowels). Even in Standard English, long vowels are often slightly diphthongized; in Cockney the diphthongs become wider, that

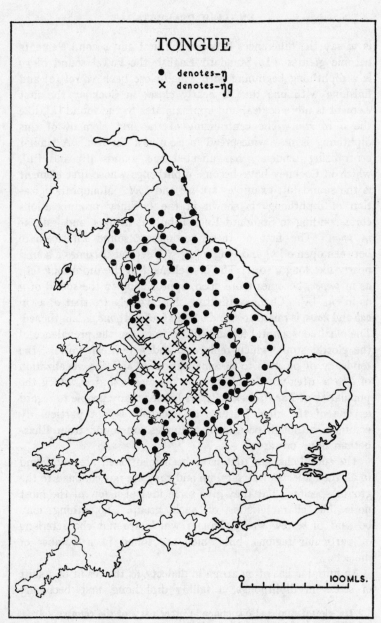

Map 5.   Pronunciation of *tongue*

is to say the differences between the first and second elements become greater. In Standard English the vowel sound of *go* is a diphthong beginning with a half-close back vowel [o] and finishing with one that is nearly close; in Cockney the first element is more central and approximates to the sound [ʌ], like the *u* in *run*. The centralizing of the first element of this diphthong is now widespread in Southern English. A similar centralizing tendency has affected the sounds [iː] and [uː], which in Cockney have become diphthongs whose first element is the sound [ə]; examples are *see* and *boot*. Monophthongization of diphthongs is shown in the Cockney pronunciations corresponding to Standard English [ai], as in *time*, and [au], as in *town*. The first of these becomes a sound intermediate between open *o* [ɔː] and long *a* [ɑː]; the second becomes a sound nearly like long *a* [ɑː]. The first element of the diphthong [ei], as in *paper*, becomes more open, approaching to the sound of *u* as in *run* [ʌ]. Changes affecting short vowels are that *a*, as in *cab* and *have*, is raised to *e*, and *o*, as in *God* and *gone*, is lengthened. The chief consonantal features of Cockney are the prevalence of the glottal stop[1], which replaces *t* and *k* between vowels, the tendency of plosives to become affricates, and the vocalization of *l* to *u* after vowels. Confusion between *v* and *w*, which the popularity of *The Pickwick Papers* has led many people to regard as one of the chief features of Cockney, is not particularly common, although occasional examples are found from Elizabethan times onwards.

The sound-changes that have been mentioned are not found in all the dialects of each group and they are not confined to the groups specified, but they give some idea of a few of the most noticeable characteristics of each group. Something may be said of a few sound-changes which are not characteristic of particular regions, but which are found in a number of dialects.

An initial *w* has often arisen in dialects, as the result of a shift of stress in diphthongs, a falling diphthong first becoming

---

[1] The glottal stop is also common in other parts of the country. It is, for example, frequently heard in Leeds.

rising and the lightly-stressed first element then becoming consonantal. Examples are *wold* 'old' and, after the loss of initial *h*, *wom* 'home' and *wot* 'hot'. This sound-change accounts for the pronunciation of RSE *one* (OE *ān*) and *once* (OE *ānes*) and the spelling of *whole* (OE *hāl*). Similar shift of stress has led to the development of initial [j] when the first element of a diphthong was pronounced in the front of the mouth. This development is common in those northern dialects in which OE *ā* was not rounded to [ɔ:]. In these dialects we find *yam* 'home' (OE *hām*) and *yan* 'one' (OE *ān*).

Initial *w* has disappeared in some dialects, as in *ooman* (for *woman*), and medial *w* has generally disappeared in the lightly-stressed second element of a compound word, as in *awkward, pennyworth, always,* and *somewhat.*

Initial *h* has disappeared in many English dialects, though words beginning with a vowel or *h* are often pronounced with initial *h* if they are emphatic. For example, in Northumberland the pronoun *it* (OE *hit*) is regularly pronounced *hit* in stressed positions.

Fricative consonants, whether voiced or voiceless, are often confused with each other, though the distinction between voiced and voiceless consonants is generally preserved. The pronunciation [wiv] for *with* is especially common in Cockney, but it is not confined to that dialect. In Northern dialects [ərə] is often used for *from.*

The assimilation of consonants is carried further than in Standard English. The place-name *Bradford* is often pronounced with a *t* in place of the first *d* because the *d* is followed by the voiceless consonant *f*. A *k* or *g* is often partially assimilated to a following *l*, with the result that we get [dlæd] for *glad* and [tlɔis] for *close.*

In many dialects the velar nasal consonant [ŋ], occurring finally in lightly-stressed syllables, has become the alveolar nasal [n], as in *evening, sending.* This sound-change is sometimes inaccurately described as 'dropping the *g.*'

The use of an intrusive *r* when a word ending with a vowel is immediately followed by a word beginning with a vowel is a characteristic of the speech of many people who would claim to speak Standard English, but it is especially common in South Midland dialects. In some dialects other consonants are used as glide-sounds before vowels. Orton records[1] that in Byers Green *v* and *n* are used in this way in such words as [frəv] beside [frən] 'from', and [tiv], [təv] beside [tin] 'to'.

A few Standard English words have acquired an intrusive *n*. Examples are *messenger* (Fr *messager*), *passenger* (Fr *passager*) and *nightingale* (OE *nihtegale*). Such an intrusive nasal occurs in dialects in other words, such as *solintary* and *skellington*. Other sound-changes affecting consonants include metathesis, as in *singify*, and the substitution of one liquid or nasal consonant for another, as in *chimbly* for *chimney*, *synnable* for *syllable* and *turmit* for *turnip*. *Hantle* for *handful* shows syncope of a lightly-stressed vowel and the subsequent loss of *f* in a heavy consonant group.

Dialectal pronunciations are often the result of a difference of stress. Many northerners, without going so far as to shift the stress, give secondary stress to the first syllables of words like *confuse* and *condemn* and to the second syllables of words like *statement* and *industry*. The result is that in the North the vowels in these syllables are often pronounced as they are spelt instead of being reduced to [ə], as in Standard English. In some dialects there is a shift of stress in polysyllabic words, and this shift generally affects the pronunciation of the vowels of the word. Thus for *interesting* we often find [intə'restiŋ] and for *advertisement* we sometimes find [ædvə'taizmɛnt].

Sometimes the difference between the dialect and the standard word may be traced back to a variation in Old English resulting in the development of two distinct types, one of which has been preserved in the literary language and the other in dialects. For example, the dialectal verb *ax*, a variant of *ask*, is from OE *ācsian*, a metathesised form of *āscian*. Similarly *wopse* goes back to OE *wæps*, while RSE *wasp* is from OE *wæsp*.

[1] Harold Orton, *The Phonology of a South Durham Dialect* (Kegan Paul, 1933), §120.

MORPHOLOGY

In word-formation the most notable characteristic of English dialects is the readiness to form compound and derivative words. Dialect speakers have not lost the art of coining vivid compound words from native elements. A *has-been* is a person or thing past its prime, and *Good owd 'as-been!* is a common expression of ironical approval, not confined in its application to the elderly. A *never-sweat* is a lazy fellow and a *rip-stitch* is a romping child. Some forceful adjectives have been formed by adding familiar suffixes to ordinary English words: the components of the word thus formed are Standard English but the compound is dialectal. Examples are *dateless* 'stupid', literally 'unconscious of time', *deedy* 'active, industrious', *easyful* 'easy-going', *sidation* 'large quantity', *muckment* 'slattern', and *hangment*, used as an oath, as in *What the hangment are you doing?* In dialects, as in Standard English, a change of suffix can cause a change of meaning. Thus, *yonderly* means 'absent-minded', whereas *yonderish* has a pejorative sense 'proud'. We also find in dialects words with suffixes different from those occurring in Standard English where the difference of suffix has not led to any significant difference of meaning. Examples are *abundation* for *abundance*, *prosperation* for *prosperity*, *timeous* (Sc, Ir) for *timely*, *timmersome* for *timorous*. Similarly the prefix *un-* is used in dialects in many words which in Standard English have the prefixes *im-* or *in-*. Examples are *unpossible*, *undecent*, *unregular*, *unperfect*. Some of these forms with *un-* were once found in Standard English and some of them express ideas which in Standard English are expressed by loan-words. Thus we find *uncome* 'not arrived', *unfriend* 'enemy', and *unfain* 'reluctant'.

Dialects have often preserved simpler forms of words which in Standard English have acquired a new suffix to replace or reinforce one which has disappeared as a result of the weakening of vowels of lightly-stressed syllables or which has been felt to be insufficiently distinctive. Thus dialectal *bread* 'breadth' is the regular development of OE *brædu*; RSE *breadth* has its *th* on the analogy of such abstract nouns as *length*. The Scottish and Irish *red(d)* 'ready' is from OE *geræde*; RSE *ready* shows the addition of the common suffix *-y*, from OE *-ig*. The dialectal adjective *slipper* 'slippery' is from OE *slipor*; RSE *slippery* has the same *-y* suffix that is found in *ready*. RSE *linen* is in origin an adjective meaning 'made of flax', formed from OE *līn* by the addition of the adjectival suffix *-en*. The word without the suffix is preserved in dialectal *lin* and in the first element of RSE *linseed*.

Even in Standard English unfamiliar words are liable to undergo corruption, but corruption is even more likely to take place in dialects, which are more free from such restraining influences as education and the written language; for example, *breakfast* becomes *bracksus*, *brecksus* and *breckwist*. Sometimes corruption is encouraged by popular etymology, with the result that *asparagus* becomes *sparrow-grass*, *rheumatic* becomes *screwmatic*, and *weekdays* become *wicked days* with an implied contrast with *Sunday*, the holy day. There are also blend-words, such as *champeron* (from Fr *champignon* and *mousseron*, which has given RSE *mushroom*), *thribble* (from *treble* and *three*), *boldrumptious* (from *bold*, *rumpus* and *presumptuous*) and *illify* (from *ill* and *vilify*). There are some dialect words, of obscure etymology, which may well be blend-words although it is not always easy to see from what words they are blended. Some of them may be regarded as being at once blend-words, corruptions and exuberant coinages. Words of this kind are always liable to be called onomatopœic, but they are not genuinely so. What these words have in common with onomatopœic words is that their meaning can often be guessed when they are heard for the first time. The difference is that onomatopœic words echo natural sounds whereas blend-words echo other words. Examples are *tranklament* 'small ornament', *catawamptious* 'bumptious', *absquatulate!* 'Get out!', *confloption* 'flurry, confusion', *fantigue* 'fussy excitement, causeless bad temper'. There is probably a good deal of sound-symbolism in dialect words, the details of which are not always clear. For example, there are in the *Concise Oxford Dictionary* only four words, apart from derivatives, beginning with *dw-*, but in *EDD* there are thirty-two, most of them indicating feebleness.

The change known as aphesis, or the disappearance of an initial lightly-stressed syllable, has affected a number of Standard English words, such as *squire* (from *esquire*) and *sport* (from *disport*), but in dialects the number of words affected is larger. Thus we find *cos* 'because', *casion* 'occasion', and *tice* 'entice'.

A number of Standard English words have gained or lost an initial *n* by the process known as metanalysis or misdivision. The final *n* of a preceding indefinite article or possessive adjective has sometimes been added to a word beginning with a vowel, and conversely a word beginning with *n* has sometimes lost that *n* as the result of a mistaken belief that it formed part of a preceding word. Examples are *newt* (OE *efete*), *apron* (OF *naperon*), and *adder* (OE *nædre*). In dialects the older form without metanalysis is sometimes preserved, as in *evet, napron* and *nadder*. On the other hand, dialects sometimes show examples of metanalysis which do not occur in present-day Standard English, such as *nurchin* 'hedgehog', *naunt* 'aunt', *nuncle* 'uncle', *neam* 'uncle' (OE *ēam*), and *nangnail* 'agnail' (OE *angnægl*). The dialectal form sometimes occurs in Elizabethan English, as, for example in the Fool's use of *nuncle* in addressing King Lear (I, iv, 114).

When we turn to accidence we find in dialects many survivals of Old English forms which in Standard English have been replaced by the operation of analogy. *Yat* 'gate' is from OE sg. *geat*; *gate* is from the plural *gatu*; the common dialect word *gate* 'road' is from Scandinavian. *Late* is often pronounced with a short *a* in dialects. This form is the regular development of OE *læt* adj.; RSE *late* is from inflected forms of the adjective or from OE *late* adv. *Clee*, a dialectal form of *claw*, is from OE *clēa* nom. sg.; *claw* is from oblique cases, such as the acc. gen. and dat. sg. *clawe*. Many Old English verbs were derived from nouns or adjectives by the addition of a suffix containing *j*, which modified the stem-vowel and afterwards disappeared. Thus we have in Old English the adjective *cōl* 'cool' and the related verb *cēlan* 'to cool'; similarly we find the noun *camb* 'comb' and the related verb *cemban* 'to comb', which has given rise to the MnE adjective *unkempt*. In Standard English the

verb has generally been re-formed by analogy to make it identical
in form with the noun or adjective but in dialects the old form
of the verb is preserved, with the result that we have the verbs
to keel and *to kemb*. Similarly the dialectal verb *mean* 'to moan'
is from OE *mǣnan* v., whereas RSE *moan* v. is a new formation
from the noun. In nearly all dialects there is a distinction in
form between *work* v. and *work* sb. There was a similar distinction in Old English (*weorc* sb., *wyrcan* v.), but in Standard English
the two forms have fallen together. Occasionally in Standard
English analogy has taken place in the other direction, as in the
noun *kiss*, with *i* from the verb (OE *coss* sb., *cyssan* v.). In
this word the dialects too show the operation of analogy: *kuss*
sb. and v. is probably from the Old English noun. The Scottish
and Irish *sealch* 'seal' is from the Old English nom. sg. *seolh*;
Standard English *seal* is from oblique cases, which had no *h* in
Old English. Similarly, Old English had variant forms of the
superlative of the word meaning 'near': *nēhst* and *nēst*. The
first of these has given Standard English *next*; the second has
given dialectal *neist*.

In Old English there was a large group of nouns known as the
weak declension, which formed their plurals in *-an*. Most of
the nouns of this declension have fallen in with the nouns which
form their plurals in *-s*, but there are a few survivals of plurals
in *-n* in Standard English. In dialects such plurals are much
more common, especially in the South and Midlands. *Een* [i:n]
as the plural of *eye* (OE *ēage*, nom. pl. *ēagan*) is common. The
plural ending *-en*, from OE *-an* is sometimes added to words
which did not belong to the weak declension in Old English, as
in *housen* (OE *hūs*, unchanged in the nom. pl.), and to loan-
words, as in *primrosen* (Med. Latin *prima rosa*). Two nouns
have double plurals in Standard English: *children* (OE *cild*;
nom. pl. *cildru*) and the archaic *kine* (OE *cū*; nom. pl. *cȳ*).
Dialects preserve forms without the second plural ending:
childer and *kye*, pronounced [kai]. On the other hand, dialects
have double plurals of some words which have regular plurals in
Standard English. Examples are [beləsəz] 'bellows' and
[galəsəz] 'braces'. The nouns of one declension in Old English

formed their plurals by changing the vowel of the stem, and from these plurals we derive such Standard English forms as *feet, lice* and *mice*. In modern dialects we find the analogical forms *foots, louses* and *mouses*.

The indefinite article is frequently *a* in dialects, even when the following word begins with a vowel. The definite article has had many developments. It has become *de* in Kent and Sussex, and *t, th* or *d* in various Northern dialects. In dialects in which it becomes both *t* and *th, t* is used before consonants and *th* before vowels. Thus, we have *t'book* beside *th'apple*. When the definite article is reduced to *t* and the next word begins with a *t* or *d*, as in *t'table* and *t'dog*, the definite article is replaced by a slight pause, of the kind used in Standard English to express the *k* in *book-case* and the first *t* in *hat trick*. Hearers who are not familiar with northern dialects often fail to notice the pause or the *t*, with the result that we find comments like that quoted by Mrs. Wright[1] from *The Times* of February 7, 1913, where Lancashire dialect is described as 'that curious lingo which seems to an outsider mainly distinguished by its contemptuous neglect of the definite article'. Even dialect speakers are not always conscious of the presence of the article, as is shown by a written notice in the window of a house adjoining the street in a Lancashire town: 'Please don't stand in front of this window. It makes kitchen dark'. In Old English the nominative and accusative singular neuter of the definite article was *þæt*, which survives as *t* in *ton* and *tother* in general dialect use.

In Standard English, adjectives are often formed from nouns by the addition of the suffix *-en*, as in *golden* beside *gold*. This practice is carried further in dialects, especially in those of the South, and we find such expressions as *tinnen pots* and *glassen bottles*.

The comparison of adjectives departs in some dialects from the rules which are observed in Standard English. Comparison by the addition of *-er* and *-est* is common in dialects even when the adjectives are polysyllabic. *More* and *most* are often used to

[1] Elizabeth Mary Wright, *Rustic Speech and Folk Lore* (OUP, 1913), p. viii.

intensify the regular comparison, producing double comparatives and superlatives of the kind which are common in Elizabethan English. Shakespeare's *most unkindest cut of all* (*Julius Caesar*, III, ii, 190) has its parallel in the dialectal *more beautifuller*. Irregular comparatives and superlatives are often replaced by analogical forms, such as *littler* for *less* and *baddest* for *worst*. Here too we find double comparison, as in *betterer*, *worser*, and *leastest*.

Both in dialects and in Standard English the development of pronouns has been influenced a good deal by variations of stress. Strongly-stressed and lightly-stressed forms existed side by side; one or other of these two forms became the ancestor of other forms, one of which was generalized and then the process was repeated. For example, Middle English had the strongly-stressed form *ich* and the lightly-stressed form [i]. *Ich* disappeared in Standard English but it is preserved in Southern dialects, while the lightly-stressed form [i] came to be used in all positions. When strongly stressed, it was lengthened to [iː], and from this form RSE *I* [ai] has developed. The lightly-stressed form [i] is preserved in dialects along with other lightly-stressed forms, such as [ə] and [ɑ]. In the South-West, forms such as *ich*, *ch*, and *utch(y)* were formerly used but they have now nearly died out. When Shakespeare wanted Edgar in *King Lear* to talk like a rustic, he put into his mouth forms like *chill* 'I will' and *che vor ye* 'I warn you' (IV, vi, 246 f.).

The second personal pronoun *thou* has undergone change both of vowel and consonant. The vowel is often reduced to [ə], and in questions, when the pronoun follows a verb, the initial [ð] often becomes [t]. Thus we get [kæntə] 'Can you?'

The pronoun *he* is generally [iː] when strongly stressed, [i] or [ə] when lightly stressed. The lightly-stressed form [ə] occurs in Shakespeare, spelt *a*. The Old English accusative form *hine* survives in Southern dialects as *en*, *un*; it is used of things as well as of persons.

The origin of RSE *she* is a much-discussed problem.[1] The Old

---

[1] See H. Lindkvist, 'On the Origin of the English Pronoun *she*,' *Anglia*, xlv (1921), pp. 1–50.

English equivalent was *hēo,* and this has survived in many Northern and North Midland dialects as [u] or [u:], usually spelt *hoo.*

The plural pronouns *they, their* and *them* are borrowed from Scandinavian. A few Midland dialects have the subjective form [ə] descended from OE *hēo* or *hīe,* and in many dialects we find *'em* [əm] as the lightly-stressed form of the objective case with [ðɛm] as the strongly-stressed form. The form *'em* is not a weakened form of *them* but is descended from the Old English dative plural form *heom,* earlier *him.*

There are several different forms of possessive pronouns. In some dialects personal pronouns, both subjective and objective, are used as possessives without any change of form. We thus get *we held we breaths* and *we want us dinner.* In other dialects the genitive ending *-s* is added to the personal pronouns both subjective and objective: *we's, us's.* In parts of Lancashire *her* (OE *heora*) is used for *their.* The neuter singular of the 3rd person possessive pronoun was in Old English *his,* like that of the masculine, and this form is still found in Hampshire dialects. In some Northern and Midland dialects the old uninflected form *it* is used as a possessive. It was occasionally so used in Shakespeare, as in *It lifted up it head (Hamlet,* I, ii, 216). In Southern and Midland dialects disjunctive forms of the possessive pronoun are formed by adding *-n* to the conjunctive form: *hisn, hern, ourn, yourn.*

Reflexive pronouns are generally formed by the addition of *self, sel* or *sen* in the singular and *selves, sels* or *sens* in the plural to the lightly-stressed form of the possessive pronoun. In dialects, as in Old English, the objective case of the personal pronoun is often used reflexively, especially in the North. We thus find *Sit thee down* beside *Sit thisen down.*

The demonstrative pronouns *this* and *that* are supplemented in all the dialects by the emphatic forms *this here* and *that there.* In South-Western dialects we find *thick here* and *thack(y).* In some dialects *yon, yond* and *yonder* are used in place of *that. Those* is rare in dialects. Even when used adjectivally or in the nominative it can be replaced by *them,* as in *them books.*

105

We also find *them there* and *they* used adjectivally, especially in the South and Midlands. In Scotland *thae* (OE *þā*) is used.

As relative pronouns we find *as, at, that* or *what*. In order to represent the genitive of the relative pronoun we find *as* or *what* coupled with a possessive pronoun, as in *That's the chap as his father went to prison*. This construction has a parallel in Old English, where the genitive of a relative pronoun could be expressed by means of the indeclinable relative particle *þe* accompanied by the possessive pronoun *his*.

In the course of the history of the English language analogy has caused many changes in verbal forms, and differences between Standard English and the dialects are often the result of unequal resistance to the influence of analogy. Thus, in Standard English several strong verbs have become weak, with the result that they now form their preterites by adding the inflexional ending *-ed* instead of changing the stem-vowel. Some verbs which have remained strong in Standard English have become weak in dialects, with the result that we find preterites like *beginned, choosed, comed, growed* and *seed*. Sometimes the ending of the weak preterite is added to a strong preterite form, giving double preterites like *begunned, gaved, knewed*. On the other hand we find *shruk* as the preterite of *shriek* and *snew* as the preterite of *snow*, no doubt on the analogy of *blew*. Dialects have preserved *wrought* as the preterite of *work* (OE *wyrcan*, pret. *worhte*) and *raught* as the preterite of *reach* (OE *rǣcan*, pret. *rǣhte*); RSE *worked* and *reached* are new formations on the analogy of the infinitive. The verb *teach* is historically parallel with *reach*, but here Standard English has kept the historically correct preterite *taught*, without resorting to analogy. Irregular weak verbs sometimes have analogical preterites newly formed from the infinitive. Examples are *catched* (beside *ketched* and *cotched*), *feeled, seeked, teached, telled* and *selled*. It was a characteristic of Northern dialects in Middle English that strong verbs formed their preterites on the basis of the preterite singular when this differed from the plural, and this characteristic is often preserved in the Northern dialects of Modern English, with the result that we find forms like *ban(d)*,

brak, fan(d) and *spak.* Forms like *we done it* and *I seen him*
are probably perfect tenses in which the auxiliary *have* has
disappeared because of lack of stress.

The past participle of strong verbs ended in *-en* in Old English.
Many past participles which have lost this *-en* in Standard
English have kept it in Northern dialects, as in *comen, cropen,
sitten, shutten,* and *getten* beside *gotten.* As the past participle
of the verb *freeze* the dialectal *afrore* (SW counties), like the
poetical *frore,* preserves the *r* of the OE *gefroren,* which in
Standard English has been replaced by *z* on the analogy of such
forms as the infinitive; a different analogy is no doubt the basis
of the dialectal *fruz,* as in *Blister my kidneys! The dahlias is
fruz.* When a past participle is used adjectivally it usually has
-en in both dialects and Standard English, and this is the origin
of the very expressive north-country adjective *brussen* (OE
geborsten, pp. of *berstan* 'to burst'). It is a derogatory adjective
used to describe anyone who has any quality or thing in excess.
A man who makes a vain parade of his learning or his wealth
will be said to be *brussen wi' it.* Some past participles have the
weak participial ending added to the strong past participle in
-en, as in *brussened,* pp. of *burst,* and *soddened,* ppl. adj. from
seethe. Strong verbs often have weak past participles, such as
knowed, drawed, throwed. Dialects have kept the historically
correct participial adjective *afeared* (OE *āfǣred*), which occurs
also in Shakespeare, whereas Standard English *afraid* shows the
influence of French *effrayer.*

The present participle is preceded by *a* in some dialects. The
a is a lightly-stressed form of the preposition *on,* and its use is
an indication that the present participle in *-ing* had its origin in
a verbal noun. Hence *What are you a-doing?* means 'What are
you engaged in the act of doing?'

SYNTAX

In some respects the syntax of modern dialects resembles
that of Elizabethan English rather than that of Standard English
of today. There is the same preference of vigour and emphasis

to logic which makes possible such constructions as the double comparative and the double negative. In modern dialects, as in Early English, we often find an exuberant piling up of negatives, but dialect speakers are sometimes capable of grim conciseness. The work of a minister who had received a unanimous call to a nonconformist church but who had not been a success was summed up in the sentence: *He came unanimous and he went unanimous.* Another general characteristic of dialect syntax is its freedom from slavish adherence to rules, though we must always be prepared to discover that this freedom is only apparent and that the dialect speaker is simply obeying different rules from those which prevail in Standard English. An example of syntactic freedom is provided by the remark of a railway porter who fell asleep by the waiting-room fire at a village station. He awoke to find that he was no longer alone and said: *Sittin' by t' fire an' gets too 'ot an' you fall asleep.*

Sometimes dialects show a departure from normal English idiom. Most dialect speakers would understand the Standard English sentence *These cows belong to the farmer*, but the word *belong* is often used in dialects in a sense which reverses the Standard English attitude to property and its possessor: *Who belongs to these cows?* Similarly, Scottish has *You suit that tie*, 'That tie suits you'.

A redundant personal pronoun is sometimes introduced after a noun, for the sake of emphasis, especially if the noun is a proper name. Thus we find: *Owd Amos, he knows nowt about it.* A particularly exuberant example of this construction occurs in *David Copperfield*:

'The old Mawther biled 'em, she did. Mrs Gummidge biled 'em. Yes,' said Mr Peggotty, slowly, who I thought appeared to stick to the subject on account of having no other subject ready, 'Mrs Gummidge, I do assure you, she biled 'em'. (Ch. 7).

Sometimes a pronoun is supplemented by a noun, which serves the purpose of identifying the subject more closely, as in *He hit him, did my uncle*.

The second person singular of the personal pronoun is used

much more frequently in dialects than in Standard English. In dialects, as in Shakespeare, *thou* is used to express familiarity. Even in dialects it would not normally be used in addressing anyone whom the speaker accepted as a superior, except in areas where there is Quaker influence. It is not much used in Scotland. In many Northern dialects *thee* or *thoo* is added before an imperative for the sake of emphasis, as in *Thee shut up!*

When the pronominal subject of a sentence is separated from its verb by a subordinate clause, *them* is often used instead of *they*, as in *Them as done her in ought to be shot*.

In most dialects the plural pronoun *us* is used as an indirect object with singular meaning, as in *Give us a bite*.

In most dialects the possessive adjectives *our* and *your* are used before proper names to indicate family relationship. A north-country way of referring to one's son or daughter is to use the phrase *yond o' yahrs* 'that one of ours'.

The pronoun *that* is used to avoid reiteration of a word used in a question. When so used it is emphatic. A common form of greeting is *It's a warm* (or *cowd*) *un,* and there are two well-established replies to this greeting: *It is that!* and *It is an' all!* Another dialectal use of *that* is as an adverb with the sense 'to such an extent', as in *he was that poorly*. When used in a negative sentence *that* is sometimes strengthened by the addition of *all*: *he wasn't all that bad*.

In verbs dialects sometimes fail to distinguish between the infinitive and the preterite. Thus, *you didn't ought* is very common in dialects. Historically, *ought* is the preterite of *owe,* but *owe* has acquired a different meaning that would make its use in place of *ought* inappropriate. Speakers of Standard English, or those who taught them, are consciously or unconsciously influenced by the fact that *ought* is preterite in form and therefore avoid using it after an auxiliary verb. Dialect speakers have no such scruples. Similarly we find *if a'd could* 'if I had been able'.

CHAPTER V

English Overseas

THE ATTITUDES OF speakers in various parts of the English-speaking world towards other varieties of English are not free from acerbity. There is a tendency among many Englishmen to disparage any forms of English speech other than British English. This attitude has led to a reaction, especially in the United States, which causes British English to be regarded with hostility, and the hostility is reinforced on both sides by the common human tendency to distrust what is unfamiliar. Side by side with this hostility, of course, there is often an affection for the speech of other parts of the English-speaking world that does not always receive such prompt expression. These attitudes are an obstacle to the serious study of the various forms of English. A good deal of the discussion of the differences between British and American English has been vitiated by attempts to show that one of these two dialects is superior to the other.

It is inevitable that there should be variations in the vocabulary of the different parts of the English-speaking world. Differences in geographical features, in flora and fauna and in the way of life all call for new words. Some of these words remain features of the local dialect and are unknown outside their country of origin, but the most important of them find their way into the general English vocabulary and some of them become so well-established that their origin is forgotten.

The pronunciation of English in the Dominions has been affected by social as well as geographical influences. The early settlers did not include a large proportion of the English upper classes, and this fact is reflected in the speech of their descendants today. In general, the English of the Dominions shows less respect for authority and precedent than does British English. It is more forthright and less sophisticated; its speakers are suspicious of any attempt at cleverness or delicately barbed insults. Highly elaborate expressions full of subtleties whose meaning is not at first apparent arouse the suspicion and hostility of hearers or readers in the Dominions, who suspect that they are being 'got at'.

Another general characteristic of the English of the Dominions is that it is being increasingly influenced by the English of the United States, and this tendency was greatly strengthened during the Second World War. Naturally, this influence is strongest on Canadian English.

Finally, in many parts of the world where English is used it has to compete with other languages, and this competition has had its effect on the local variety of English, especially on the vocabulary. The study of the English of Canada and South Africa has to concern itself very much with the problems of bilingual speakers, and in India and many parts of Africa there is the additional problem that English, while remaining a convenient *lingua franca*, is spoken by only a very small proportion of the inhabitants of countries of which it is an official language.

IRELAND

As far back as the Middle English period there was a distinctive Anglo-Irish dialect, represented by sixteen English poems in MS. Harley 913 in the British Museum, a manuscript written at the beginning of the fourteenth century. It is probable, but not certain, that the poems were written or collected at Kildare, and they are generally known as *The Kildare Lyrics*. Their dialect has many points in common with the dialects of South-West England, but differs from them in the loss of final lightly-stressed -*e*, a characteristic which, at the date of the Kildare manuscript, was a feature of the Northern dialects of English.

It is not possible to establish continuity of development from the dialect of *The Kildare Lyrics* to the Anglo-Irish dialects of today, although Irish pronunciations are satirized in English plays from the seventeenth century onwards. The Anglo-Irish dialects of today[1] preserve some characteristics, such as the voiceless pronunciation of *wh* and the retention of a short *a* before *f, s* and voiceless *th*, which are no longer found in Standard English, although they are common in Northern English dialects. Some of the characteristics of the Irish pronunciation of English are:

1. An unrounded vowel *a* is found after *w* in words, such as *want*, in which British English has a rounded vowel, pronounced [ɒ] though usually spelt *a*.

2. ME open *ē* has not been raised to [iː] in words like *leaf*. This was regarded in the nineteenth century as one of the most noticeable features of Irish pronunciation, but it is now dying out.

3. Consonants are often unvoiced finally, and in other positions voicing of consonants is often so weak as not to be noticeable to English ears.

4. Off-glides are prominent, especially after voiceless plosives.

5. The distinction between the alveolar plosives [t], [d] and the pre-dental fricatives [θ], [ð] tends to be lost. This confusion is due in part to the influence of Gaelic in which *t* and *d* are dental, not alveolar, consonants. For both plosives and fricatives, affricate consonants, with slow separation of the organs of speech, are often heard. As a result of the falling together of these sounds, we find in English representation of Irish speech such spellings as *dere* for *there* and *trote* for both *throat* and *troth*.

6. Plosive consonants are often aspirated.

7. The so-called 'dark *l*', which is used in English after vowels, is not generally used in Irish pronunciation; 'clear *l*',

---

[1] For details of Anglo-Irish pronunciation I am especially indebted to Jeremiah J. Hogan's *The English Language in Ireland* (Educational Company of Ireland, 1927).

which is used in English before vowels, is used by many Irish speakers in all positions.

8. The consonant *r* is pronounced in all positions, whereas in English it is generally silent before consonants. In Anglo-Irish a vowel often develops between the *r* and a following *m*, as in [ɑrəm] 'arm'. A similar glide develops between *l* and *m*, as in [filəm] 'film'.

Many of these characteristics of the Irish pronunciation of English are due to the influence of Irish Gaelic pronunciation on bilingual speakers. This influence is especially strong on the consonants. The pronunciation of vowels often shows a compromise between English and Gaelic pronunciation, with the complication that English vowels, unlike the consonants, have undergone many changes during the last few centuries, and Irish speakers sometimes preserve pronunciations that are no longer current in British English.

Apart from differences of pronunciation, there are differences in accidence and syntax that can be traced to Gaelic influence. One of the best known of these is the use of *after* with a verbal noun to express the perfect tense. *I'm after doing it* means 'I've done it' just as *I'm after my dinner* means 'I've had my dinner'. Another common Anglo-Irish construction is the use of *be* and *do be* to express the continuous present, as in *he do be cutting corn every day* and *I be going to school early*.

THE UNITED STATES

A good deal of the rancour which disfigures many pronouncements on the differences between British and American English is the result of a failure to compare like with like. Englishmen denounce vulgarisms that they have heard in American gangster films without realizing that most educated Americans would share their distaste, and Americans ridicule the affected mannerisms of a stage stereotype of an English aristocrat, whose speech is quite unlike that of ninety-nine per cent of the inhabitants of the British Isles. It is important to remember that there are class dialects in both British and American English, and there are very few features of good American speech that are demonstrably either better or worse than the corresponding features of good English speech. Another source of antipathy is unfamiliarity, and if an Englishman dislikes American speech, his dislike does not as a rule survive a visit to the United States. It is difficult to make any general statement about American English that would not be equally true of British English, but it is perhaps true to say that American English shows a greater disregard for precedent than does British English and that it also shows a greater capacity for word-formation.

VOCABULARY

There are differences in vocabulary between British and American English, but there is such frequent interchange of books and ideas between England and America and words are so easily borrowed that differences of vocabulary very quickly cease to have dialectal significance. The early settlers in America borrowed many words from native American languages. Many of these, such as *cannibal, canoe, chocolate, cocoa, potato,* and *tomato,* are now in general use in both British and American English. Others describe distinctively American animals or things: names of trees and plants such as *hickory, persimmon* and *sequoia,* names of animals such as *moose, opossum, raccoon, skunk* and *terrapin,* and words used to describe various aspects of the American Indian way of life such as *moccasin, papoose, squaw, tomahawk, totem* and *wigwam.* A further group of American English words consists of words borrowed from the languages of other European settlers in America; examples are *chowder, gopher, prairie,* and *picayune* from French, *alfalfa, armadillo, coyote, mustang, lasso, ranch, rodeo, cinch, adobe, dago* and *pickaninny* from Spanish, and *cole-slaw, cookie, boss, dope, snoop, spook* and *waffle* from Dutch. Among the words borrowed from Dutch we may include *Yankee* if we accept the likely etymology of the word from *Janke,* a diminutive of *Jan.* German words were introduced rather later, for the most part in the nineteenth century; they include several words dealing with food and drink, such as *delicatessen, frankfurter, hamburger, sauerkraut* and *schnitzel*.

Another group of words consists of words formed in America from well-established English words and suffixes. Such words are *influential, lengthy, reliable* and *talented*. Such words are now perfectly well-established in both British and American English and no longer have any dialectal significance, but in the nineteenth century they met with stiff opposition in British English because they were regarded as Americanisms.

American influence on the vocabulary of British English is particularly noticeable in certain fields, notably politics, drinking and commerce. In each group of words it is possible to make the distinction between words which have been so completely assimilated into British English that those who use them are hardly conscious of their transatlantic origin, and those which are still thought of as Americanisms. Political terms include *caucus, filibuster* and *carpet-bagger*; names of drinks include *cocktail, high-ball, coke* and *apple-jack*; commercial words include coined names of products which have become household words, such as *kleenex, cellophane, kodak* and *vaseline*.

SEMANTICS

The differences between British and American English often result from the use of the same word in different senses in the two dialects. Words of this kind cause a good deal of trouble because their use may lead to undetected errors. No great harm is done if an Englishman says *fortnight* where an American says *two weeks* or if he speaks of a document as *cyclostyled* when an American can see at a glance that it is really *mimeographed*, but there is real danger if *public schools* are mentioned because the term is used in completely different senses in England and America: American public schools correspond to English primary and secondary schools, whereas English public schools would in America be described as private. Other examples of words whose different meanings could give rise to misunderstanding are *billion*, which means a thousand million in America but a million million in England, and *a contested election*, which in England is merely one in which there is more than one candidate, whereas in American use the phrase means one in which the result is challenged.

One British manufacturer of motor-cars has brought out a short glossary for the use of British tourists in America. The British driver needs to know that *petrol* is *gas*, *mudguard* is *fender*, *gearbox* is *transmission*, and *boot* is *trunk*. The greatest source of confusion is *hood*, which is the American English equivalent of BE *bonnet*, whereas in England the hood is the adjustable roof of a touring car; in the United States this is known as a *convertible top*.

Two groups of words can be distinguished among those whose meanings differ in England and America: those which are used in American English in senses that are archaic or obsolete in British English, and those which are used in American English in senses that are preserved in English dialects. To the first group belongs *guess* in the sense of 'think', a sense found in Chaucer. Similarly *sick* in the unspecialized sense 'ill' is common in American English, though in British English it is an archaism except when used attributively, as in *a sick man, on the sick list* and *sick leave*. Other examples are *fall* in the sense 'autumn', and *bug* with the unspecialized meaning 'insect'.

The group of words that are in general use in American English while they are provincialisms in British English overlaps with these archaisms because it is not uncommon for a word to pass out of general use while surviving as a provincialism. We occasionally find such words re-establishing themselves in general use as a result of American influence. Thus the verb *to wilt* is described by Ray (1691) as a north-country word. It is common in nineteenth-century American English and is now non-dialectal in British English. *Chore* 'task' is returning into use in British English, perhaps as a result of American influence. Other words have remained dialectal in British English: *shoat* 'young weaned pig' is recorded from the fifteenth century though by the nineteenth century it is thought of as a Norfolk or Wiltshire word; *deck* 'pack of cards' is common in sixteenth-century British English but is now a northernism; *cater-cornered* (or *kitty-cornered*) is now dialectal in British English. All three words are current in American English. Sometimes it is one particular meaning of a word that is dialectal in British English, as *mad* in the sense 'angry' and *pig* in the sense 'young pig'.

PRONUNCIATION

There are many differences of pronunciation between American and British English. American intonation does not rise or fall so suddenly as that of British English and the intonation pattern of sentences tends to be simpler. These differences may well be regarded as characteristics of British, rather than of American, speech, since the intonation of Australians, South Africans and Canadians resembles that of Americans. The pitch of the voice varies a good deal from one individual to another, but, in general, American voices have a higher pitch than British. In British English high pitch is usually a sign of emphasis, but this is not necessarily so in American English. Consequently to British ears American English often seems unduly emphatic. Another cause contributing to the same effect is that American voices are often louder than British, especially in casual conversation.

The tempo of American speech is rather slower than that of British speech. Consequently Englishmen tend to speak of 'the American drawl' and Americans often refer to the clipped speech of Englishmen. One reason for the clipped effect is that the lightly-stressed syllables of polysyllabic words are very much reduced and sometimes disappear altogether in British English, whereas in American English they often receive secondary stress, and even syllables of very little stress are pronounced with care. The difference between British and American treatment of words like *temporarily* and *extraordinarily* is very noticeable. In such words American secondary stress avoids the huddle of several consecutive lightly-stressed syllables that

117

is found in British English, and the same tendency leads to the preservation of the *a* in *secretary* and the *o* in *explanatory*, which many British speakers drop altogether. On the other hand, American English prefers a short *i* in the lightly-stressed second syllable of words like *hostile*, *missile*, *futile*, and *fertile*, whereas British English has the diphthong [ai], a comparatively recent development that would be more appropriate in a strongly-stressed syllable. In general, American pronunciation tends to follow spelling more closely than does British, and there are fewer silent consonants. The loss of *d* in *kindness*, of *t* in *often* and at the end of *trait*, and of the medial *l* in *fulfil* is common in British but rare in American pronunciation.

Sometimes American English agrees in pronunciation with Northern dialects of British English more closely than with Standard English. One of the most easily recognizable characteristics of Northern English speech is the use of a short front vowel for *a* before [f], [s] and [ɵ], as in *laugh*, *ask* and *path*, where Southern English has a long back vowel. American English has the so-called 'flat *a*', which is close to the Northern English vowel, though generally rather longer. Another marked difference between British and American English pronunciation is the loss of *r* before consonants in British English. In American English, as in many Scottish, Irish and Northern English dialects, *r* generally remains when followed by a consonant, though there are differences in the quality of the *r* in the various dialects. Many speakers in Eastern and Southern regions of the United States give *r* the same treatment that it receives in British English. There are historical reasons for the variations within American English: the Southern and Eastern states were colonized first, and the settlers came in the main from Southern England, whereas the nineteenth-century settlers in the Middle and Far West included a larger proportion of northerners, Scots and Irish. In the development of the diphthongs found in such words as *great* and *home* American English agrees with Northern English in keeping the first element of each diphthong half-close whereas in the South of England the first element of the diphthong in *great* is tending to become open *e* and the first element of the diphthong in *home* is tending to become a centralized vowel. These changes are not always recorded in pronouncing dictionaries because they are still taking place, but they are very widespread. In all these sound-changes the reason for the resemblance between American and Northern English is that these dialects have been conservative and have resisted the influence of sound-changes taking place in Southern English.

American English shows the results of other sound-changes that are not normal in Northern English, although partial parallels can often be quoted from British English of the past or present. Vowels, both long and short, tend to be lengthened in strongly-stressed syllables in American speech, though the distinction between vowels historically long and those historically short is usually preserved. In Southern dialects of American English short vowels are not only lengthened but diphthongized by the addition of the central vowel [ə]. Nasalization of vowels is common in American English, especially next to nasal consonants. The frequent unrounding and lengthening of short *o* is a distinctive feature of American English pronunciation. It may be an independent American development or it may have had its origin in a fashionable pronunciation in seventeenth-century British English that has had a few survivals, such as 'Gad, sir' today. Another American characteristic is the use of [uː] in many words which in British English have [juː]. British English normally has [uː] after certain consonants, especially *l, r,* [tʃ] and [dʒ], as in *lute, rule, chew* and *judicial,* but many American speakers use [uː] in such words as *due, dew, news, duke* and *duty.* Another group of words in which there is a twofold development in both British and American English, but with a greater preference for one development in America, consists of words which in Middle English contained the group *er.* In such words in both British and American English *er* has sometimes remained, as in *servant,* and has sometimes become *ar,* as in *carve,* and there is a small group of words which have *er* in spelling but, in British English, *ar* in pronunciation. In American English in words of this group, such as *clerk, Derby* and *Berkeley,* the *er* is pronounced as in *servant.*

119

MORPHOLOGY

The differences in word-formation between American and British English do not provide any clear-cut basis for differentiation between the two dialects. For the most part American English has indulged more freely in practices that are fairly common in British English. Americans are particularly good at coining picturesque compound words, and many of these have been borrowed into British English and are not thought of as Americanisms. *Highbrow* is now so well established in the language that it probably comes as a surprise to many people that its earliest occurrence recorded in the *Supplement* to *OED* is dated 1911. Many American compounds are still felt to be slang but some, such as *skyscraper* and *killjoy*, may be regarded as having been assimilated into the standard language.

Blend-words are common in American English, and many of these have been borrowed into British English. Sometimes the origin of the blend is obvious, as in *travelogue* and *Aframerican*, but there is sometimes less certainty: *boost* may be a blend of *boom* and *hoist*, and more than two words may have contributed to produce *blizzard*.

Back-formations, resulting from a misunderstanding of the function of part of a word, are fairly common in British English; examples are the verb *to sidle*, resulting from a misunderstanding of the adverb *sideling*, and *pea*, which arose when the older form *pease* was wrongly taken to be a plural. They are even more common in American, especially in sub-standard dialects; examples are *corp*, from *corpse*, and Bret Harte's *The Heathen Chinee*.

Shortenings, of the kind deplored by Swift, who fought a losing battle against such words as *mob*, from *mobile vulgus*, are perhaps even more common in American than in British English; examples are *gas* from *gasoline*, *movie* from *moving picture*, *auto* from *automobile*, and *cuss* from *customer*.

In accidence American English sometimes keeps past participles in *-en* which have disappeared in British English. The historically correct past participle *stricken* is more common in

American than in British English, where it has been replaced by the analogical *struck*, except in set phrases like *stricken in years*. The past participles *got* and *gotten* are both analogical, but *gotten* preserves the old participial ending in *-en*. Its use in American English involves a distinction which British speakers often fail to understand: *gotten* is used only in the sense 'acquired' or 'become', and is not used to replace *got* when *to have got* means 'to possess'. The latter sense of *got* is less common in American than in British English; corresponding to BE *he hadn't got a dog*, AE has *he didn't have a dog*.

SYNTAX

In syntax American English shows a greater willingness than British English to rebel against the rules imposed by grammarians. In so rebelling Americans are often restoring or preserving syntactic usages which have an older standing in the language than the rules which forbid them. One of the syntactic features of Elizabethan English was the freedom with which one part of speech could be used for another, and this same freedom is a characteristic of the American English of today. We have grown accustomed in British English to the use of short native nouns as verbs, since the decay of inflexional endings in early Modern English often removed the difference in form between a noun and its cognate verb. Thus, the noun *love* (OE *lufu*) is identical in form with the verb *love* (OE *lufian*). There is, however, generally an outcry when abstract nouns of foreign origin, such as *sabotage* and *contact*, are used as verbs, and the usage is often attributed to American influence. The loss of final *-e* in early Modern English led too to the falling together of adjectives with their cognate adverbs. Hence we find that adjectives are often used in place of adverbs, and this process has been carried further in American than in British English. The best-known American examples are *sure* and *real*.

British subtleties in the use of *shall* and *will* are not always observed in American English, where *will* is normally used to

121

express futurity while *shall* is used to express purpose or authority, whatever the person of the subject.

In British English *either* and *neither* generally stand alone in pronominal use; in American English they are often followed by the pronoun *one*.

One characteristic of American English syntax that is often noticed by British visitors is the use of a verb followed by an adverb and a preposition in place of a simple verb. There is often a good deal of argument whether the additions earn their keep by modifying the meaning of the verb. It may be that there is a slight difference in meaning between *check* and *check up on* and between *meet* and *meet up with*, but the longer expressions often seem to have no better justification than exuberance.

DIALECTS

The dialects within American English have a special interest for students of English dialects. These dialects are both regional and social, and it is possible to notice parallel developments in Britain and America, though it is not always certain whether the parallels are due to independent developments or to the influence of one form of English on the other.

Writers on American English have often commented on its comparative freedom from dialects, and the greater mobility of Americans, leading to a mixture of dialects, has undoubtedly had the effect of encouraging uniformity of speech. It may well be, however, that this freedom from dialects has been exaggerated, and fuller investigation is already beginning to reveal dialectal variations within the huge dialect which used to be known as General American and which was said to be spoken by something like two-thirds of the population of the United States. Instead of the older division of American dialects into General American, Southern and New England, it is now usual to recognize three main dialects, Northern, Midland, and Southern, each of them having sub-dialects, among which may be included the dialects of New York City and Eastern New England as subdivisions of the Northern area. The Northern region 'extends westward in an area bounded on the south by a line beginning a little below Sandy Hook in New Jersey, veering somewhat to the North and running along the northern tier of counties in Pennsylvania—settled from New England and New York—and from there pursuing a slightly southerly course through Ohio, Indiana, and Illinois. Its divagations west of the Great Lakes Basin cannot at present be determined with any degree of certainty.'[1]

The boundary between the Midland and Southern areas 'begins at a point somewhat below Dover in Delaware, sweeps through Baltimore in something of an arc, turns sharply south-west north of the Potomac, follows the crest of the Blue Ridge in Virginia, and south of the James River swerves out into the North Carolina Piedmont. As we approach the lower part of South Carolina and Georgia the boundary is as yet unknown'.[2]

The dialect criteria upon which the classification of American dialects is based are concerned with both vocabulary and pronunciation, but so far it is the lexical material collected for the linguistic atlases that has been analysed most thoroughly. Characteristic words of the Northern dialect include *white bread* and *poison ivy*, corresponding to *light bread* and *poison vine* in the other dialects. In the Midland dialect we find *armload* for an armful of wood (compared with *turn* in the South), and 'a quarter *till* the hour' is a typical Midland expression. In the South we find such words as *lightwood* for firewood and *snap beans* for string beans. It is interesting to note that some words which are thought of in England as non-dialectal are current only in certain dialects of the United States. Thus *pig-sty* is a characteristic New England term to describe what would elsewhere in the United States be described as a *pig-pen*; *brook* is Northern; and it is in the Southern States that cows are said to *low* at feeding time. Other words such as *chittlins*

---

[1] Thomas Pyles, *Words and Ways of American English* (Andrew Melrose, 1954), p. 197.

[2] Albert H. Marckwardt, *American English* (New York, OUP, 1958), p. 135.

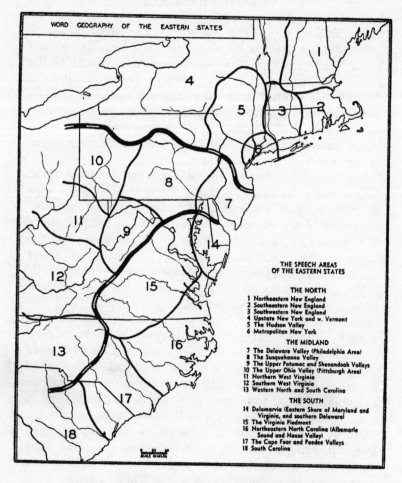

THE SPEECH AREAS
OF THE EASTERN STATES

THE NORTH

1 Northeastern New England
2 Southeastern New England
3 Southwestern New England
4 Upstate New York and w. Vermont
5 The Hudson Valley
6 Metropolitan New York

THE MIDLAND

7 The Delaware Valley (Philadelphia Area)
8 The Susquehanna Valley
9 The Upper Potomac and Shenandoah Valleys
10 The Upper Ohio Valley (Pittsburgh Area)
11 Northern West Virginia
12 Southern West Virginia
13 Western North and South Carolina

THE SOUTH

14 Delamarvia (Eastern Shore of Maryland and
   Virginia, and southern Delaware)
15 The Virginia Piedmont
16 Northeastern North Carolina (Albemarle
   Sound and Neuse Valley)
17 The Cape Fear and Peedee Valleys
18 South Carolina

Map 6. The Speech Areas of the Eastern United
States, reprinted from Map 3 of Hans Kurath,
A Word Geography of the Eastern United States,
University of Michigan Press, by permission.
Copyright 1949 by the University of Michigan.

or *chitterlings* 'the small intestines of pigs' are dialectal in both England and the United States.

Distinctions in pronunciation include the Northern use of [s] in *greasy* and the verb *grease*, whereas in many parts of the United States [z] is used and *greasy* rhymes with *easy*. In the sub-dialects of the Northern area, the most noticeable characteristic of Eastern New England is the use of a long back vowel in words like *path* and *half*, and the best-known feature of the dialect of New York City is the use of a diphthong something like *oi* to represent the *ir* of *bird* and the *ear* of *earth*. The Northern dialect is distinguished from the Midland by its treatment of short *o* in words like *fog* and *hog*: the vowel is unrounded in the North but not in the Midland area. A characteristic of the Southern dialect, which it shares to some extent with Eastern New England and New York City, is the use of [ju:] instead of the Northern and Midland [u:] in words like *Tuesday*, *due* and *new*; in this it resembles British English. Another characteristic of the same group of dialects is the loss of *r* before consonants, as in *card*, *word* and *for*. In New England pronunciation no *r* is normally heard in the sentence *Park your car in Harvard Yard*, although in New England, as in Great Britain, intrusive *r* is frequently used to avoid hiatus between two vowels.

The Southern dialect is frequently used in novels and plays to add local colour, not always accurately. H. L. Mencken calls attention to its misuse:

> Southern speech has suffered cruelly on the stage and in talkies, where kittenish actresses from the domain of General American think that they have imitated it sufficiently when they have thrown in a few *you-alls* and *honey-chiles* and converted every *I* into a long *ah*.[1]

The incorrect use of *you-all* is regarded by Southerners as a particularly offensive mistake when it occurs in the portrayal of Southern speech. *You-all* did not become common until the last quarter of the nineteenth century; it is a plural pronoun and its use in the singular is a solecism.

[1] H. L. Mencken, *The American Language: Supplement II* (Alfred A. Knopf, 1948), pp. 124 f.

The variations among the dialects of the United States are not for the most part so great as to interfere with mutual intelligibility, but there is one dialect which has such strongly marked individual features that it cannot easily be understood by people from other parts of the country, and it can therefore be regarded as a language rather than a dialect. This is the Gullah or Geechee language spoken by a quarter of a million Negroes along the coast of South Carolina and Georgia, both on the Sea Islands and on the mainland. It is basically English, but it shows the very marked influence of African languages not only on its vocabulary but also on its system of sounds, its syntax, its morphology and its intonation.

One of the problems to be investigated by students of American dialects is the extent to which the English settlers in America brought with them dialectal variations that already existed in England. Professor W. N. Francis has pointed out[1] that the Quakers who settled in Pennsylvania came from both Yorkshire and East Anglia, with the result that traces of both Yorkshire and Norfolk dialects are to be found in Philadelphia. Professor Francis further points out that it is possible to see a historical reason for the resemblances between British English and the New England dialect of American English in that the westward-moving pioneers severed their ties with England whereas the New Englanders did not. Hence New England kept up with the changing fashions of speech in England whereas the rest of the United States pioneer communities kept earlier pronunciations with little change. The dialects of East Anglia have often been suggested as the basis of American English, and this view accords well with what is known about the original homes of the earliest settlers, but it is doubtful whether we know enough about the dialects of British English in the seventeenth century to allow us to establish any but the most general links between British and American dialects. Many claims are based on the accidents of recording and preservation or of the range of knowledge of the person making the claim. If a word or a

[1] W. N. Francis 'The Present State of the American Dialect Atlas' in *TYDS* lvii (1957), p. 36.

pronunciation is found both in a provincial English dialect and in American English or in one of the sub-dialects of American English, it does not provide evidence of a special link with that dialect unless it can be shown that it does not occur in other British dialects, and British dialects have not yet been surveyed with a sufficiently close network to allow negative statements of much value to be made. A further difficulty is that allowance must be made for changes that have taken place in British dialects since the seventeenth century.

CANADA

Canada is officially a bilingual country; about one-third of its population is French-speaking. Speakers of French are most numerous in Quebec, and the English spoken there includes many French loan-words. The first important group of English-speaking settlers in Canada consisted of Loyalists at the time of the War of American Independence who wished to continue to live in a British colony. Until the last quarter of the nineteenth century immigration into Canada was mainly from the United Kingdom with a high proportion of Scotsmen and Irishmen. From about 1880 onwards there were large-scale immigrations from many European countries, but these did not significantly affect Canadian English.

The great majority of Canadians live within a hundred miles of the border with the United States, and by far the most important influence on Canadian speech is the English spoken in the United States. This influence is encouraged by constant travel across the border between the two countries, by radio and cinema, and by newspapers and commercial links. At the same time there are pockets of resistance where British English is still influential: fashionable private schools and, to some extent, universities encourage British English usages, and there are official and social groups, especially in the larger cities, where the influence of British English is strong. A further source of British English has been provided by two World Wars, in the course of which large numbers of Canadians spent some time in

England. The regions where the influence of United States English is weakest are the Maritime Provinces and Newfoundland. The speech of Scottish immigrants has been influential in Ontario. Some Canadians deplore the influence both of the English of the United States and of the more noticeably Southern features of British English, and in course of time Canada will no doubt evolve its own variety of English, but it seems likely that this will closely resemble the English of the United States.

One sometimes finds contradictory statements about Canadian usage on specific points where British usage differs from that of the United States. Such contradictions are generally the result of assuming that the speech of a small number of Canadians is typical of the country as a whole. There is room for research to find out how widespread is the use of such British English words as *pram* (AE *baby-carriage*), *tin* (AE *can*), *sweet* (AE *dessert*), and *braces* (AE *suspenders*). Such an investigation might well extend to pronunciations, such as that of *schedule* (*sh* or *sk*), *lieutenant* (*left-* or *loot-*), *duke* (*oo* or *you*), and *vacation* (neutral or long vowel in first syllable). Only after research on a large scale has been carried out will it be possible to say how far the variations in Canadian pronunciation are dialectal and how far they are idiosyncrasies of individual speakers which cannot be assigned to particular regions or social groups.

SOUTH AFRICA

In South Africa English has to compete with Afrikaans, which is gaining ground, and it is to be expected that the process will continue at a greater rate now that South Africa has left the Commonwealth. In the country districts speakers of Afrikaans greatly outnumber those who speak English, but English is in general the language of commerce and industry and it flourishes chiefly in the towns. In spite of the numerical preponderance of Afrikaans-speakers, immigrants from Great Britain have often been in positions, as teachers or employers, which made their opinions influential, and such immigrants have sometimes discouraged the development of a distinctively South African

128

variety of English. There are many bilingual speakers and there is a good deal of Afrikaans influence on South African English in vocabulary, idiom and pronunciation. Many of the loan-words from Afrikaans are understood outside South Africa, but they are generally associated with South African life and they can therefore be regarded as features of South African English. They include words used by the early settlers, such as *voortrekker* 'pioneer', *trek* 'journey, migration', *inspan* 'to yoke (oxen) to a vehicle' and *outspan* 'to unyoke', geographical features, such as *veldt* 'grass country', *kopje* 'small hill', *kloof* 'glen, ravine' and *bosch* 'bush', and names of local fauna, such as *hartebeest* and *klipspringer*, the names of two different kinds of antelope, and *aardvark* (literally 'earth-pig'). Some words with strong African associations are borrowed from Hottentot; among these are *gnu* 'oxlike antelope' and *karoo* 'elevated plateau'.

One reason for the tendency among some British speakers to disparage South African English is that a few South African pronunciations happen to be similar to pronunciations which in British English are regarded as features of class dialect. For example, the diphthong in words like *day* and *gate* is pronounced in South African English with a very open first element, which to British ears resembles the Cockney pronunciation. The South African pronunciation will probably seem less strange to Englishmen in the future than it has done in the past, since in British English, especially in the South, there is an increasing tendency to pronounce this diphthong with an open first element.

AUSTRALIA

Well over ninety per cent of the population of Australia is of British origin, and bilingualism is therefore not a problem. The only foreign languages that have exerted much influence on the distinctively Australian vocabulary are those of the aborigines, from which are borrowed such words as *boomerang*, *kangaroo*, *corroboree* (originally meaning 'dance' but now meaning a tumult or noise made by a group of people), and *billabong*, a branch of a river forming a backwater. In view of the great differences in natural features and flora and fauna between Australia and Great Britain, there was scope for much more borrowing than actually took place, but the early settlers preferred when possible to adapt English words to make them meet the new demands made on them. Sometimes the adaptation was infelicitous, as in the use of *laughing jackass* to describe the bird which is now more often called by its native name *kookaburra*. The adaptation of English words affected both form and meaning. New compounds were formed, such as *the outback*, to describe the country remote from towns, and *ropeable* 'angry', originally applied to cattle so wild that they could be controlled only by roping. Some of these compounds and the phrases formed from them describe aspects of the relations between the settlers and the aborigines; an example is *blacktracker*, a native used by the police to track down criminals and people lost in the bush. The discovery of gold in 1850 led to a new influx of words and adaptations, such as *diggings* 'mine, goldfield', *mullock* 'rock or refuse containing no gold, rubbish' and *fossick* 'to search', and other aspects of Australian history are reflected in such words as *squatter* and *bushranger*. *Squatter* is in origin an Americanism and was used to describe a man who occupied land to which he had no legal claim. During the early nineteenth century the word was used in this sense in Australia but there it later came to mean a man who held pastoral land as a tenant of the government. Life on sheep and cattle stations today is reflected by such words as *jackaroo*, a trainee manager who is learning every aspect of the job, *offsider* 'assistant' and *rouseabout* 'handyman'. A *wowser*, 'a puritanical person' is of Australian origin but has spread to other parts of the English-speaking world.

There has been loss as well as gain in the adaptation of the English vocabulary to Australian use. It has often been pointed out that many English words describing the countryside have almost passed out of use in Australia. This is true not only of words like *copse* and *spinney*, *thicket* and *dale*, which are little used by town-dwellers even in England, but it applies also to such everyday British words as *field, meadow, wood, forest, brook, stream* and *village*. On the other hand, Australian English uses words like *bush, scrub* and *creek* that are little used in England and gives to *paddock* a wider sense than it has in England. In Australia any enclosed piece of land, of whatever size, can be described as a paddock. The noun *bush* has given rise to the participial adjective *bushed*, literally 'lost in the bush' and figuratively 'lost, bewildered'.

One source of the Australian vocabulary has been the local dialects of British English. Some of the most familiar Australian words may have this origin, and there are many words of uncertain etymology which resemble British dialect words closely enough for some connexion to be possible though not certain. Some of these words have been re-introduced into British English from Australian and their ultimate dialectal origin has been forgotten. Possible examples are: *to barrack* 'to jeer' (cf. N. Irish *to barrack* 'to brag, to be boastful'), *cobber* (cf. Suffolk *to cob* 'to take a liking to', although this verb (*EDD cob* v.²) is not very well authenticated), *dinkum* 'honest, genuine' (cf. Lincs. *fair dinkum* 'fair play'), *to fossick* (cf. Cornish *fossick* 'to obtain by asking, ferret out') and *skerrick* 'small amount' (generally used with a negative; cf. *EDD skerrick* 'particle, morsel'). Many Australian wool-terms are from British English dialects; in Australia these are technical terms generally used only by workers in the wool industry. Examples are *cot* 'matted fleece of wool', *fadge* 'a loosely packed sack of wool', *kemps* 'coarse hairs amongst wool', and *noil* 'short wool left after combing'.

Sometimes the difference between British and Australian English is one of idiom.[1] Corresponding to British English *You'll be all right*, Australian English has *You'll be right*; corresponding to *You'll be in trouble*, it has *You'll be in strife*; corresponding to *to give up* it has *to give away*. A common Australian comment on something marvellous or incredible is *You wouldn't read about it*. Some characteristically Australian

---

[1] For the examples in this paragraph I am indebted to Professor and Mrs A. C. Cawley, of the University of Queensland.

idioms result from the use of one part of speech for another, as in *to fine up* 'to become fine (of the weather)' and *to rabble* 'to behave in a disorderly manner'. As in British and American English, polysyllabic words are often curtailed in Australia, with the result that *university* becomes *uni* and *beauty* and *beautiful* both become *beaut*.

When Englishmen describe Australian pronunciation, the most frequent summing-up is to say that it is like Cockney. Australians generally resent this description, and the resentment has a good deal of linguistic interest as evidence of the disparaging attitude towards the Cockney dialect which underlies it and of the emotion which statements about speech are liable to arouse. Sidney J. Baker, who himself calls attention to points of resemblance,[1] such as the tendency away from the back of the tongue (p. 335) and the raising of [ɛ] to [ɪ] and of [æ] to [ɛ] (p. 330), takes the view:

> Since no observer has yet been able to produce more than a few superficial resemblances between the Australian and the Cockney accent, the allegation that Australians talk like Cockneys must be regarded as little more than one of the unfortunately popular myths to which we, as a young nation, are susceptible' (p. 323).

The truth is that there are some points of resemblance and many points of difference between the two dialects. The point of resemblance that is most often quoted is the development of the diphthong [ei] in words like *day* towards [ai], but, as we have seen, this development is found in South African English and in other dialects, and the quality of the first element of the diphthong is not identical in Cockney and Australian English. Many differences between the two dialects have been pointed out: the intonation differs considerably, Cockney has a quicker rhythm, and the glottal stop and development of plosive consonants to affricates, which are frequent in Cockney, are not Australian characteristics.

In the development of vowels in Australian English some general tendencies are for vowels to become more front and

[1] In *The Australian Language* (Angus and Robertson, 1945).

132

more close and for them to be diphthongized. In these respects Australian English is simply carrying further the tendencies that have affected British English vowels since the Middle English period. Sometimes the Australian vowels develop not only to diphthongs but to triphthongs, and a sound that frequently occurs as one element of the diphthong or triphthong is the centralized vowel [ə].

Some of the more noticeable Australian developments of particular sounds may be mentioned:

1. The sound [ɑː], as in *father* and *half*, is generally fronted to [aː].

2. The sounds [iː], as in *sea* and *feel*, and [uː], as in *too* and *you*, become diphthongs with a centralized first element: [iː] becomes [əi] and [uː] becomes [əu].

3. The diphthongs [ei], as in *lady* and *day*, and [ou], as in *go* and *home*, both have a more open and somewhat centralized first element. The lowering of the first element of the diphthong [ei] does not lead to confusion with the diphthong [ai], found in *fine* and *ride*, because the first element of [ai] is in Australian English often retracted and slightly rounded so as to approach [ɔ]. The two diphthongs are thus quite distinct to an Australian ear.

4. The diphthong in words like *poor* tends to be replaced by the monophthong [ɔː]. It may be noted that many British speakers use this pronunciation.

5. The most notable variation in lightly-stressed syllables is concerned with the vowel which in British English is pronounced [ɪ], though it is often spelt *e*. In Southern English the vowel in the final syllable of *pocket*, *palace*, *offices* and *appointed* is [ɪ]. Australians, like many northern speakers of British English, generally use [ə]. When the [ɪ] occurs at the end of a word, it is in Australian generally lengthened and raised to [iː] and this long vowel is then often diphthonigized to [əi].

133

NEW ZEALAND

New Zealand has often been called the most British of the Dominions and, in spite of the distance from Great Britain, the linguistic divergence has not been great. New Zealand has shown stronger resistance than Australia to the influence of American English, although such usages as *sick* in the sense 'ill' are common in New Zealand, and it has also put up some resistance to Australian influences. Some resemblances between Australian and New Zealand English may be due to parallel trends rather than to direct influence. For example, the virtual disappearance from Australian English of a number of common English words describing scenery has its parallel in New Zealand, where such words as *moor, heath, brook, copse* and *meadow* are not in current use.

Not many Maori words have passed into the vocabulary of New Zealand English. *Whare* 'hut' is well established, but others, such as *kit* 'basket' and *hoot* 'money' are now obsolescent. Some Maori words are in use as proper names, such as Ngaio, from the Maori name of a kind of tree.

Since many New Zealanders both aim at speaking like Englishmen and succeed in doing so, it is possible in speaking of New Zealand pronunciation only to indicate some tendencies which are fairly widespread in New Zealand, without suggesting that the pronunciations indicated are invariable:

1. In New Zealand, as in Australia, the *a* in words like *calm* and *father* is pronounced further forward than in Standard English. In parts of New Zealand, as well as in Australia, there is a tendency to use a short front vowel in words like *dance* and *slant*, which in Standard English have [ɑː], although northern speakers of British English pronounce these words with [æ].

2. The sound [uː], as in *too* and *you*, is sometimes fronted.

3. There is a tendency, as in Australia, to raise and lengthen the sound [ɪ] when it occurs finally in lightly-stressed syllables, as in *city* and *likely*. A similar lengthening of [ɪ] (spelt *e*) takes place in syllables preceding the one which bears the chief stress

134

of the word. Examples are *before, belong* and *eleven.* When [ɪ] is followed by a consonant in a lightly-stressed syllable it is centralized to [ə], as in *Alice, Latin, rabbit* and *take it.*

4. The sibilant [ʃ] is often voiced to [ʒ], as in the names *Asia* and *Persia.*

5. Words which in British English are stressed on the second or third syllable are in New Zealand English often stressed on the first syllable, as in *magazine* and *mankind.* A similar shift of stress often takes place in phrases, as in *after all, all the same.*

6. Words like the conjunction *and* and prepositions, which are generally lightly stressed, receive more stress than in British English. Similarly in the names of the days of the week the final syllable is in New Zealand and Australia generally pronounced like *day,* whereas in British English it is reduced to [-dɪ].

INDIA AND PAKISTAN

In India and Pakistan the chief question concerning English is whether it shall be used at all as an official language. It has been found to be a convenient *lingua franca* for communication among the many linguistic groups in India and Pakistan, but only a very small proportion of the population of the two countries speak English.[1] The Constitution of the Republic of India, adopted in 1950, laid down that Hindi should be the official language of India but that English should continue in use for a further fifteen years. The replacement of English by Hindi is proving a slower process than was expected, but it is less true today than it was fifty years ago that a knowledge of English is essential for advancement in India. Since most Indians and Pakistanis who speak English use it as a second language, they normally aim at speaking the British variety of

[1] In 1958 it was officially estimated that English was then written and read up to school-leaving standard by four million people in India (*The Times,* March 17, 1958).

135

English, without feeling pride in developing a distinctively local form of the language.

Indian English tends to be bookish and not sufficiently in touch with the living English of today. This characteristic is a natural result of the method of teaching. The number of Englishmen available to teach English to Indians is quite inadequate in comparison with the huge population of the country. Hence, most English-speaking Indians have been taught English by other Indians, and both teachers and taught have too often had to rely on books for their knowledge of the language. They have therefore often modelled their style on that of English classic authors. Indians have a good deal of difficulty in distinguishing between one level of English and another, and many of the examples of what has come to be called Babu English are the result of uncertainty about what is the appropriate level of language—poetic, archaic, literary, colloquial, or slang, to mention only some of the possibilities— to suit a particular occasion. A similar uncertainty is likely to exist whenever a foreign language is studied through the medium of books without the opportunity of hearing it spoken as a living language. It has been suggested that even the best pieces of Latin composition which schoolboys of today produce, basing them on the most approved models, would probably have much the same effect on an educated Roman of the time of Cicero as that which a piece of Babu English has on an Englishman.

After the First World War less attention was paid to English grammar in Indian schools and the direct method of teaching became more common. There was an increasing feeling that English was a foreign language whose use in India was merely a temporary expedient. There has consequently been an increase in the number of Indians who feel that there is no point in striving hard to achieve accuracy or literary quality in the use of English: it is enough if one can make oneself understood. There has been a serious decline in the standard of English taught in schools in both India and Pakistan. An attempt was made to stem this decline by the establishment in 1955 of an English Language Institute at Allahabad with a £20,000 grant from the

Nuffield Foundation. Three years later this was followed by the founding of a Central Institute of English at Hyderabad in India and a 'language unit' at the University of the Punjab at Lahore in Pakistan. All of these ventures have been assisted by the British Council.[1]

OTHER OVERSEAS TERRITORIES

Problems similar to those which arise in India and Pakistan arise in other parts of the British Commonwealth when they cease to be Crown Colonies. In Nigeria English serves the same purposes as in India: it is not only a useful second language serving as a means of communication with other countries but it is also a valuable means of communication among Nigerians who speak different languages. Where there is a national language currently used over a wide area, the footing of English as an official language is less secure, although it is likely to remain in use as a second language. The 1957 Independence Constitution of the Federation of Malaya set a ten-year target for the establishment of Malay as the sole official language of the Federation, but it is unlikely that the use of English in Malaya will completely die out.

One English dialect, used in many different parts of the world, remains to be mentioned: Pidgin English. It differs so much from the other varieties of overseas English described in this chapter that it is well on the way to becoming a separate language or group of languages, and an Englishman who has not the slightest difficulty in understanding American or Australian English may very easily be baffled by a piece of pidgin.

Pidgin English is a class dialect of a standing inferior to most other varieties of overseas English and its use in conversation with an educated non-European is likely to cause offence. It originated in China as a means of communication between English-speaking people and the natives of China, and the name *pidgin* is derived from the Chinese distortion of the English word *business*. Another variety, which had its origin in the

[1] *The Times*, February 18, 1959.

need for a means of communication between English settlers and the aborigines of Australia, has now become established in the islands of the Pacific and is known as Beach-la-mar. Other varieties are used in different parts of Africa.

Pidgin English represents an attempt to make English easier for a non-European to use and to understand, partly by the introduction of loan-words from non-European languages and partly by the distortion or simplification of English syntax and word-forms. Certain English words, such as *belong*, tend to recur with monotonous frequency. Clearly pidgin serves a useful purpose as a *lingua franca* for speakers of many different languages, but it may perhaps be doubted whether it is much easier to learn than British English, from which it differs very considerably in syntax. One cannot help feeling that it is a travesty of a language which English sailors and traders have imposed on non-Europeans in much the same way as adults impose 'baby-talk' on babies. Many of the non-English words in pidgin have been taken from other aboriginal languages and are now learnt by both European and non-European speakers of pidgin who both think, mistakenly, that each of them is conversing in the other's language. It would have been just as easy for the native to learn the normal English word.

Pidgin English has not much to recommend it, but it is interesting and often amusing to observe the ingenuity shown in using a simple vocabulary to express new ideas. Jespersen[1] has quoted as examples the phrases used to describe a piano (*big fellow bokus* (i.e., *box*) *you fight him he cry*) and a concertina (*little fellow bokus you shove him he cry you pull him he cry*). These are ingenious inventions, but they may well be nonce-usages which can hardly be regarded as a normal part of the Pidgin English vocabulary. Some of the widely used pidgin expressions, however, show a similar, if less strongly marked ingenuity together with a willingness to sacrifice conciseness. Examples are *lamp belong Jesus* 'the moon', *missionary belong soldier* 'army chaplain', and *small doctor* 'medical orderly'.

[1] Otto Jespersen, *Language, Its Nature, Development, and Origin* (George Allen and Unwin, 1922) pp. 217 f.

Pidgin English is essentially an oral dialect, but it has some-times been reduced to writing, especially by missionaries, and simplified spelling then adds to the effect of strangeness. The following example is the Lord's Prayer as rendered by the Alexishafen Catholic Mission:

> Fader bilong mifelo, yu stop long heven—Ol i santuim nem bilong yu—Kingdom bilong yu i kam—Ol i hirim tok bilong yu long graund olsem long heven. Tude givim mifelo kaikai bilong de—Forgivim rong bilong mifelo—olsem mifelo forgivim rong—ol i mekim long mifelo. Yu no bringim mifelo long traiim—tekewe samting no gud long mifelo. Amen.[1]

The following passage is a more easily intelligible example of pidgin as used in the Cameroons.[2]

> Dis ole woman, sah, she be mammy for dat picken woman. Dat picken woman be wife for dat man. Dat man 'e done go for bush all day, an' when 'e done come back 'e find 'e wife never make him food. 'E belly de cry out, an' de man angry too much, so he like beat 'e wife. De wife 'e run, de man 'e run, for beat 'e wife, an' de ole woman 'e run for beat dis man.

[1] Quoted from Sidney J. Baker, *The Australian Language* (Angus and Robertson, 1945), p. 235.
[2] Gerald Durrell, *The Bafut Beagles*, Penguin edition, 1958, Ch. 8.

CHAPTER VI

Dialect Research

DIALECT RESEARCH MAY have a significance far wider than it seems to have at first, since every new discovery throws some new light on such problems as the nature of dialect or of dialect boundaries. When two dialects belong to the same geographical area and are distinguished from each other only by a difference in time, there is the additional link that the same feature or its development may have been preserved, and it is possible to find in English dialects of the present day many survivals of Old and Middle English dialectal variations. There are nevertheless clear differences between the methods of investigating Early English and those required by Modern English dialects, differences that are imposed by the nature of the material to be investigated.

When we study Early English dialects we are deprived of the opportunity of first-hand observation of spoken dialects; we have to study them through the distorting medium of the written language in which they have been preserved. There is, too, an enormous difference in the amount of material available for study: the amount of extant evidence about Old English dialects is meagre; the material for the study of Middle English dialects is greater in bulk but still hard to use because vital pieces of information are often missing; the evidence for the study of Modern English dialects is almost infinite. The student of present-day dialects enjoys a further advantage in that he can make use of scientific experimental techniques and he can ask his informant questions in order to elicit particular facts.

In view of these advantages, it might seem reasonable to expect that present-day dialects would have attracted much more attention than those of the past. In fact, they have not done so because the advantages that have been mentioned are counter-balanced by disadvantages. Perhaps the chief of these arises from the changed status of dialects since the rise of Standard English. Old and Middle English dialects have been carefully studied because they are the key to Old and Middle English literature; Modern English literature can be studied without any attention being paid to dialects, and even those who study the spoken language are often interested only in Standard English. Then, too, written records are much easier to consult than records of speech. The study of present-day spoken dialects must be based upon field-work, and the recording of dialects, although it has made great progress during the last two decades, is still in its infancy in comparison with the recording of the written word. Finally, the very wealth of material available for the study of the spoken English of the present day presents a problem; the dialects of today present a picture so complicated that it is difficult to distinguish significant trends.

There is still plenty of work to be done on Old and Middle English dialects. The first requirement is the editing of texts. For the student of dialects a critical edition of a work that exists in several manuscripts is not enough; he needs to be able to consult all the extant manuscripts, since Old and Middle English scribes made no attempt to preserve the spellings of the manuscripts that they copied. Several Middle English texts have been preserved in a large number of manuscripts, and it seems likely that in future increasing use will be made of micro-films, since the cost of printing all these manuscripts would be prohibitive.

The next requirements are a study of the language of each manuscript and an adequate glossary of each text. Here too microfilms can prove useful in reproducing the typescript records of research needed by only a small number of other workers.

In a good deal of this research the dialectal interest would be only incidental, since there are several linguistic characteristics which apparently have no dialectal significance.

The art of dialect research consists in the main of the ability to detect significant trends when confronted with a mass of detailed information. The chief problem is to know how far it is legitimate to ignore isolated occurrences of forms that resist the general trend. Unless some isolated forms are ignored, no general statement about dialect is possible. On the other hand, some of the pioneers in the study of Old and Middle English dialects have made general statements which later research may well show to have been oversimplified. The study of dialects of the present day has shown that different words containing the same sound may show differing developments of that sound, and it is therefore necessary to remember this possibility when we are investigating problems of Old and Middle English dialectology, such as the threefold development of OE $\check{y}$.

One branch of Old and Middle English dialect studies that has yet to be fully explored is the dialectal distribution of vocabulary. There is a need for fairly full glossaries, recording the number of occurrences of words in each text, since a decided preponderance of a particular word in one dialect can be regarded as significant, whereas isolated occurrences cannot. In this branch of dialect study it is particularly important to beware of drawing conclusions from negative evidence; when texts are few, a good deal may depend on the accident of survival.

There is no lack of material for the investigation of present-day dialects, but the material is not always of the kind that we should like. The speech of any one person is known as an idiolect, and the best way of beginning the study of a dialect is to study a number of idiolects in order to see whether any consistent pattern emerges. Unfortunately, people now move about so much and come under so many different influences that very often no consistent pattern does emerge. Most of the studies of English dialects that have so far been published are archaistic in their approach: they seek for survivals in present-day speech of dialectal variations that we know to have existed in the past. This bias is understandable and desirable in so far as this is the kind of dialectal research that most urgently needs to be undertaken. The number of speakers who preserve the old dialects is rapidly diminishing, but even if such speakers completely disappear, there will still be scope for dialect research, though the nature of the research will change. Instead of seeking in dialects for survivals of the past, investigators will study the speech of individuals or groups of people in order to find out what are the realities of contemporary speech as distinct from the picture presented in grammars. The effects of mixed backgrounds on speech may profitably be investigated and more attention may be paid to the differences that occur in the speech of one person according to varying environment or occasion. The very complicated nature of the material to be investigated adds to the difficulty of the research but it also adds to its interest.

Research into dialects can follow the established divisions of linguistic study: it can deal with vocabulary, semantics, pronunciation, word-formation, accidence, and syntax, and each of these main groups can be subdivided. For example, a study of dialectal pronunciation must necessarily deal with the quality of vowels and consonants but it should also include a study of such features as intonation. In the early days of the study of English dialects it was vocabulary that attracted most attention; today a good deal of attention is being paid to the phonology of dialects. Two aspects of dialect study that have been neglected in the past are intonation and syntax. One reason for the neglect of intonation may have been that its serious study calls for a good ear for variations of pitch, and this is not a very common gift. Another is that subtle differences of intonation are not easy to record except by means of a tape-recorder, and portable tape-recorders have not until recently been available. There has been some research in this field at the University of Leeds, where an M.A. dissertation on the intonation of Lincolnshire dialects has been completed.[1] Syntax

[1] Cynthia Haldenby, *Intonation in Lincolnshire Dialect*, Leeds M.A. Dissertation, 1959.

cannot be studied at all thoroughly by means of a questionnaire. Its investigation calls for an ability to take part in the free and easy conversation of dialect speakers. Nothing is so likely to interfere with the natural syntax of dialect speech as the knowledge that the investigator is particularly interested in details of syntax.

There is still much work to be done on English dialect vocabulary. A good deal remains to be discovered about the distribution of dialect words that are already known, and a promising field for the discovery of new words is in the technical vocabulary of particular trades. The etymology of a dialect word must be known before its varying pronunciations can be used to illustrate the phonology of dialects, but there are many dialect words whose etymology has yet to be discovered, and there is plenty of work to be done on the semantic development of dialect words.

In phonology and accidence the boundaries between different dialects need to be fixed with greater precision than has been attained in the past. There is undoubtedly a need for a complete survey of English dialects of the kind that is now in progress at the University of Leeds, but there is a danger in assuming that such a task can be completed once and for all. It was such an approach to dialect study that led to the closing down of the English Dialect Society after the publication of Wright's *English Dialect Dictionary* on the grounds that there was then no more work for the Society to do. Any dialect survey is based upon a small selection from a vast mass of available material. An investigator ought to make some attempt to discover whether the sample that he has chosen is large enough to be representative. Naturally he will make this attempt when he is making preliminary plans for the survey, but it is a question to which no final answer is possible and the answer to it will vary in different parts of the country. When a survey of English dialects has been completed, it will be well worth while to cover selected areas again with a closer net, and in course of time a new survey will become necessary in order to find out in what ways the picture has changed. In the same way it is instructive to compare the information revealed by surveys taking place at present with the picture presented by A. J. Ellis in his *Early English Pronunciation* (1889). In selecting areas to be investigated with a closer net, it will be useful to concentrate on those parts of the country which seem to constitute border areas. In order to find out how close the net should be, it is profitable to undertake an intensive study of a few small areas in order to find out whether the results differ materially according to the number of informants in each place. Dialect surveys are often based upon information obtained from one informant in each village. Results obtained in this way are valuable in countries where the speech of the inhabitants of each village is homogeneous, but English dialects are now so mixed that we cannot assume that one informant, however carefully selected, can be regarded as typical of a whole village. In choosing informants for the preparation of a dialect atlas, preference is normally given to people with an uncomplicated history. The number of such persons is rapidly diminishing, and one way in which dialect research might profitably develop in the future is by investigating the dialect of speakers specially chosen for their complicated speech-history. The result would be worthless as a basis for the compiling of a dialect atlas, but it would throw useful light on such questions as the permanence of speech-habits and it would have the advantage that it would be a study of the sort of dialect that is spoken by the great majority of English dialect speakers today. It is more difficult than the traditional kind of dialect investigation, and it is possible only when dialect research of the traditional kind has prepared the way by establishing the chief characteristics of a number of dialects.

When dialect boundaries have been discovered there is an opportunity to link up dialect studies with other branches of knowledge by trying to find a reason why the boundaries occur where they do. Sometimes the reason is to be found in the geographical features of the district, such as a river or a patch of hilly country. Sometimes the reason may be historical, and the cause of dialectal variation may sometimes be traced very far back in the past, to the fluctuating boundaries of the

Anglo-Saxon Heptarchy or to the Danelaw. Sometimes economic factors play a part: areas which share a common main industry or which look towards the same market town are liable to have some dialectal characteristics in common. Sometimes a knowledge of the method employed in local industries is necessary to an understanding of the meaning of dialect vocabulary. To anyone brought up in a sheep-farming district, a word like *sheep* has insufficient defining value; he will use many different words to describe different kinds of sheep.

One of the chief difficulties of dialect research is how to collect the material without distorting it. It is essential that the recorded speech should be natural, but, if the speaker knows that what he says is being recorded, that knowledge is almost sure to interfere with the naturalness of his pronunciation or of his choice of words. On the other hand, any attempt to record speech without the knowledge of the speaker is liable to cause resentment. This is one of the objections to the use of recorded telephone conversations as material for research; other objections are that telephone conversations tend to develop a syntax and an articulation of their own and that the telephone is not a very accurate instrument. An attempt has sometimes been made to use conversations in novels as evidence of contemporary speech, but the question at once arises how far the novelist is an accurate reporter. Such conversations cannot be regarded as primary sources of evidence about actual speech, and, if they are investigated at all, their interest is literary rather than linguistic. The most favoured way of collecting evidence for dialect research is the questionnaire, but it is not the only way and it has obvious limitations. It can be used very effectively for the investigation of vocabulary and pronunciation, but it is less useful for the investigation of syntax, and its use nearly always involves a loss of naturalness of speech. Some preliminary investigation of a dialect is necessary before a questionnaire can be prepared. Probably the best way of obtaining a natural record of speech is to secure the co-operation of a group of people who are discussing a subject of general interest and to disregard the earlier part of the recording, during which the speakers are most likely to suffer from a self-consciousness that may affect their speech. This body of material may be supplemented by reports from field-workers of remarks made to them or overheard by them. A field-worker collecting material of this kind needs to have a good memory and to record conversations as soon as possible after they have taken place; any production of a note-book is liable to lead to a drying-up of the sources of material, if not to active expression of resentment of the kind produced by Mr Pickwick, a pioneer in this branch of linguistic research: 'Would any body believe as an informer 'ud go about in a man's cab, not only takin' down his number, but ev'ry word he says into the bargain?' (*The Pickwick Papers*, Ch. 2).

The tape-recording machine has a useful part to play in dialect research, though, like all machines, it is sometimes in danger of being regarded as a substitute for, rather than as an aid to, research. The important question is what use is going to be made of the recordings when they have been collected. As an aid to research, tape-recordings have two obvious advantages. They make it possible to record an informant's answers with greater accuracy, since an investigator can transcribe the recordings unhurriedly when he is alone and can repeat the playing back of the recording until he is satisfied with the accuracy of his transcript. A second advantage of tape-recordings is that they make division of labour possible. A good ear for sounds is not a common qualification, and a field-worker who possesses the other necessary qualities but who has not a very good ear for sounds is able to enlist the help of some-one who has, or even of phonetic instruments, to analyse the sounds that he has recorded. A disadvantage of a recording machine is that it may arouse the suspicion or hostility of some informants and make others self-conscious. On the other hand, some informants rather like to hear a recording of their own speech, and the prospect of hearing a recording can be used as an inducement to compensate for the quite considerable sacrifice of time that working through a questionnaire involves. Here, as on so many points, a decision has to be left to the judgment of the field-worker.

Apart from its value to the field-worker, the tape-recording machine is a useful means of preserving dialects for posterity or for the general public who find the reading of phonetic script uncongenial. The invention is still so recent that it is not yet possible to say how permanent tape-recordings will be and there is much to be said in favour of transferring selected recordings on to gramophone records. The value of the tape-recording machine as a way of satisfying and encouraging popular interest in dialect is illustrated by an experiment that has been tried at the Castle Museum at York, where a press-button tape-recording machine has been installed. The record consists of a dialect passage, lasting for forty-five seconds, from each of the three Ridings and one from the City of York. No doubt the novelty and ingenuity of the experiment did much to stimulate public interest, but the figures quoted to describe the use made of the machine provide remarkable evidence of the widespread interest in dialect. During the first six months after the installation of the machine, the recording was played 17,800 times and was heard by approximately 236,000 people.[1]

In dialect research as it is conducted today the field-worker is of fundamental importance. His importance was not so fully recognized during the nineteenth century and Joseph Wright, in compiling his *English Dialect Dictionary*, made a good deal of use of information supplied by local residents, often a village schoolmaster or clergyman with an interest in dialect, but the tendency today is to emphasize that the collection of information about dialect is a highly skilled task. The advantages of the postal questionnaire are its cheapness and the speed with which material can be collected, but the use of postal methods involves a number of restrictions and uncertainties. There is a good deal of chance about the location of informants who return a postal questionnaire, whereas a field-worker's informants normally come from places carefully selected in the light of a knowledge of local geography and history, and a field-worker can exercise more care in checking the qualifications of his informants than

---

[1] R. Patterson, 'Dialect as a Museum "Display"', *TYDS* lv (1955), pp. 46-8.

can the organizers of a postal questionnaire. The need for a field-worker is most apparent when pronunciation is being investigated, since so much depends on the accuracy of the investigator's hearing and on his freedom from preconceptions based on the written form of the word in question. Even when research is concerned with the choice of words rather than with their pronunciation, however, information obtained from a trained field-worker is more reliable than information from an unknown source, since the field-worker is more likely to have satisfied himself that his informant is a native whose speech can be regarded as typical of the place where he lives, and not a speaker who has introduced words from other dialects. A good deal, too, depends on the way in which a question is framed. A trained field-worker is less likely than an amateur enthusiast to suggest one particular answer to his informant. There have been instances of interesting words being reported when what the informant in fact said was 'Aye, that's right'. A field-worker has to resist the temptation to urge his informant to speak more plainly, and requests for repetition, though sometimes necessary, are always liable to elicit a distorted pronunciation. A similar distortion may take place if the informant is given the chance to correct the field-worker's imitation of his pronunciation, but the risk is worth taking, since it improves the accuracy of the field-worker's transcription. The postal questionnaire need not be entirely ruled out as a means of obtaining information about dialects. It is a useful way of making the net closer by supplementing the information collected by field-workers. A long and complicated questionnaire needs a field-worker to use it, but a few short and simple questions can be answered by post. Quite apart from the value of the information obtained, public appeals for information on specific points serve a useful purpose by arousing interest in dialects and making informants think about things that they have previously taken for granted. This aspect of dialect research is particularly important in connexion with the collaboration of schools. School-children have provided much valuable information about field-names which has been incorporated in the publications of the English Place-Name

Society. There are many problems of dialect research where their help might be equally useful.

A field-worker needs to possess a rare mixture of personal qualities and technical skill. He must be friendly and able to get on good terms with strangers. He must be patient and tactful, content to listen to a good deal of information that does not interest him in order to elicit the items of information that he is seeking, but careful not to waste time. He needs to have good health and stamina, since his work is physically tiring. Above all, he needs to have a good ear for varieties of speech-sounds and enough technical knowledge to enable him to transcribe sounds quickly and accurately in phonetic symbols. If he can himself speak a form of English that does not sound offensively 'la-di-da' to dialect speakers, he will find it easier to get on good terms with them. Lastly, he must have a sense of vocation and a genuine interest in dialect, for with all these qualities he could earn very much more in other occupations than he is likely to be paid as a dialect field-worker.

One of the field-worker's most important tasks is the choice of suitable informants to answer the questions contained in the questionnaire. The most important requirement is that the informant shall be a native of the village in which he lives. It is desirable that both his parents should have been natives of the village and that he should have spent most of his life there. Elderly informants are generally to be preferred because they are more likely to remember the older forms of the local dialect. Working through a questionnaire takes several hours and an informant who has retired from his work is most likely to be willing to spare the time, but the informant should still be fairly active, with good sight and hearing. As a rule farmers and farm labourers, especially those who have worked on small farms, make good informants. The informant must always be regarded as the teacher and the field-worker as his pupil. The role of instructor is one which the informant generally enjoys.

One problem which confronts a field-worker is whether he should allow more than one informant to contribute the answers to a single questionnaire. Ideally he should not, especially if pronunciation is in question. If a second informant is used, he should answer the whole questionnaire and he then acts as a very valuable check on the first informant. There may, however, be occasions when the rigorous application of this rule would prevent a field-worker from collecting valuable information, since many informants whose other qualifications are ideal may be unwilling to spare the time or may not have the technical knowledge necessary to answer a whole questionnaire. When a questionnaire is divided into sections it is perhaps legitimate to regard some of the more technical sections as appendices that can be omitted or answered by a different informant when necessary, but one requirement should be regarded as indispensable: every answer should be from a specified informant about whose linguistic background the field-worker has adequate information.

Another question of method that has to be decided is whether a field-worker should be allowed to revise the material that he has collected. The best solution of the problem would seem to be that if further experience makes a field-worker want to revise his material, it is an indication that he or another field-worker should return to the place for further investigation, possibly with a different informant.

When information about dialects has been collected by field-workers and reduced to manageable proportions by an editor, it is necessary to decide how the results of the research shall be presented. The usual method is by means of maps on which each recorded occurrence of a word or a linguistic usage is represented. A vast amount of information has to be recorded and these maps are necessarily large and expensive to produce. Moreover, if the network is at all fine, there is so much material that a reader examining a detailed map may find it hard to see the wood for the trees, and, even so, a map inevitably presents an over-simplified picture of dialect. It does not, for example, give any information about the age or the social standing of the speaker, and this information is often important. In view of the very high cost of maps, it seems likely that in future the organizers of dialect surveys will pay increasing attention to other methods of presenting their results. One suggestion that has been made is to make use of the grid which is now superimposed on one-inch Ordnance Survey maps. If every dialect form is accompanied by a grid reference indicating where it was heard, the recorded forms can be set out fairly cheaply on printed or cyclostyled sheets in the order of the grid references. Sheets can then be set out side by side presenting the sort of picture that can be represented by a map. Whatever method of presentation is adopted for the main bulk of the material, however, there will always be a use for small-scale maps to present summaries of the most important pieces of information.

Although English dialects are full of interest, England has lagged behind some continental countries in dialect research. It may be that the work done by British scholars in the nineteenth century has received insufficient recognition abroad because its bias was mainly lexical, whereas continental scholars are more interested in the distribution of dialectal features, but a country which has produced Joseph Wright does not need to be too modest about its achievements in dialectology. Since the Second World War a good deal has been done to belie the reproach that the serious study of dialects is neglected in this country.

The earliest important study of the phonology of English dialects was that of A. J. Ellis, who devoted the fifth volume of his *Early English Pronunciation* (1889) to a detailed study of the phonology of Modern English dialects, with illustrative specimens in phonetic script. Ellis's work can still be used with profit, although the presentation of his results is not easy to follow and the 'palaeotype' that he used for the transcription of specimens now seems antiquated.

The publication of Joseph Wright's *English Dialect Dictionary* in six volumes from 1898 to 1905 was a landmark in the history of the study of English dialects. Wright had access to manuscript collections which had been prepared by W. W. Skeat and A. Smythe Palmer and to the publications of the English Dialect Society, but the work carried out by Wright himself and by his wife Elizabeth Mary Wright was quite outstanding. Wright

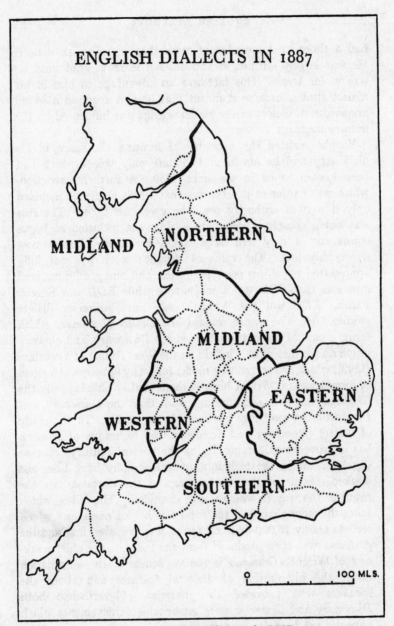

ENGLISH DIALECTS IN 1887

MIDLAND

NORTHERN

MIDLAND

WESTERN

EASTERN

SOUTHERN

0   100 MLS.

Map 7.   English Dialects in 1887

153

had a thorough knowledge of more than one English dialect. He was largely self-taught and did not learn to read until he was in his teens. This fact was an advantage to him in his dialect studies because it meant that he had acquired a sound knowledge of dialect before his knowledge was influenced by the literary language.

Wright realized the necessity of limiting the scope of his dictionary and he aimed at including only words which had been known to be in use since 1650. A further restriction, which was harder to justify, was that words would be included only if written authority could be given for them. The rule was not a complete protection against the inclusion of bogus words and it may well have excluded valuable material now irrevocably lost. The value of Wright's work was not fully appreciated by all his contemporaries, and one good-humoured gibe was that *OED* was Don Quixote while *EDD* was Sancho Panza. *EDD* was not Wright's only contribution to dialect studies. He also wrote an *English Dialect Grammar*, which forms a part of the sixth volume of the *Dictionary*, and a monograph on the dialect of Windhill, in the West Riding of Yorkshire (1892), which has served as a model for many subsequent writers of monographs. Wright himself thought that philologically the *Grammar* was a more important work than the *Dictionary*, but the *Dictionary* probably has more lasting value. In the study of dialect phonology and accidence, the technique of research has improved considerably during the present century, whereas developments in the technique of lexicography have been less marked. Some of the shortcomings of the *Grammar* are the result of the way in which it was compiled. The index, which takes up more than half the total number of pages and which records nearly 16,000 dialectal forms, was prepared first and the grammar was then produced from the index. The chief weakness of Wright's *Grammar* is the vagueness of the information about the distribution of dialectal features and about the speakers who provided the material. Nevertheless both *Dictionary* and *Grammar* were remarkable achievements which have not yet been superseded.

Dialect societies have played an active part in encouraging research into English dialects. The earliest of these was the English Dialect Society. The first proposal towards the foundation of a Society for collecting and preserving provincial words was made by Aldis Wright in *Notes and Queries* for March 12, 1870. Striking a note that was to become familiar, Wright said:

> *In a few years it will be too late.* Railroads and certificated teachers are doing their work. Let each provincial word, and usage of a word, be recorded, with an example of its application if necessary, and a note of the place where it is so used; but of etymologies let collectors beware.

Aldis Wright's suggestion was taken up by A. J. Ellis in the Introduction to Part III of his *Early English Pronunciation* (1871). The Society came into being two years later with W. W. Skeat as its secretary. It undertook an ambitious programme of publications, which can still be used with advantage. The Society's publications were in four series: bibliographies, reprinted glossaries, original glossaries, and miscellanies. In the last group were included a few specimens of early dialectal texts and reports on dialect research. One drawback of the Society's publications is that the material is too often arranged by counties. It is only rarely that county boundaries coincide with dialect boundaries, and county glossaries include in the same alphabetical list words that have a very limited local currency and words that are in general dialect use. A good deal of the information contained in the Society's publications was incorporated in *EDD*, which gives a better idea of the distribution of dialect vocabulary, although Wright's summary of distribution by counties is necessarily vague.

Aldis Wright's warning that collectors should beware of etymology was followed up in the *Rules and Directions for Word-Collectors* which the Society issued in the first year of its life, and in the Second Annual Report Skeat defended the policy of asking word-collectors not to concern themselves with etymology. He suggested that etymology should be left until a later stage, after the material had been collected, and pointed out that there was a danger that speculation about the supposed etymology of a word might distort a collector's definition of its meaning. Although he was writing during the pioneer days of dialect research, Skeat showed that he realized that the word-collector's task was no simple matter. Many later investigators could have profited by his reminder that the investigator should describe not only the sense and the use of a word and the exact locality where it is used, but should say whether it is common or uncommon and what class of people use it. He realized that the study of regional dialects cannot be divorced from the study of class dialects.

In 1876 the headquarters of the Society were transferred to Manchester, where they remained until 1893, when they were transferred to Oxford, shortly before the Society ceased to exist. One result of the Society's long association with Manchester was that its library, consisting of more than eight hundred books and pamphlets, was presented to the Manchester Free Libraries Committee, and the Manchester Central Library today is consequently particularly rich in works on dialect.

The closing down of the English Dialect Society left a gap which has been partially filled by the foundation of county dialect societies in those parts of the country, chiefly the northern counties, in which interest in dialects is strongest. The county society which has had the longest life and which has done most to encourage the study of dialect is the Yorkshire Dialect Society, founded in 1897 and still flourishing. It grew out of the activities of the Yorkshire Committee of Workers set up to collect material for *EDD*. This committee had come into existence in October 1894 at the suggestion of Joseph Wright. Other societies with similar aims are the Lakeland Dialect Society (founded in 1939) and the Lancashire Dialect Society (founded in 1951). Each of these societies publishes an annual volume of transactions in which are included original prose and verse in dialect and articles on various aspects of dialect research. These articles cover a wider field than might be supposed from the names of the societies which publish them. Thus, *The Transactions of the Yorkshire Dialect Society* has included studies of such subjects as William Barnes, the Dorset poet (1917),

Essex dialect (1918), the dialects of Northumberland (1930), slang, cant and jargon (1935), and Shakespeare's use of dialect (1950). *The Journal of the Lakeland Dialect Society* has concentrated on the publication of work in dialect to a greater extent than the other societies, but it has included such articles as 'Lakeland Dialect Study' (1953) and 'The Linguistic Survey of Scotland and its Activities in Cumberland' (1955), a title which shows that dialect research does not slavishly accept political boundaries. *The Journal of the Lancashire Dialect Society* has included articles on the Leeds survey of dialectal English (1952), the study of dialect in Germany (1954), the study of German dialect in Switzerland (1955), linguistic geography (1956), Cheshire place-names (1956), and the study of American dialects (1959 and 1960). The county dialect societies have undertaken the investigation of certain aspects of dialect by means of postal questionnaires. The results of these investigations are recorded in such articles as Harold Orton's 'Yorkshire Terms for Earwig and for the Mid-Morning Meal' (*TYDS*, lviii (1958), 52–55) and A. W. Boyd's 'Farming Terms' (*JLDS*, viii (1959), 19–31). Appeals for information of this kind often receive publicity in local newspapers, and the enquiry for local names for an earwig produced about 130 replies. One feature of the work of the county dialect societies is that they help to act as a link between the academic study of dialect and its day-to-day use and their transactions include articles by many university teachers.

Beside the county societies there are other societies which do a good deal to encourage the study of dialect. The American Dialect Society was founded in 1889 and had the support of such eminent scholars as F. J. Child and J. M. Manly. It was revived in 1941 and its publications are of importance to all who take an interest in American English. The Philological Society was established in 1842 and has included English dialects among the wide range of subjects whose study it has encouraged. The Society's publications include such studies as R. B. Peacock's 'Glossary of the Dialect of the Hundred of Lonsdale in Lancashire', published in the Transactions for 1867, and B.

Brilioth's *Grammar of the Dialect of Lorton (Cumberland)*, published in 1913. The Philological Society joined with the Early English Text and Chaucer Societies to publish A. J. Ellis's monumental *Early English Pronunciation* (1869–1889), the fifth volume of which is a survey of English dialects. There are also non-academic societies, like the flourishing Edwin Waugh Society of Rochdale, which do not publish transactions but which encourage an interest in dialect.

Two systematic surveys of the dialects of Great Britain are in progress, with headquarters at the Universities of Leeds and Edinburgh.

The director of the Leeds survey is Professor Harold Orton, who worked in collaboration with Professor Eugen Dieth, of the University of Zurich, until the death of Dieth in 1956. The aims of the survey have been described by Professor Orton:

> Our task, as it presented itself to us in 1946, fell into several stages. First, there was the production of a comprehensive questionnaire, to reveal the distinctive lexical, phonological, morphological and syntactical features of all the main English dialects; second, the selection of an adequate network of rural localities with enough dialect-speaking informants of the right kind; third, the selection and training of competent fieldworkers to use the Questionnaire for securing the responses wanted from informants; fourth, the editing of all this material preparatory to publication; fifth, the publication of the results of the Survey in a suitable form, whether maps, or lists, or both; sixth, the provision of the necessary accommodation from which to carry on the Survey; lastly, the requisite money to finance the project had to be assured.[1]

Work on the survey began in 1946 and the field-work in the network of 311 localities spread over the whole of England was completed in 1961. The aim of the survey is archaistic; it is to investigate the traditional vernacular as reflected in the speech of the oldest generation of surviving dialect speakers and it concentrates on farmers and farm-workers of sixty years of age or more. The reasons for the agricultural bias are that traditional regional dialects are best preserved in farming

[1] Harold Orton 'An English Dialect Survey: Linguistic Atlas of England', *Orbis*, ix (1960), p. 333.

communities and that farming, as a universal industry, provides a larger amount of comparable material for the whole country than would be provided by more localized industries, such as mining or seafaring. The questionnaire used for the survey was published in 1952 by the Leeds Philosophical and Literary Society. It comprises about 1300 questions, dealing in the main with farming and the home, and is divided into nine sections, each of which can be answered in about two hours. Of the questions 365 are designed to throw light on the sound-system of any given dialect, 62 on its morphology, 41 on its syntax, and 730 on its lexical features. The compilers of the questionnaire resisted the temptation to ask informants to translate Standard English words into their own dialects, and care was taken to avoid using in a question any word or sound that might form part of the reply. The questionnaire was devised for the use of skilled field-workers who realize the necessity of adhering rigidly to the exact wording of each question. The replies of informants are transcribed by field-workers in phonetic symbols and the field-worker is also asked to record incidental material arising out of his conversations with informants. The localities which have been investigated are mainly rural, preferably with 400 to 500 inhabitants, and not as a rule more than fifteen miles apart. Although the survey covers the whole of England, the northern counties have been surveyed first and the material from these counties has now been published.

The Linguistic Survey of Scotland is remarkable for the wide range of interests which it represents, a range which is enlarged by the existence in Scotland of a Celtic language side by side with the English dialect commonly known as Lowland Scots. The survey is directed by Professors Angus McIntosh, Kenneth Jackson and David Abercrombie. One difference in method between the Leeds and Edinburgh surveys is that the latter has made use of postal questionnaires as well as investigation by field-workers. The Scottish survey began in 1949 and questionnaires were sent out in 1951 and 1953, each asking for information about 207 linguistic points chiefly of lexical interest. The questionnaire was sent to head teachers of schools with a request that it should be passed on to some native of the district who would be able and willing to fill it up and return it. The appeal met with a good response and 1336 completed copies of the first questionnaire were received from Scotland alone. In addition, 234 copies were received from Northumberland, 72 from Cumberland, 198 from Northern Ireland, and 16 from the Isle of Man.

The postal questionnaires of the Edinburgh survey have been supplemented by another questionnaire intended for the use of field-workers. This consists of 982 items, the main purpose of which is to discover the phonological structure of the various dialects; 'it is designed to discover how many different vowels and consonants are used in each particular dialect, what these are, and in which contexts of neighbouring sounds each of them occurs'.[1] This method shows the application to dialect study of a structuralist technique that has been used very effectively in the study of foreign languages of whose previous history nothing is known, and it is to be contrasted with the approach to the phonology of dialect found in most published monographs, which are chiefly concerned with tracing the development in modern dialects of the sounds which are believed to have existed in earlier periods of the history of the English language. The decision of the directors of the Scottish survey to include neighbouring areas of England is to be welcomed, since linguistic boundaries do not necessarily correspond with those of political units, and the historical causes of linguistic boundaries form a particularly fruitful field of dialect research. It is, for example, interesting to try to discover the reasons why, in the distribution of dialect vocabulary, the linguistic boundary in the East is often well down in Central or South Northumberland, whereas in the West, Northern English words tend to spread North into Dumfriesshire.[2]

Two important lexicographical projects are in progress at

---

[1] John S. Woolley, 'The Linguistic Survey of Scotland and its Activities in Cumberland', *Journal of the Lakeland Dialect Society*, xvii (1955), p. 10.
[2] Woolley, *op. cit.*, p. 11.

Edinburgh and are housed in the same building as the Linguistic Survey of Scotland: the preparation and publication of the *Scottish National Dictionary* and the *Dictionary of the Older Scottish Tongue*. These two dictionaries are being edited under the general supervision of the Scottish Dictionaries Joint Council, on which the Scottish universities are represented, and they continue the work begun by the late Sir William Craigie, one of the editors of the *Oxford English Dictionary*, and by the late William Grant, Convener of the Scottish Dialect Committee.

The links between history and dialect boundaries form an important part of the research that is in progress into the dialects spoken in the United States. Another feature of American dialect research is that it pays attention to the study of social levels of dialect as well as to regional variations. *The Linguistic Atlas of the United States* has to deal with a population four times that of England spread over an area sixty times as great. The survey has therefore been organized as a group of semi-autonomous projects, using the same methods but independently administered and financed. The survey of the New England states is complete; the field-work was carried out in 213 places between 1931 and 1933 and the results were published in 1939–1943 in a handbook and six volumes of maps recording the phonetic spellings of all the replies. The questionnaires used in the American survey contain from 500 to 800 items, a much smaller number than in the English or Scottish surveys. On the other hand in the American survey two informants have been used in each place, one of them old and not highly educated, the other middle-aged with at least a high school education. Hence it is possible to obtain a contrast between two generations and two social levels.

The questionnaires are designed to investigate pronunciation and grammar as well as vocabulary. The investigators are concerned not only with relics of the past but also with innovations; for example, one of their tasks has been to record the various local terms used to describe what in British English is called paraffin and in American English is generally called kerosene.

The choice of communities to be investigated was determined largely by historical considerations. All the earliest permanent settlements were included; some were chosen because they were established on routes of migration or communication, others because they were isolated by natural features such as rivers or mountains; some were chosen because they had been settled by more or less compact bodies of immigrants, like the Cornish miners who settled in the copper country of Northern Michigan.

Most of the field-workers engaged in the American survey have had some experience of investigating and recording American Indian languages. In the New England survey two field-workers conducted three-fifths of the interviews. In the Middle and South Atlantic states there were two field-workers. In the other regions field-workers have been more numerous, but it has been the normal practice for a new field-worker to accompany an experienced one on a field trip before undertaking interviews on his own and in this way the dangers arising from the use of a large number of inexperienced field-workers have been lessened.

Although the American survey is not complete, it has already made it necessary to revise traditional views of American dialects. The old threefold division into New England, Southern and General American has been found to be a serious over-simplification.

CHAPTER VII

Class and Occupational Dialects

THE BASIS OF subdivision of a language into its dialects need not necessarily be regional, and speech-habits are shared not only by those who come from the same place but also by those who belong to the same social class. The existence of class dialect is recognized by many dictionaries. Thus, *OED* says of *lady* (sense 4 b): 'The uneducated, especially in London, still often use "Lady" in the singular as a term of address for "Madam" or "Ma'am"'. Deep feeling underlies H. C. Wyld's description of the word *bloody* in his *Universal English Dictionary* as a 'low, vulgar, blasphemous epithet; also meaningless adjective much used among very low persons'. The editors of *OED* seem to share this emotion in their comment on the same word: 'Now constantly in the mouths of the lowest classes, but by respectable people considered a horrid word'.

The same linguistic characteristic may be a feature of both regional and class dialect. Professor T. H. Pear has pointed out that one of the difficulties in separating geographical and social dialects is that the public schools spread one particular social dialect all over England.[1] The use of a long or short *a* in words like *path* and *grass* is primarily a regional characteristic: it is normal in the South, but in the North a short vowel is more common. Such is the prestige of Southern English, however, that in the North a long *a* in such words has come to be a feature of class dialect. Speakers often become proud of their own

[1] T. H. Pear, *English Social Differences* (George Allen and Unwin, 1955), p. 70.

163

dialect, and the distaste which many southerners feel for the short *a* is exceeded only by the contempt which many northerners feel for the long vowel. It is reassuring to find that the same tendency to make a moral issue of dialectal differences exists in Scotland, as in the remark of the Fifer who said to the Aberdonian, 'Onywye, we're no the fowk that caas *fush* feesh'.[1]

Just as many people speak a regional dialect without being conscious of doing so, there are many who speak an easily recognizable class dialect without realizing the extent to which their vocabulary and pronunciation reveal their social class. A well-born Englishman, trying to establish friendly contacts in a village pub, is reported to have said 'Don't call me sir, my good man'.

There is no doubt that there is a widespread interest in class dialect today, and it is equally true that to many people the interest seems unhealthy. It is worth while to examine why the discussion of what constitutes upper-class usage should be distasteful to some people while it is a subject of enthralling interest to others. One reason for distaste is the suspicion that the wide interest that the subject arouses does not spring wholly from disinterested love of knowledge. If it did, one would expect interest to be aroused equally by other aspects of sociology or linguistics which quite conspicuously are not subjects of general interest. Interest in upper-class speech is too often the result of a desire to acquire the externals of upper-class behaviour so as to give the impression that one belongs to that class oneself. Although the writers of books and articles on upper-class speech are usually anxious to claim that their works are purely factual, the impression that they make on the reader is very similar to that produced by a nineteenth-century book of etiquette. For example, in *Noblesse Oblige*[2] Professor A. S. C. Ross claims that his whole article is purely factual (p. 12), but we find the injunction 'Letters to ambassadors whom one does

[1] Angus McIntosh, *An Introduction to a Survey of Scottish Dialects* (Nelson, 1952), p. 53.
[2] *Noblesse Oblige: An Enquiry into the Identifiable Characteristics of the English Aristocracy*, by Alan S. C. Ross, Nancy Mitford and others (Hamish Hamilton, 1956).

not know should begin *Dear Excellency* and the envelope should be addressed. . . .' (p. 17). For at least one of Professor Ross's readers the distinction between ambassadors that one knows and those that one does not know simply does not arise, and such crumbs of information seem to belong to the sphere of prescriptive, rather than descriptive, linguistics.

One reason why the discussion of the differences between upper-class and lower-class English seems so unsatisfactory is that to divide linguistic usages into two groups, one labelled U and the other non-U, involves serious over-simplification. If there are social classes at all, there are far more than two of them, and the student of class dialects is not concerned merely with the speech-habits of that small fraction of the population which belongs to the upper classes. Moreover, it is an over-simplification to regard upper-class speech as homogeneous. Anyone who listens regularly to BBC news bulletins has little difficulty in identifying the speech of several different announcers even though he may not know their names, and the study of class dialects might well begin with the detailed study of such idiolects.

A further difficulty is one of definition. The serious study of class dialect must be preceded, or at any rate accompanied, by very great advances in the science of sociology. Until social classes can be defined with some degree of precision, it is unprofitable to try to achieve precision in describing the speech-habits of those classes. The lack of precision is not entirely due to the fact that the science of sociology is still in its infancy; it is due also to the scarcity of clearly-defined social groups in English society of today. The rigidity with which social groups can be defined varies in different parts of the country. In County Durham the degree of rigidity of both social and regional groups is high, if we are to believe an article in *The Economist*:

Perhaps the greatest deterrent to firms from the south is that immigrant executives and their wives might not mix well with their native counterparts, who are inclined, in the presence of southerners, to stress their flat A's. The local hunting and shooting milieu is said to be impenetrable to those of under fifty years' standing in the county: the many technologists and executives at the ICI works at Billingham appear to move very largely in ICI circles only.[1]

The development of a new dialect even in a close community takes some time, and it is therefore too early to explore the possibilities of the development of an ICI dialect in County Durham, but the writer of this paragraph calls attention to an interesting social aspect of regional dialect: its use to emphasize the solidarity of a group and to warn outsiders to keep their distance. The description of the behaviour of northerners in this paragraph shows dialect speakers hitting back at the speakers of Standard English. It is more common to find Standard English used as the unifying bond by a process similar to that described in the passage in *The Book of Judges* which has given the word *shibboleth* to the English language:

> . . . the men of Gilead said unto him, 'Art thou an Ephraimite?' If he said 'Nay', then said they unto him, 'Say now Shibboleth'; and he said 'Sibboleth', for he could not frame to pronounce it right. Then they took him and slew him. . . . (*Judges*, xii, 5 f.)

It is interesting to find the Authorized Version here using the verb *frame* in a sense familiar to dialect speakers but not now normally current in Standard English.

A good deal has been written about social classes and their characteristics, but the subject is so complicated that much remains to be done before the necessary degree of precision is attained. Classes can easily be recognized in English social life; the difficulty arises when one tries to indicate the boundaries of those classes. There is perhaps a parallel between social classes and regional dialects, whose boundaries are similarly difficult to define. The boundary between one regional dialect and another is a belt which is formed when the boundaries of a number of dialect features approximately coincide with each other. Corresponding to the features of regional dialects there are the constituent elements of social classes, such as birth, education, wealth and occupation. Homogeneity of any one of these elements is not enough to constitute a social class, though it may constitute a group, sometimes called a stratum, whose

[1] *The Economist*, April 8, 1961, p. 105.

characteristics, including speech, can be studied. Many occupations, such as the teaching profession, are internally stratified. One man may belong to several different strata, some of which have homogeneous speech-habits while others have not. For example, those who went to the same public school are likely to share the same speech-habits; those whose only link with each other is that they each earn £1,000 a year are not. In seeking groups whose members share a common dialect, it is possible to choose either strata, such as occupations, or the more complicated social classes that combine several strata, but the study of social dialect can most profitably begin with groups which can be defined with a fair degree of rigidity, and one of the tasks of an investigator is to discover how great a degree of uniformity exists within such groups. The boys, especially the senior boys, at Eton or Winchester probably constitute groups which, if they could be induced to co-operate, would be as useful to a field-worker studying class dialect as elderly villagers, who have never left their native village, are to the student of regional dialect.

When we leave such social groups, difficulties of definition at once begin to arise. When anyone speaks about the characteristics of upper-class speech, it is legitimate to ask, in the most respectful manner possible, 'But how do you know?' The answer that is usually implicit in such pronouncements, and one that is sometimes given explicitly, is that the speaker is describing the usage of himself and his friends. It is difficult, without discourtesy, to pursue the subject further, but it is clear that the size and nature of the group in question must be defined before it is possible to say anything of value about the speech-habits of the members of the group. When one examines a list of the supposed characteristics of upper-class speech, it becomes clear that the size of the group of upper-class speakers varies with each of the characteristics mentioned. The number of speakers using many so-called upper-class expressions must be very much larger than the group of people that could properly be described as upper-class. For example, Professor Ross claims (*Noblesse Oblige*, pp. 25 ff.) that it is U (i.e. upper-class)

to say *'yesterday* and *'int'resting* but non-U to say *yester'day*
and *inte'resting*; it is U to make *acknowledge* rhyme with *college*
but non-U to make the second syllable rhyme with *bowl*; it is
U to pronounce *vase* to rhyme with *bars* but non-U to make it
rhyme with *cause* or *maize*; it is U to pronounce *spoon* to rhyme
with *boon* but non-U to make it rhyme with the Yorkshire
pronunciation of *bun*; it is U to pronounce *also* as if it were
spelt *awlso*. We are told that non-U speakers hardly use the
word *sponge-cake* but substitute *sponge* for it. If we accept
these distinctions, we must be struck by the thought how very
numerous the English upper classes are. There must be many
people who do not think of themselves as belonging to the upper
classes who not only habitually use what is described as the U-
pronunciation, but who are not conscious of having heard any
other. Of course, once a speech-habit comes to be generally
accepted as upper-class, it is always likely to spread, but it is
doubtful whether any of the pronunciations now under discussion
has acquired any *cachet* of that kind.

It is not only the size of the group of 'non-U speakers' which
varies but its composition. For example, Professor Ross says
(*Noblesse Oblige*, p. 26) that it is non-U to pronounce *ride* as if
spelt *raid* and rightly adds that this kind of pronunciation is
often called *refained*, but those who use it constitute quite a
different group from those who indulge in the other pronunciations which Professor Ross describes as non-U.

The discussion of the differences between upper- and lower-
class speech is usually little more than a list of supposed
vulgarisms. This is understandable, because one of the characteristics of upper-class speech is that it does not call attention
to itself, whereas vulgarisms do attract attention. Pre-
occupation with class-indicators is not as a rule an upper-class
characteristic, and it is significant that a list of English vulgarisms
would include such phrases as *quite a gentleman, so thoroughly
the gentlewoman*, and *she has class*. Other phrases that might
be said to be vulgarisms are *of a morning* and *I was that
aggravated*. A number of English words arise from curtailment
of longer words, and some of these spend some time as vulgarisms

before being accepted; Swift's antipathy to the word *mob* is well-known. Today such curtailments as *chocs* for *chocolates* and *advert* for *advertisement* are vulgarisms; no one can say what will be their ultimate fate. *Telly* for *television* is perhaps less clearly a vulgarism; the shortened form is used informally or playfully by many educated speakers, often with a half-apologetic smile that serves as the spoken language's equivalent of quotation marks. Some words which are certainly not vulgarisms when properly used become vulgarisms when used with particular meanings. There is often room for differences of opinion on such words, but it is perhaps reasonable to include in this category such words as *mental* in the sense 'mentally deficient' and *gastric* in the sentence *He has a gastric stomach*. Certain pronunciations, such as *Gawd* for *God*, may perhaps be said to be vulgarisms, and such actions as a nudge or placing the forefinger by the side of the nose are the vulgarisms of gesture language.

One characteristic which may perhaps be associated with upper-class speech, although it is found among only a small proportion of speakers, is the preservation of some old-fashioned pronunciations, such as [liːʒə] for *leisure*. A novelist, recording the speech of an aristocratic character, uses such spellings as *hijjus* for *hideous*, *ojus* for *odious*, *insijjus* for *insidious* and even *djew* for *do you*. These spellings record pronunciations which are now old-fashioned. Upper-class speakers often feel that it is bourgeois to take too much trouble to achieve careful pronunciation, and their pronunciation therefore often seems careless. The pronunciations *huntin'*, *shootin'*, and *fishin'* have become notorious class-indicators; one sometimes hears *mornin'* for *morning*. The treatment of initial *h* is another class-indicator. The loss of *h* has come to be regarded as a sign of lower-class speech. Those who feel insecure about their social position are usually careful to pronounce it, but upper-class speakers are generally much less anxious, and are more ready to drop initial *h* when there are good historical reasons for doing so, as in words like *historian* and *hotel*, with lightly-stressed first syllables, or in words like *humour* and *humid*, where the first element of the diphthong following the *h* has been raised to a semi-vowel.

In the latter part of the nineteenth and the early part of the present century the loss of initial *h* was a fashionable affectation. A member of the House of Commons offended the Senior Common Room at Christ Church, where he was dining as a guest, by his lengthy descriptions of men and debates in the House. An elderly don finally administered the reproof: 'I would 'ave the gentleman know that in this place the 'Ouse means 'ere'.[1]

Sometimes an upper-class pronunciation is both old-fashioned and apparently careless, since upper-class speakers have resisted the tendency to restore the pronunciations of certain words to bring them into conformity with the spelling. Thus, upper-class speakers are more likely than middle-class speakers to say *weskit* for *waistcoat* and *forred* for *forehead*. Another example of this tendency is *feller* for *fellow*. If we are to judge by eighteenth-century rhymes, the pronunciation *feller* preserves the older development of the vowel of the lightly-stressed syllable which in Standard English has been replaced by a spelling pronunciation. This is one of a number of words in which extremes of class dialect meet. Since *fellow* is the Standard English pronunciation, it is used by speakers of all social classes, but side by side with it we find *feller* used frequently by lower-class and occasionally by upper-class speakers, but very rarely by speakers of the middle classes.

Certain words and phrases have become famous as class-indicators. Examples are words such as *serviette* and phrases such as *Pleased to meet you*. It has been said that the best answer to *Pleased to meet you* is *Glad to have you know me*. Unlike many linguistic class-indicators, the expression *Pleased to meet you* is open to objection on grounds that are not purely arbitrary, since it says explicitly something which it would be more courteous to take for granted. Similarly, the use of the expression *Excuse my glove* when shaking hands has been described as non-U. It would be more accurate to describe it as discourteous. The use of this expression means: 'I think

[1] J. C. Masterman in *Sunday Times*, October 9, 1960.

that it is discourteous to offer a gloved hand for you to shake, but I don't think that you are sufficiently important to warrant the very slight trouble that it would cause me to remove my glove'.

This distinction between what is discourteous and what is lower-class is one that must be made. It would be rash to assume that the upper classes are never guilty of discourtesy; it would be more true to say that, when discourtesy is involved, upper and lower classes are discourteous in different ways. The lower classes may be more likely to show discourtesy by means of a loud voice or by flat contradiction; the upper classes by means of arrogant or patronising intonation or the use of expressions like 'these people' to describe individual members of lower-income groups. The use of *Pardon!* if the hearer does not hear the speaker properly has been stigmatized as lower-class and *What?* has been said to be the normal upper-class equivalent. There is an interesting parallel to *What?* in the north-country *You what?* which always seems rather truculent. All of these expressions seem to be open to objection. They have been defended on the grounds of brevity, but their brevity is part of the objection to them. They cause little trouble to the speaker but a good deal of trouble to the person addressed. *Pardon!* is technically an apology but really it is a request or a command: 'Say that again'. The real objection to it is that some people use it too readily when, by taking a little more trouble, they could avoid the demand implicit in the use of the word. Something a little more prolix might serve to make it clear that the speaker realizes that he is asking a favour and that his apology is not merely off-hand or formal.

A good example of the large number of different factors that enter into quite an everyday feature of class dialect is illustrated by the practice of calling people by their surnames without any title. It is to some extent a feature of regional dialect, since the practice is more common, and less discourteous, in British English than in American English. The sex of the speaker and that of the person addressed are clearly significant, since the practice is more common among men than women. The social class of the speaker and that of the person addressed are also relevant. A man who feels that his social position is insecure is likely to use the title 'Mr', and to expect others to use it to him. Many people have no objection to being addressed by their surname by an equal but resent the dropping of the 'Mr' by a supposed superior or inferior. The practice of calling a woman servant by her surname is probably especially common among those who belong, or wish to belong, to the upper classes, but it is often resented by the person who is so addressed. The relative ages of the speaker and the person addressed will often determine whether one says 'John', 'Smith', or 'Mr Smith'. Fashions in such matters change, and the use of Christian names instead of surnames has probably become more common in recent years. Finally, something depends on the personality of the person concerned ('After all, no one uses a pet name for the east wind'), and it is a fairly common experience after a week at a summer school to find that one knows only the Christian names of half one's fellow-students and only the surnames of the other half.

Class dialect plays its part in the various ways of speaking of one's wife. 'Mrs Smith' (now not often heard), 'my wife', and 'Mary' indicate different degrees of informality or intimacy, but 'Mrs S.', 'the wife' and 'the missus' are vulgarisms.

In order that class dialects may be studied profitably, it is necessary to resist the assumption that social classes are a number of horizontal layers, each of which is inferior to some other classes and superior to others. The distinction between one class and another may be vertical, not horizontal. The sort of investigation that is most likely to be profitable is one which is based on a social classification that can be applied objectively without the use of vague terms like 'upper classes' and 'lower classes'. For example, classification can be based upon the kind of school which the informant attended or upon his occupation. It may be objected that such a classification will have results not very different from those which follow from the horizontal division of society into layers, but there will at any rate be a gain in precision. One might, for example, try to find out whether clergymen have distinctive speech. Other objective classifications that are possible are according to the age or sex of the speaker. An extreme example of a dialect based on age is baby-talk, and here it would be necessary to distinguish two dialects which do not overlap as much as they should: the language of babies and the language used by adults when talking to babies. Certain words and certain intonations are more often used by women than by men and *vice versa*. Similarly, certain expressions are felt to be appropriate to particular age-groups and if they are used by others the hearer is conscious of a feeling of incongruity. Sensitiveness to such details of usage is an important asset in a novelist in his handling of conversations, and the point may be illustrated by a sentence from a letter which Charles Reade wrote to his publisher, John Blackwood: 'I will not alter the word "lovely", because the speaker is not my good J. Blackwood, but a girl, and this is a girl's favourite adjective, and they continually apply it to men'.[1]

A beginning has been made in the study of both class dialects and occupational voices by a number of highly skilled critics of speech who are as a rule without professional training in either phonetics or linguistics, namely by actors and music-hall comedians. So far as special characteristics can be recorded by means of the printed word, novelists might be added. There are certain groups whose linguistic characteristics are recognized objects of mimicry. Beside the regional groups, such as Scotsmen and Welshmen, there are occupational and social groups, like the young man about town, the clergyman and the retired Army officer. In course of time stereotypes have been developed for all these categories, and it is part of the task of the student of class dialect to discover how far these stereotypes have counterparts in reality. It may well be that they are badly out of date: if they reflect reality at all they reflect the reality of half a century or more ago, though to music-hall and radio addicts they are probably more familiar than the reality. One is reminded of the young man who had to admit that he

[1] Quoted from Malcolm Elwin, *Charles Reade* (Jonathan Cape, 1931), p. 311.

was a failure as an actor and that he couldn't even play the part of a Cambridge undergraduate, and then he added: 'And the worst of it is, I *am* a Cambridge undergraduate'. The sort of question that has to be investigated here is: 'Do rich young men have difficulty in pronouncing their *r*'s and do they replace final [ə] by [ɑː]?[1] Do clergymen lengthen their vowels and make use of exaggerated variations of intonation? But it is only part of the investigator's task to find out whether this mimicry is true to life. A more important part of his task is to analyse it, to find out by what linguistic variations a particular effect is achieved. The means that can be used include variations in the quality of vowels and consonants, in intonation and in loudness, and the use of pauses. For example, women assistants in post offices have the reputation of being haughty. Two characteristics contribute to this impression. One is the loudness of their voices; the other is the clearness of their articulation in contrast to the rather blurred and hesitant effect that most of us achieve. It may be noticed that both of these characteristics can be acquired by assistants who are really very well-disposed to their customers and who are not in the least haughty. They are useful ways of making oneself heard against a background of competing noises and the natural result of speaking to a succession of customers many of whom are hard of hearing.

Each profession tends to develop its own linguistic idiosyncrasies, of which its members are usually unconscious. There is the high-pitched academic voice, which is often accompanied by a fondness for long and involved sentences with frequent qualifying phrases and pauses during which the speaker seeks for the right word. For many people the speech of a radio announcer represents an ideal which it would be disrespectful to describe as dialectal, but, in both its virtues and its defects, it tends to develop distinctive characteristics. Sir George Clark has pointed out that the physical conditions of the apparatus of

---

[1] The raising of this question in a lecture produced from one member of the audience the comment: 'I should just like to say that it isn't only wich young men that have twouble with their *r*'s.'

broadcasting make a high-pitched and monotonous voice more audible than one of more weight and variety and that the announcer's effort to speak clearly and correctly tends to produce an artificial accent which 'has a mincing refinement empty of character and colour'.[1] This criticism is perhaps less true now than when it was made in 1929, and some voices heard on radio and television today go too far in the effort to avoid colourless monotony. A common mannerism is the enthusiastic shout of triumph with which, after a slight pause, a compere announces the name of a variety artist. Television commercials go much further than the BBC in their quest for variety of intonation, ranging as they do from the cooing to the gloating, from the languorous to the coy.

The linguistic idiosyncrasies of the legal profession have been discussed by Mr Geoffrey Lincoln,[2] who speaks of the 'local dialect', which could more properly be called an occupational dialect, of the Law Courts. He points out that this special language is reserved for the use of barristers and judges and adds by way of illustration: 'A witness who suddenly said "In my humble submission" would be instantly and laughably shown up as some kind of imbecile' (p. 67). Some of the expressions mentioned by Mr Lincoln are *I'm much obliged, with the greatest respect, if your lordship pleases, grow to the point, I agree with every word that has fallen from my lord.*

One occupation that is said to have developed its own special form of language is that of commercial traveller, although the phrase 'commercial travellers' English' is often used as a snobbish synonym for 'vulgarism'. In a short story by Dorothy L. Sayers one exasperated Oxford undergraduate says to another: 'And, for the Lord's sake, stop talking about "undergrads", like a ruddy commercial traveller'. A commercial traveller who overhears asks mildly if the expression is offensive in any way, and the undergraduate, full of penitence on account of his 'beastly brick', explains that 'nobody says "undergrads" except townees

---

[1] G. N. Clark, *The Bull's Bellow and the Ratton's Squeak*, SPE 33 (OUP, 1929), p. 415.
[2] Geoffrey Lincoln, *No Moaning of the Bar* (Geoffrey Bles, 1957), p. 72.

and journalists and people outside the university'.[1] One phrase
that has been quoted as a typical example of 'commercial
travellers' English' is 'Take a pew, old man', and this phrase
will serve to illustrate the combination of bonhomie, facetiousness
and out-of-date slang that is generally found in the dialect
which is, rightly or wrongly, associated with the less successful
commercial traveller.

The speech of actors and actresses is, understandably enough,
often loud and clear, even when they are off the stage. The
distinctive pronunciations of certain words that are favoured
by some actors are generally associated with old-fashioned
actors not of the highest standing. One producer is said to have
complained when an actor rolled the *r* in *children*: '*Childrrren* is
the illegitimate plural of *cheeyild*'.

One class dialect that has grown to enormous proportions,
although it is found only in the written, not in the spoken,
language is the commercial language which is not confined to
any one trade or business. We tend to think of commercial
jargon as a characteristic vice of the twentieth century, but it
has its roots in the past. Thus, in Sir Walter Scott's *Rob Roy*
(1818) Francis Osbaldistone speaks of the delight which his father
took in sentences such as 'Your's received, and duly honoured
the bills inclosed, as per margin' (Ch. 1). Part of the explanation
of the rise of this special language is that frequently recurring
situations call forth responses which in time become conven-
tionalized. Another contributory cause is a kind of mechanical
courtesy, which has the result that a letter becomes *your esteemed
favour*. The unthinking use of these verbal counters sometimes
produces gems like 'We have the pleasure to inform you that the
shoes that you have ordered are not available' or letters refusing
a piece of easily-obtainable information and concluding with
the words 'Assuring you of our best attention at all times'. It
is an interesting pastime to translate some of these conventional
commercial phrases into colloquial English. Translations that
have been submitted by contributors to newspapers include:
The matter is receiving attention 'We've lost the file', *The matter*

[1] Dorothy L. Sayers, *Hangman's Holiday* (Gollancz, 1933), p. 102.

is receiving active attention 'We are trying to find the file', *We are making exhaustive enquiries* 'You'll wait a long time for the answer to this one', *Thank you for your further esteemed favour* 'We are getting about tired of you and your troubles'.

Words indicating smallness tend to disappear from the vocabulary of trade, and this tendency has apparently received official sanction in that there seems now to be no such thing as a small egg; one has one's choice of *standard, medium* or *large* eggs. One customer who asked for a small tube of tooth-paste claims to have been told rather reproachfully that there were no small tubes; the three sizes were *Large, Super Large* and *Jumbo*. For similar reasons evening newpapers have a bewildering variety of descriptions, all of which are designed to disclaim early publication. An edition which appears about noon will be described as the *city edition*, but it needs an expert to sort out the relative priority of the *late night final, last edition*, and *last extra*. Sometimes the language of commerce seems to be based on snobbishness. A request for socks will produce a tactfully worded correction to *hose*, and a reference to hire purchase has been known to elicit the rebuke: 'We prefer to call it deferred payments'.

Wine merchants achieve startling results by the use of adjectives which would be more appropriate in other contexts; this practice has been satirized in James Thurber's 'It is a naïve domestic burgundy without any breeding, but I think that you'll be amused at its presumption'.

One group of occupational dialects with which we are all familiar consists of the written dialects used in newspapers. Writers on language often refer to journalese as though the word described a single homogeneous way of writing, but there are several different kinds. The term *journalese* nevertheless serves a useful purpose as a description of the kind of writing which became widespread as a result of the journalistic revolution brought about by Alfred Harmsworth, later Lord Northcliffe, when he founded the *Daily Mail* in 1896. The chief aim of this kind of writing is to catch the attention of the reader and to cater for readers who find sustained attention difficult. Long paragraphs are avoided, and it is not uncommon to find a paragraph consisting of a single sentence. There is a tendency to combine many incongruous pieces of information in a single sentence. Examples are:

> Born on May 2, 1904, pipe-smoking Bing is 5 ft. 9 ins. tall, has blue eyes, and brown hair, thinning on top. Always casually and informally dressed, he invariably wears a smile.

> The left-handed Davis Cup player, a 25-year-old bachelor, has been ill since Friday.

> Of Irish birth, benign in manner, with the pink complexion and white hair which would as well become a business executive, Mr Thompson does not prevaricate.

Certain tricks of expression, such as inversion of the normal order of subject and verb, are common, and there are unusual titles, such as 'Reader Jones', which is no doubt useful when the writer does not know whether the person to whom he refers is Mr, Mrs, or Miss. A typical example of this kind of journalese is:

> Said newsagent Mrs May Rigby, of Renshaw-street: 'We believe that many motorists use this route into town to avoid Oxford Road'.
> Added grocer Mrs Jean Ruddy: 'It's a terrible spot. We get accidents galore. Something should be done about it'.

Another common practice, which is no doubt a debasement, at several removes, of Bunyan's coinage of names like Mr Worldly Wiseman, is the coining of nicknames preceded by 'Mr'. Thus a pianist is called 'Mr Piano', a professor whose research is conducted at Jodrell Bank is described as 'Mr Jodrell', and a man who is charged with failing to maintain his family is 'Mr Lazybones'. These nicknames are especially common in headlines, which have developed their own special language.[1] The chief cause of its special features is the limitation of space, which

[1] See Heinrich Straumann, *Newspaper Headlines* (George Allen and Unwin, 1935).

leads to a preference for very short words, like *wed* for the more idiomatic *marry*, *bid* for *attempt*, and *Red*, used to describe anyone whose politics are left of centre. The same shortage of space often leads to the replacement of the conjunction *and* by a comma. Special features of syntax develop, such as the use of the infinitive instead of the future ('Film Star to Wed'), and a fondness for strings of nouns in apposition, a practice which sometimes leaves the meaning obscure, since the reader has to pause to decide which words are nouns and which verbs. An example is: 'University Pay Rises Burden'.

Miss Marghanita Laski[1] has called attention to the specialized grammar and vocabulary of the fashion-writer in the glossy monthlies. Such language includes a large number of glamour-words, 'extremely evocative in the right context and of no real meaning whatsoever'. Examples of such words quoted by Miss Laski include *bold, crisp, important, jaunty, significant*, and *subtle*. Any regular reader of advertisement columns would find it an easy matter to provide further examples. Such language makes very free use of euphemisms. We have grown so accustomed to such euphemisms that most people will be rather startled by the deliberate avoidance of euphemisms in the title of Miss Laski's article, *Cheap Clothes for Fat Old Women*, but will recognize the style of the translation: *Limited Income Clothes for Dignified Maturity*. The idea of cheapness is one that is very productive of synonyms in commercial writing; these include such words and phrases as *less expensive, democratic, realistic*, and *at keenest prices*.

Fashion journalists are only one group of writers who have developed their own special language. Financial journalists have done the same. Apart from technical terms, such as *bull, bear* and *stag*, certain phrases tend to recur because the conditions which they describe tend to recur. In order to avoid repetition journalists dealing with subjects such as finance and sport make frequent use of 'elegant variation'. The following

---

[1] In 'Cheap Clothes for Fat Old Women' in *The New Statesman and Nation*. Quoted from Michael Barsley, *A Book of Wit and Humour* (Pan Books, 1954), pp. 224–226.

extracts are all from the financial column of a single issue of
an evening paper:

> . . . gilts went up. War Loan plussed 7s. 6d. to £52 17s. 6d.
> and others followed. Elsewhere prices shrugged off recent
> nervousness and edged higher. Steels looked more cheerful
> and United, Summers and Stewarts and Lloyds made a bright
> trio. Leading industrials to notch small gains included Turner
> and Newall, ICI, Boots and Dunlop. Top stores moved up . . .
> Whiteley's spurted 2s. 6d. . . . Banks managed plusses of up to
> 1s. 9d., in Barclays. Insurances, too, regained some ground.
> . . . Beer and "baccy" shares joined in the general cheer. Oils
> rallied from a dull start with Shell touching 121s. 9d. Tins
> made fresh headway with gains of up to 3s. Golds moved in a
> similar vein. . . .

The author has succeeded in finding sixteen different ways of
saying that prices rose.

Literary criticism has its special vocabulary of vogue-words
like *ambivalent, immediacy*, and *integrated*. It is of the nature
of such terms that they change with the changing fashions of
literary criticism, and every reader of such works could probably
compile his own list of words which tend to recur. One such
list includes the terms *ambience, ambiguity, imagery, symbolism,
polarity, the death wish, involvement, commitment, the human
situation, the human predicament*.[1]

One class dialect that can be distinguished among the multi-
tude of dialects that flourish in newspapers is that used in the
fourth or fifth leaders of *The Times*. This can reasonably be
called a class as well as an occupational dialect, since it is
especially associated with a newspaper which makes no secret
of its appeal to 'top people'. It is a dialect with a long tradition
of culture behind it, and some of its characteristics may well be
due to the influence of Latin. The style might be described, by
those whose sympathy with it is imperfect, as playfully academic,
and it has something in common with the kind of language used
in presenting candidates for honorary degrees at universities.
The sentences are long and the writers are not afraid of using

---

[1] A. C. Ward, 'Language and the Community' in *Essays and Studies
Collected for the English Association*, New Series 14 (John Murray, 1961),
p. 77.

polysyllabic words. Effects are carefully built up, in contrast to the concise 'throw away' style of much American journalism. Anticlimax is achieved by the deliberate use of slang and colloquialism, which is all the more marked by contrast with the rather formal diction which is normal in this dialect. The following is an example:

> What happens—to take a hypothetical case—when the puissant territory of Rumpongo throws off the shackles of what-have-you and becomes a fully fledged republic? At any moment the exigencies of the international situation may oblige the Prime Minister to fly to Washington or the Foreign Secretary to London. Neither can be suitably received or entertained without their country's national anthem being played at some stage of the proceedings. How on earth are the necessary arrangements made? . . . So rapidly, moreover, are new countries coming off the conveyor-belt that there is precious little to prevent an unscrupulous composer from flogging the same dignified and relevant melody to two or even more of them. This patriotic babel cries out for coordination and control. What is really needed is an international anthem, a sort of 'Happy Birthday to You' tune which could be easily played and easily recognized and would serve as a universal sop to national pride.[1]

One style of writing which deserves the name of class dialect flourishes in school magazines and other books and magazines written for boys; it has been described as Old Boy English. A good example is quoted in a life of Baring-Gould[2] with the comment that the specialized style and diction of this kind of writing never change:

> And then there was the master whose name is now a household word, known all over the world, Sabine Baring-Gould, a layman then. Everybody liked him, although he took no part in games. But the yarns which he used to spin to a favoured few up in his rooms on winter nights were inexhaustible and all of them absolutely impromptu. What a brain! I stand astonished at the thought, and proud I was once his pupil. Baring-Gould was popularly known among the boys as Snout.

[1] *The Times,* August 12, 1960.
[2] William Purcell: *Onward Christian Soldier: A Life of Sabine Baring-Gould* (Longmans, 1957), p. 56.

The workers in particular industries often develop phrases whose meaning is so obvious to those who are familiar with the conditions of the industry that the speakers do not always realize that their meaning is not equally clear to everyone. For example, Lancashire cotton workers will speak of being *stopped for bobbins* when their work is held up because they need a new supply of bobbins. A less well-known idiom in the same industry is *for sick*, as contrasted with *for constant*. The first phrase describes the work done on behalf of a worker who is ill; the second is used of a worker in regular employment. The most distinctive features of occupational dialects are generally words rather than phrases. Each trade or profession tends to have its own technical terms, and sometimes particular technical terms tend to be confined to one particular part of the country, with the result that regional and occupational dialects cut across each other. Writing that makes use of technical terms not commonly intelligible is known as jargon, and writers on what constitutes good English urge their readers to avoid the excessive use of such words. The advice is sound, but it is well to remember on the other hand that technical terms, when properly used, perform a very useful function. How useful they are can be illustrated by quoting an extract from a letter to a plumber in which the writer has got into serious difficulties which he would have avoided if he had known and used the appropriate technical terms. The passage will serve as an example of class dialect; it shows a writer struggling heroically with a medium which is almost too much for him:

> The bit what the water comes out of has come out of the bit what the water passes through before passing into the bit what it should come out of with the result that the water now comes out of the bit what it used to pass through on its way into the part what it should come out of instead of coming out of the bit what it should come out of.[1]

The meaning attached to the word *dialect* in this chapter may seem to some readers to be too wide. It can, however, be justified in the light of the definition of dialect given in the first

[1] Quoted in *The Daily Telegraph*, December 30, 1957.

chapter, and it may well be that the subordinate varieties of English that are mentioned here will receive more attention in the future than they have received in the past. The old regional dialects, which most of us think of when dialects are mentioned, still have plenty of vitality in them, but it is only to be expected that in course of time they will lose most of their distinctive features. Class and occupational dialects and the dialects spoken in towns have not the historical interest of the old country dialects, but they may be expected to have a strong appeal for the linguistic pioneer, in that serious study of these forms of speech has hardly begun.

CHAPTER VIII

Dialect and Literature

THE STANDARDIZATION OF written English began earlier and has proceeded much further than that of spoken English, and consequently English dialects today are generally associated with speech much more than with writing. There are, however, several links between dialect and literature, and some of these links will be considered in this chapter. The first link to be discussed here is the way in which dialects can throw light on the interpretation of literature. The remaining links will be considered under two heads: literature in dialect and dialect in literature.

The help afforded by modern dialects in the interpretation of Old and Middle English texts is particularly welcome when an Early English text contains a word which is unique or so rare that its meaning cannot be deduced from the literary contexts in which it occurs. An example occurs at v. 1363 of the Old English poem *Beowulf*, where *hrinde bearwas* are described as overhanging a pool. *Bearwas* means 'woods' or 'groves' but *hrinde* is not recorded elsewhere in Old English, and Richard Morris suggested emendation to *hrimge*, a contracted form of *hrimige* 'rimy'.[1] This emendation was widely accepted until the publication of the fifth volume of *EDD* in 1904. Joseph Wright there showed that in Scottish and Northern English dialects a common word for hoar frost is *rind* and that from it has been formed the adjective *rindy* with the same meaning as

---

[1] *The Blickling Homilies*, ed. by Richard Morris (EETS 1880), pp. vi f, 209.

rimy. He pointed out that emendation is unnecessary: the MS reading *hrinde* is simply a contraction of *hrindge* or *hrindige*, the plural of an adjective *hrindig*.

When we come to Middle English literature, examples of the help offered by dialects in the interpretation of texts become more numerous, partly because Middle English literature is much more extensive than Old English. Mrs Wright calls attention to many examples in the fourteenth-century poem *Sir Gawain and the Green Knight*,[1] the vocabulary of which includes a large number of unusual words. The Green Knight's horse has *molaynes* (v. 169), which are probably the same as the South Midland *mullen*, the headgear or bridle of a horse. *Toppyng* (v. 191) is shown by dialects to mean a horse's fore-lock. The adjective *wysty* (v. 2189) is used to describe the green chapel; it is probably the same word as *wisty* (Lancs, Ches) 'spacious, bare'. The verb *mynteʒ* (v. 2290) 'aims a blow' survives in *mint* (Scotland, Ireland, North Country). In the poem *Purity*, which is preserved in the same manuscript as *Sir Gawain and the Green Knight*, there occurs the word *trasches* (v. 40) which has been glossed as 'trousers', but it is probably the same word as *trash* 'a worn-out boot or shoe' (*EDD* TRASH *v.*[1] and *sb.*[2] sense 9). The use of *shepe* for 'shepherd' in the second line of *Piers Plowman* puzzles many readers, who are liable to mistake it for *sheep*, but *shep* is a common dialect word for 'shepherd' recorded in Cumberland, Lincolnshire, Somerset and Devonshire.

The word *barlay*, which is still frequently used in children's games, is used in *Sir Gawain and the Green Knight*, v. 296 in the sense 'I claim'. Professor J. R. R. Tolkien[2] has pointed out that the formula *Fain I*, as used in children's games, may throw light on a line in Chaucer's *Clerk's Tale*: 'That lordes heestes mowe nat been yfeyned' (v. 529). The line means that lords' orders must be obeyed, i.e. they cannot be treated with a 'Fain I' ('I decline').

[1] Elizabeth Mary Wright, *Rustic Speech and Folk Lore* (OUP, 1913), pp. 69 f.
[2] Quoted by Iona and Peter Opie, *The Lore and Language of School-children* (OUP, 1959), p. 151.

The examples that have been quoted show that dialects can help in the study of Early English texts. Conversely familiarity with Old and Middle English can often help anyone who is unfamiliar with modern dialects to understand words which might otherwise puzzle him. There is a proverb *The healer's as bad as the stealer*, which at first seems to cast an undeserved slur on the medical profession. Its true meaning is clear to those who are familiar with the dialectal verb *heal* meaning 'hide, conceal' and to those who know that there is an Old English verb *helian* 'to conceal', which would become *heal* in Modern English. A *healer* is thus a receiver of stolen property. The expression *to dree one's weird* 'to endure one's fate', is now practically confined to Scottish dialect, but it occurs in Middle English (*Purity*, v. 1224) and the two words in the expression which are unfamiliar in Modern English are familiar to students of Old English as *drēogan* 'to endure' and *wyrd* 'fate, destiny'. A very expressive Lancashire word is *witchert* 'with wet feet'. The meaning and etymology of the word are more clear in the Middle English form, which occurs in *Piers Plowman*: 'wo-werie and wetschod' (C-Text, Passus xxi, v. 1).

It is not only on Old and Middle English texts that modern dialects can throw light; they are valuable also as aids to the understanding of Shakespeare's plays. Hamlet says of the play performed before Claudius: 'This is miching mallecho; it means mischief' (III, ii, 148). The word *miching* has puzzled many commentators but it is probably from *mich* 'to play truant from school'. In *King Henry V* England is described as 'that nook-shotten isle of Albion' (III, v, 14). Modern dialects provide two different meanings that have been used to explain the much-discussed word *nook-shotten*. In Cheshire the word has the sense 'shot into a corner' and is used of cheese put aside from the rest as inferior. Another north-country sense is 'having many sharp turns and angles' and the word is applied to a house that is all holes and corners. Either of these senses would suit the derogatory use of the word in *King Henry V*.

Many words are used by Shakespeare in senses which still survive in dialects. *Inkle* is used by Autolycus in *The Winter's*

Tale to describe a kind of tape (IV, iv, 208); there is a common dialect phrase 'as thick as inkle-weavers'. The Shepherd in the same play, on finding Perdita, speculates 'A boy or a child, I wonder?' (III, iii, 70); in dialects *child* is still used in the sense 'girl' and *EDD* quotes from Shropshire the question 'Is it a lad or a child?' *Mobled* is used in dialects with the meaning 'muffled'; Hamlet expresses doubt about the suitability of the word when it is used by one of the players (II, ii, 534), perhaps because it is felt to be provincial. When Thersites in *Troilus and Cressida* (V, iv, 10) speaks of *a sleeveless errand* he is using *sleeveless* in the sense 'useless', a meaning to which there are many parallels in Elizabethan drama; the word is so used in many north-country dialects, and the Shakespearean phrase survives in dialects. Three further examples all occur in *Macbeth*. The phrase *the baby of a girl* (III, iv, 106) is sometimes taken to mean 'infant of a very young mother', and is so glossed by C. T. Onions in *A Shakespeare Glossary*, but it may be noted that *babby* is commonly used in dialects in the sense 'doll', and several editors take *baby* in *Macbeth* as having that meaning, which suits the context very well. Macbeth speaks of 'the blood-bolter'd Banquo' (IV, i, 123); in Shropshire tangled or unkempt hair is called *bautered* and in Warwickshire snow is said to *balter* on horses' feet. The Doctor, after seeing Lady Macbeth sleepwalking, says 'My mind she has mated, and amaz'd my sight' (V, i, 75); the word *mated* survives in modern dialects with the meaning 'confused, bewildered'. Other examples are *darkling* 'in the dark', *fond* 'foolish', *malkin* 'slattern', *nayword* 'byword', *ort* 'fragment, especially of food', *pick-thank* 'flatterer, mischief-maker', *urchin* 'hedgehog', *yare* 'ready'.

Sometimes words which have survived in present-day English in a different form are used by Shakespeare and his contemporaries in forms which still survive in dialects. Examples are: *ballet* for *ballad*, *brinded* for *brindled*, *crowner* for *coroner*, *haviour* for *behaviour*, *margent* for *margin*, and the verb *owe* for *own*.

A number of idiomatic phrases used by Shakespeare are still current in dialects. Examples are: *we burn daylight (Romeo and Juliet*, I, iv, 43) 'we light candles before they are needed', hence used figuratively in the sense 'we waste time'; *by inchmeal* (*The Tempest*, II, ii, 3) 'little by little'; *to make a coil* (*King John*, II, i, 165) 'to make a fuss'; *a thing of naught* (*A Midsummer Night's Dream*, IV, ii, 14) 'a worthless thing'; *ha' done* (*The Taming of the Shrew*, III, ii, 118) 'cease'.

There is a sense in which all English literature is dialect literature, since Standard English is simply one dialect that has acquired more importance than the other dialects. One aspect of this importance is that it is the normal medium of written communication all over the country, and there are many people whose speech shows all kinds of regional and social variations who use the written language with virtually complete uniformity. There is, therefore, a very marked difference in kind between the conception of dialect literature in Old and Middle English and that from the sixteenth century onwards. In Old and Middle English a writer would use the dialect of the part of the country where he happened to have been brought up or to live, and an account of the works written in the various Old and Middle English dialects belongs to the history of English literature rather than to the history of English dialects.

From the fifteenth to the eighteenth century there was a gap during which very little English literature was written in dialect. In the eighteenth century we find the beginnings of a revival of interest in the writing of dialect literature; this revival gained momentum during the nineteenth century and it is still active today. In Scotland there has been a continuous vernacular literary tradition from the time of Barbour's *Bruce* until the present day. From a linguistic point of view Lowland Scots is simply a dialect of English, but it is a dialect that has preserved more of the characteristics of a literary language than have any of the dialects spoken in England, with the exception of Standard English. It is therefore reasonable to regard literature written in Scottish dialects as an independent national literature, although the use of Scottish dialects in novels and plays written for the most part in Standard English can properly be considered, along with the use of English dialects in the same way, as an aspect of dialect literature. The occasional use of dialect in this way serves several purposes: it can serve as an element of local colour, it is a way of individualizing characters, and it is sometimes introduced for humorous effect.

For the reader of the present day, dialect literature suffers under serious handicaps, which have been pointed out by Sir William Craigie.[1] The most obvious of these is the difficulty of understanding it. Inevitably dialect literature cannot appeal to a wide audience. Even if a reader unfamiliar with the dialect is willing to go to the trouble of looking up in a dictionary the meanings of unfamiliar words, he cannot appreciate the author's full effect. To do this it is necessary for the reader to be so familiar with the dialect words used that they have rich associations for him. The number of such readers is small and constantly diminishing.

Another disadvantage of dialect literature arises from the colloquial nature of most dialect. Written dialects do exist, but most English regional dialects belong essentially to the spoken language, and those who are best able to appreciate them are often not very much in the habit of reading or may not even be able to read at all. English spelling has no claim to be regarded as phonetic, and the representation of pronunciation by means of writing involves many inconsistencies and compromises. In the writing of dialect there is the special drawback that the compromises are unfamiliar ones. Most readers of dialect literature find their attention distracted by the necessity of translating the written symbols into sounds without any of the direct association between the written symbol and the idea to be expressed that is found in more familiar forms of English. The difficulty of reading dialect literature would be even greater if dialect authors attempted to record dialectal pronunciation with any exactness, but fortunately they do not; they are content to suggest dialectal pronunciation by the use of a few semi-phonetic spellings. Unfortunately, however, writers of dialect literature are often

[1] 'Dialect in Literature' in *Essays by Divers Hands*, xvii (OUP, 1938), pp. 69-91.

unskilled in the art of representing sounds and consequently vary the spelling needlessly. Such spellings as *wot, ov, sed* and *menny* for *what, of, said* and *many* do not represent dialectal pronunciations; they are simply phonetic or semi-phonetic spellings of the Standard English pronunciation of these words. Their use in dialect literature serves no useful purpose and makes it look needlessly difficult. Tennyson's *The Northern Cobbler* has a footnote which shows that he was aware of some of the difficulties of representing dialectal pronunciation in literature. The note reads: 'The vowels *aï*, pronounced separately though in the closest conjunction, best render the sound of the long *i* and *y* in this dialect. But since such words as *craïin', daïin', whaï, aï* (I), etc. look awkward except in a page of express phonetics, I have thought it better to leave the simple *i* and *y*, and to trust that my readers will give them the broader pronunciation'. Tennyson's description of the sound which he calls 'long *i*' applies not only to the Lincolnshire dialect but also to Standard English. No doubt the first element of the diphthong had a distinctive pronunciation in Tennyson's dialect, but the spelling which he rejected because it looked awkward was open to the even more serious objection that it did not indicate in what way the dialectal pronunciation of the word differed from that current in Standard English. Even a dialect speaker has difficulty in either appreciating or reproducing passages that are written in a dialect other than the one with which he is familiar.

A third disadvantage of dialect literature is that the range of dialect vocabulary is less wide than that of Standard English. The vocabulary of dialect is extraordinarily rich and vigorous in certain fields, but it is usually confined to the affairs of everyday life and is inadequate for the expression of many of the abstract ideas that need to be expressed in literature. It may be objected that a dialect author never tries to confine himself exclusively to a dialect vocabulary, but the mixture of dialect words and literary words can easily produce incongruous effects.

These disadvantages are serious, but they do not mean that dialect literature is unworthy of serious study. They are limitations of the field of dialect literature, but within that limited field a high order of achievement is possible. Dialect literature makes a simple and direct appeal to the feelings of those who are familiar with the dialect used. It gains its effects by its associations with the everyday life of those by whom and for whom it is written and it deals with emotions that are not the less deeply felt for being universally experienced. It deals with homely things in a homely way and is appreciated most by readers with few literary interests.

One of the best dialect poems surviving into the Modern English period is the traditional *Lyke-wake Dirge*, which was sung at wakes for the dead. Its composition cannot be exactly dated, but the earliest recorded version was printed in the seventeenth century. Another version was included by Sir Walter Scott in his *Border Minstrelsy*, and a third version is quoted here[1]:

THE LYKE-WAKE DIRGE

This yah neet, this yah neet,
  Ivvery neet an' awl,
Fire an' fleet an' cann'l leet,
  An' Christ tak up thi sowl.

When thoo fra hither gans awaay,
  Ivvery neet an' awl,
Ti Whinny Moor thoo cum'st at last,
  An' Christ tak up thi sowl.

If ivver tho gav' owther hosen or shoon,
  Ivvery neet an' awl,
Clap tha doon an' put 'em on,
  An' Christ tak up thi sowl.

---

[1] Quoted from Richard Blakeborough's *Wit, Character, Folklore and Customs of the North Riding of Yorkshire* (OUP, 1898), pp. 123 f. The earliest version is printed in *The White Rose Garland*, ed. by W. J. Halliday and A. S. Umpleby (Dent, 1949).

Bud if hosen or shoon thoo nivver ga' neean,
    Ivvery neet an' awl,
T' whinnies 'll prick tha sair ti t' beean,
    An' Christ tak up thi sowl.

Fra Whinny Moor that thoo mayst pass,
    Ivvery neet an' awl,
Ti t' Brigg o' Dreead thoo'll cum at last,
    An' Christ tak up thi sowl.

If ivver thoo gav' o' thi siller an' gawd,
    Ivvery neet an' awl,
At t' Brigg o' Dreead thoo'll finnd footho'd,
    An' Christ tak up thi sowl.

Bud if o' siller an' gawd thoo nivver ga' neean,
    Ivvery neet an' awl,
Thoo'll doon, doon tumm'l tiwards Hell fleeams,
    An' Christ tak up thi sowl.

Fra t' Brigg o' Dreead 'at thoo mayst pass,
    Ivvery neet an' awl,
Ti t' fleeams o' Hell thoo'll cum at last,
    An' Christ tak up thi sowl.

If ivver thoo gav' owther bite or sup,
    Ivvery neet an' awl,
T' fleeams 'll nivver catch tha up,
    An' Christ tak up thi sowl.

Bud if bite or sup thoo nivver ga' neean,
    Ivvery neet an' awl,
T' fleeams 'll bo'n tha sair ti t'beean,
    An' Christ tak up thi sowl.

The theme of the poem is similar to that of the medieval play *Everyman*: good deeds while a man is alive will help to alleviate the terrors of death. Attempts have been made to localize Whinnymoor but such localization is pointless. It is simply a moor full of whins and brambles in the crossing of which a pair of shoes would be very useful. The word *fleet* in the third line has caused discussion and Scott printed it as *sleet*. The basic meaning of the word is 'floor' but it is often used with the meaning 'part of a house' or 'house-room'. (See *EDD* s.v. *Flet*).

The writings in English dialects that have survived from the seventeenth and eighteenth centuries are few in number and, for the most part, poor in quality. Their interest is chiefly for the philologist and the social historian. There are a few dialogues from Yorkshire,[1] and two Devonshire texts, *The Exmoor Scolding*[2] and *The Exmoor Courtship*, were published in the *Gentleman's Magazine* for June and July 1746. In the same year was published *A View of the Lancashire Dialect* by 'Tim Bobbin', who was John Collier (1708–86), born at Urmston, near Manchester, and for most of his life a schoolmaster at Milnrow, near Rochdale. The *Gentleman's Magazine*'s comment on Tim Bobbin shows that its interest in dialect was mainly lexical. Collier's work was disparaged because 'the peculiarity of it consists chiefly in a corrupt pronunciation of known words with few originals'. This is the comment of an antiquary, but it may well be that Tim Bobbin owed some of his enormous popularity to his unwillingness to make much use of a special dialect vocabulary. Such a vocabulary makes a strong appeal to the philologist, but the general reader, even if he has some knowledge of dialect, is soon deterred if the number of unfamiliar words is too large. The first edition of *A View of the Lancashire Dialect* was short but the author later added several episodes. The book belongs to the literature of low life and roguery. The two characters are Tummus and Meary, but Meary is clearly subordinate, as may be seen by her comparative taciturnity: she has 44 lines to Tummus's 320. The book was remarkably popular and had a good deal of influence on later Lancashire dialect authors; more than sixty editions have been published.

During the nineteenth century dialect literature flourished in the North of England because it satisfied the needs of the new

---

[1] Reprinted by Skeat, *EDS* 76 (1895), pp. 109, 149, 176 ff.
[2] Reprinted by Elworthy, *EDS* 25 (1879).

industrial communities that were then coming into existence. One of the most popular and prolific dialect authors was Edwin Waugh (1817–90), the son of a Rochdale shoemaker. There is still a flourishing dialect society in Rochdale called the Edwin Waugh Society. Perhaps his best-known poem is *Come whoam to thi childer an' me*, a wife's appeal to a drunken husband, first published in 1856. A feature of this poem, as of many dialect poems, is the strongly didactic tone. Waugh wrote poems in Standard English as well as in dialect, but, as often happens when a dialect author writes in Standard English, these poems are conventional and derivative.

Samuel Laycock (1826–93) was born in Marsden in Yorkshire but most of his life was spent in Lancashire. He became a cotton worker and was unemployed during the Cotton Famine of the early 1860's. The Cotton Famine is the background of his best-known poem *Welcome, bonny brid*, addressed to a new-born baby daughter. Like Edwin Waugh and many other dialect authors, Laycock is at his best in portraying strong family affection against a background of poverty.

Of Lancashire writers of dialect prose during the nineteenth century the best is perhaps Ben Brierley (1825–96). He began his literary career with sentimental tales of village life but he later turned to comic sketches, which are his best work, although they are rather repetitive.

During the present century Thomas Thompson did much to exploit the comic possibilities of Lancashire dialect. Most of his work consists of short sketches which appeared originally in the *Manchester Guardian*. They are an excellent portrayal of some aspects of Lancashire character: its impatience with pretentiousness, its fondness for good-humoured banter, and its grim humour in the face of adversity.

There is a healthy tradition of writing in dialect in Yorkshire, a tradition which has close links with that of Lancashire in that some of the best-known poets, such as Samuel Laycock and Ammon Wrigley, were born in the moorland villages of the Pennines and spent part of their lives in Yorkshire and part in Lancashire.

Of the large number of Yorkshire dialect poets of the nineteenth century two from the West Riding may be mentioned. Ben Preston (1819–1902) was born at Bradford and was a worker in the woollen trade. His best poems are full of pathos and show the author's sympathy with the struggles of poor people. *Owd Moxy* describes the death of an old dry-waller in a winter storm on the moors, and *I Niver Can Call Her My Wife* is a monologue by a weaver, earning eight shillings a week, who refuses to marry because marriage would cause the woman he loves to share his own wretched poverty:

> An' Aw said as Aw thowt of her een,
>   Each breeter fur t'tear at wur in't;
> It's a sin to be niver forgeen,
>   To yoke hur ta famine an' stint;
> So Aw'll e'en travel forrud throo life,
>   Like a man throo a desert unknawn;
> Aw mun ne'er hev a hoam an' a wife,
>   Bud my sorras will all be my awn.

The most prolific and versatile of all Yorkshire dialect writers was John Hartley (1839–1915), who was born at Halifax. He is best known as the editor, for a period of nearly fifty years, of the *Original Clock Almanack*, the most famous of the many almanacks which have kept alive the tradition of Yorkshire dialect writing. Most of Hartley's stories, essays and poems were first published in the *Clock Almanack*, and the best were collected in book form, notably in *Yorkshire Lyrics* (1898). The first poem that he ever wrote is also his best-known. Its title, *Bite Bigger*, is derived from the words spoken by a child who, having found an apple in the street, is urging a smaller child to have a larger share. The poem has the characteristics that recur again and again in dialect poetry: sentiment, strong affection, a winter setting, and interest in the doings of very poor people. *Nelly o' Bob's* is a love song on a more cheerful note than is usual in dialect poetry. *To a Daisy* belongs to

another very popular poetic tradition, but it strikes a new note
of affectionate raillery:

> Aa, Aw'm feeared tha's come too sooin,
> Little daisy!
> Pray, whativer wor ta doin'?
> Are ta crazy?
> Winter winds are blowin' yet.
> Tha'll be starved, mi little pet.

The northern counties have been most productive of dialect
literature, but other counties have produced outstanding dialect
poets. It is not always realized that Tennyson has to be included
among the number of poets who wrote in dialect. Many people
who have been brought up as dialect speakers become increasingly
fond of dialect in later life, and Tennyson, who all his life spoke
with traces of his native Lincolnshire dialect, included among
his later works a series of dramatic monologues in dialect. These
are generally described as humorous poems, but the humour, as
often in dialect literature, is of a rather grim kind. The poems
are chiefly valuable as character-studies of the supposed speakers.
Northern Farmer: Old Style and *Northern Farmer: New Style*
depict different kinds of toughness of character. The first is
spoken by a dying farmer with a stern sense of duty and a good
sense of his own worth: 'Do godamoighty knaw what a's doing
a-taäkin' o' meä?' He has a poor opinion of the doctor and the
parson, but he is very worried about the difficulty that the
Squire will have in getting a successor to look after the eight
hundred acres that he farms for him: 'An' Squire 'ull be so mad
an' all'. *Northern Farmer: New Style* represents another aspect
of character by means of a familiar situation: a self-seeking
farmer is threatening to disinherit his son if he marries a penni-
less parson's daughter. The farmer's contempt for poverty and
his placid assumption that wealth is the only real good are well
portrayed:

> Feyther 'ad ammost nowt; leästways 'is munny was
>   'id,
> But 'e tued an' moil'd 'issen deäd, and 'e died a good
>   'un, 'e did.

The Village Wife: or The Entail shows more subtlety of characterization and tells more of a story than either of the Northern Farmer poems. A village gossip, describing the decline and fall of the late Squire and his family, lays bare her own callousness, ignorance and conceit. She shows a suspicious attitude towards bookishness that is not uncommon among dialect speakers. The old Squire is reported to have paid £30 and more for an old book and even to have written a book himself,

> An' 'e niver knawd nowt but booöks,
> an' booöks, as thou knows, beänt nowt.

The characters depicted in Tennyson's dialect poems are convincing but not on the whole very attractive. In his latest dialect monologues the atmosphere and the characters are rather less grim. *The Northern Cobbler* describes a man's successful fight to overcome the craving for drink. *The Spinster's Sweet-Arts* is a good-humoured monologue by a spinster who has rejected many suitors in order to keep control of her two hundred a year; she is addressing her tom-cats, named after her rejected suitors.

Tennyson's dialect poems are not all in his native Lincolnshire dialect. One of his later poems, *Tomorrow*, is a monologue written in an Irish dialect, but it is chiefly of interest as showing, by comparison with the Lincolnshire poems, that a dialect author is more likely to produce good work in his native dialect than in one which he knows only by observation from outside.

One of the best-known dialect writers of the nineteenth century was the Dorset poet William Barnes (1801–1886), a friend and neighbour of Thomas Hardy. Barnes was a philologist as well as a poet, and he took an active part in the movement, to which William Morris gave his support, to get rid of loan-words from the English language and to replace them by newly-coined compounds made up of native elements. In its revolt against pretentiousness the movement had much to recommend it, but it led to eccentricities like *fore-say* for 'preface', *wort-lore* for 'botany', *rede-craft* for 'logic', and *folk-wain* for 'omnibus', that have taken no root in the language. One of Barnes's many books was *A Grammar and Glossary of the Dorset Dialect* (1863), and it is easy to see how his philological and literary interests met in his *Poems of Rural Life in the Dorset Dialect* (1844) and *Hwomely Rhymes* (1859). These poems show the author's understanding of the countrymen among whom he worked as a clergyman. The picture that he presents is an idealized one; he has none of Crabbe's remorselessness in the depicting of common life. His humour, too, is of a gentle unsophisticated kind, dealing with such subjects as a shy bridegroom (*The Shy Man*). His favourite theme is married happiness, and it is not surprising that Coventry Patmore thought highly of his work. The first stanza of *The Bachelor*, in spite of the bathos of the fourth line, strikes a note that recurs again and again:

> No! I don't begrudge en his life,
> Nor his goold, nor his housen, nor lands;
> Teäke all o't, an' gi'e me my wife,
> A wife's be the cheapest ov hands.
> Lie alwone! sigh alwone! die alwone!
> Then be vorgot.
> No! I be content wi' my lot.

Barnes's wife died in 1852. Her death was a crushing blow and it led him to write *The Wife A-Lost*, a deeply moving poem, which describes how a bereaved husband cannot bear to remain indoors:

> Since I noo mwore do zee your feäce,
> Up steäirs or down below,
> I'll zit me in the lwonesome pleäce,
> Where flat-bough'd beech do grow:
> Below the beeches' bough, my love,
> Where you did never come,
> An' I don't look to meet ye now,
> As I do look at hwome.

When we turn to the second type of dialect literature, that in which dialect speakers are introduced as characters in novels and plays, it is clear that authors vary a good deal in the extent to which they aim at complete realism in the use of dialect. At one extreme we have Wilkie Collins, who, in *The Moonstone*, is content to say that one of his characters speaks in dialect but disclaims any attempt to reproduce it:

> '(Nota bene—I translate Mrs Yolland out of the Yorkshire language into the English language. When I tell you that the all-accomplished Cuff was every now and then puzzled to understand her until I helped him, you will draw your own conclusions as to what *your* state of mind would be if I reported her in her native tongue)'.[1]

At the other extreme is Mark Twain, who adds a prefatory note to *Huckleberry Finn* which shows that he takes dialectal differences seriously:

> In this book a number of dialects are used, to wit: the Missouri negro dialect; the extremest form of the backwoods South-Western dialect; the ordinary "Pike-Country" dialect; and four modified varieties of this last. The shadings have not been done in a haphazard fashion, or by guess-work; but painstakingly and with the trustworthy guidance and support of personal familiarity with these several forms of speech.
> I make this explanation for the reason that without it many readers would suppose that all these characters were trying to talk alike and not succeeding.

Most novelists and dramatists who introduce dialect-speaking characters steer between these two extremes. They do not as a rule try to reproduce dialect exactly, but are content to use occasional dialectal spellings, leaving the filling in of further details to the imagination of the reader or the skill of the actor.

The most effective examples of the use of dialect in literature are those in which dialectal words and pronunciations are introduced unobtrusively in such a way that a reader completely ignorant of the dialect has no real difficulty in understanding the meaning while a reader who is familiar with the dialect derives added enjoyment. A good example is the passage in *The Mayor of Casterbridge* which describes the reception of

[1] *The Moonstone:* Gabriel Betteredge's narrative, Ch. 15.

Donald Farfrae's patriotic and emotional song by the Caster-bridge townsfolk. Hardy prepares the reader for their comments by describing them as a 'set of worthies who were only too prone to shut up their emotions with caustic words'.

> 'What did ye come away from yer own country for, young maister, if ye be so wownded about it?' inquired Christopher Coney, from the background, with the tone of a man who preferred the original subject. 'Faith, it wasn't worth your while on our account, for, as Maister Billy Wills says, we be bruckle folk here—the best o' us hardly honest sometimes, what with hard winters, and so many mouths to fill, and God-a'mighty sending his little taties so terrible small to fill 'em with. We don't think about flowers and fair faces, not we—except in the shape o' cauliflowers and pigs' chaps'.
>
> 'But, no!' said Donald Farfrae, gazing round into their faces with earnest concern; 'the best of ye hardly honest—not that surely? None of ye has been stealing what didn't belong to him?'
>
> 'Lord! no, no!' said Solomon Longways, smiling grimly. 'That's only his random way o' speaking. 'A was always such a man of under-thoughts'. (And reprovingly towards Christopher): 'Don't ye be so over-familiar with a gentleman that ye know nothing of—and that's travelled a'most from the North Pole'.
>
> Christopher Coney was silenced, and as he could get no public sympathy, he mumbled his feelings to himself: 'Be dazed, if I loved my country half as well as the young feller do, I'd live by claning my neighbour's pigsties afore I'd go away! For my part I've no more love for my country that I have for Botany Bay!' (Ch. 8).

This passage shows how effective dialect can be as a means of deflating high-flown sentiments. When a dialect speaker suspects insincerity he reacts against it by the deliberate use of anticlimax, but dialect literature does not always shun the expression of emotion. Many dialect poems are very sentimental, and a skilful craftsman can use dialect without incongruity even in highly emotional or rhetorical passages. This mixture is particularly common in Scots dialect which has never lost the characteristics of a literary language. A good example of the rhetorical use of dialect is the famous passage in *Guy Mannering*

in which Meg Merrilies addresses the laird who has evicted the gipsies from their cottages:

> 'Ride your ways', said the gipsy, 'ride your ways, Laird of Ellangowan—ride your ways, Godfrey Bertram!—This day have ye quenched seven smoking hearths—see if the fire in your ain parlour burn the blyther for that. Ye have riven the thack off seven cottar houses—look if your ain roof-tree stand the faster.—Ye may stable your stirks in the shealings at Derncleugh—see that the hare does not couch on the hearthstone at Ellangowan.—Ride your ways, Godfrey Bertram—what do ye glower after our folk for?—There's thirty hearts there, that wad hae wanted bread ere ye had wanted sunkets, and spent their lifeblood ere ye had scratched your finger. Yes—there's thirty yonder, from the auld wife of a hundred to the babe that was born last week, that ye have turned out o' their bits o' bields, to sleep with the tod and the blackcock in the muirs! —Ride your ways, Ellangowan.—Our bairns are hinging at our weary backs—look that your braw cradle at hame be the fairer spread up—not that I am wishing ill to little Harry, or to the babe that's yet to be born—God forbid—and make them kind to the poor, and better folk than their father!—And now, ride e'en your ways; for these are the last words ye'll ever hear Meg Merrilies speak, and this is the last reise that I'll ever cut in the bonny woods of Ellangowan'. (Ch. 8).

One of the earliest English works to introduce characters speaking a distinctive dialect is Chaucer's *Reeves Tale*, where the dialect used by the two clerks is so markedly different from the dialect of the rest of the tale that it is quite clear that the differences are deliberate. The clerks speak northern English, and their use of this dialect undoubtedly adds to the effectiveness of the tale. It gives life and realism to a conventional fabliau, and it helps to individualize the two clerks. It is always dangerous to apply present-day standards of humour to the literature of the past, but it is hard to resist the view that northern dialect is used in the *Reeves Tale* for the purpose of humour, just as in modern plays actors, both amateur and professional, often achieve a humorous effect by the use of an exaggerated northern accent, an effect that is sometimes, but not always, intended by the author.[1]

[1] On the use of dialect in the *Reeves Tale* see J. R. R. Tolkien, 'Chaucer as a Philologist', *TPS*, 1934, pp. 1–70.

The Reeves Tale is not an isolated example in medieval English literature of the use of dialect for humorous effect and as an aid to characterization. One of the best-known medieval English plays is the Second Shepherds' Play of the Towneley Cycle. This is written in a northern dialect, but one of the characters, called Mak, speaks in a southern dialect on his first appearance, although he soon lapses into the northern dialect of the other characters, perhaps becuse one of the shepherds quickly protests against his unfamiliar speech: 'Now take outt that Sothren tothe'. Professor A. C. Cawley points out[1] that Mak's southern speech must have had for a northern audience the same comic appeal that the northern dialect of John and Aleyn in the *Reeves Tale* had for a southern audience.

Dialect was occasionally introduced into Elizabethan and Jacobean drama, but no great subtlety was shown in its use and realism was not aimed at. The most famous example is that used by Edgar in *King Lear*, with such forms as *chill* (OE *ic wille*) and *chud* (OE *ic wolde*) and with the voicing of initial fricatives in *zwaggered* and *vortnight* (IV, vi, 242-7), but this was probably a conventional stage dialect with features from various southern dialects.

One group of dialects which has found frequent literary expression in English during the last three or four centuries, especially on the stage, is that provided by foreigners with an imperfect command of English. Stage Scotsmen, Welshmen and Irishmen form a group intermediate between foreigners and the speakers of English dialects, since some of their linguistic characteristics are features of English regional dialects and some are due to the influence of Celtic languages. In comic scenes characters of several different nationalities are often contrasted with each other. Thus in *King Henry V* (III, ii) we have Fluellen, Macmorris and Jamy using the Welsh, Irish and Scottish stage dialects and in *The Merry Wives of Windsor* (III, i) the Frenchman Dr Caius is contrasted with the Welshman Sir Hugh Evans. The following extract from another play

---

[1] *The Wakefield Pageants in the Towneley Cycle* (MUP, 1958), p. 131.

shows Welsh used side by side with the stage dialect of a Welshman speaking English:

> *Sir Owen.* *Belly the ruddo whee: wrage witho, Manda gen y
> Mon du ac whelloch en wea awh.*
>
> *Gwenthyan.* *Sir Owen gramarcye whee: Gwenthyan Manda
> gen y, ac welloch en Thlawen en ryn mogh.*
>
> *Farneze.* *Mandage Thlawen,* oh my good widdow gabble
> that we may vnderstand you, and haue at you.
>
> *Sir Owen.* Haue at her: nay by Cod is no haue at her to,
> Is tawge in her prittish tongue, for tis fine delicates tongue, I
> can tell her. Welshe tongue is finer as greeke tongue.
>
> *Farneze.* A bakte Neates tongue is finer than both.[1]

Convention plays a large part in these portrayals and the
conventions become increasingly rigid during the eighteenth and
nineteenth centuries. Producers and actors enter into the spirit
of the thing, and today films about spies generally include
characters whose usefulness as spies must be greatly lessened
by their imperfect command of English. The powerful influence
of convention goes even further, at the expense of realism, and
it is not uncommon to find scenes in which foreigners, speaking
to one another in their own country, will do so in English with
a marked foreign accent, to make it quite clear to the audience
that they are not English.

In the United States today the linguistic difficulties of immigrants from various European countries contribute to the
variety of dialects spoken and are often reflected in literature,
notably in Leo Rosten's Hyman Kaplan, whose difficulties are
full of interest for the student of the English language:

> Mr Kaplan was not in the slightest impressed by precedent.
> He seemed to take the position that each rule of grammar, each
> canon of syntax, each convention of usage, no matter how
> ancient or how formidable, had to prove its case anew—to him.
> He seemed to make the whole English language start from
> scratch.[2]

The English language has so many irregularities that one can

---

[1] *Patient Grissil,* by Thomas Dekker and others, II, i, 165–174, in *The
Dramatic Works of Thomas Dekker,* ed. Fredson Bowers, vol. 1 (CUP, 1953).
[2] Leo Rosten, *The Return of Hyman Kaplan* (Gollancz, 1959), pp. 58 f.

sympathize with Hyman Kaplan's view that the superlative of *good* is *high-cless* and that the plural of *sandwich* is *delicatessen*.

The English spoken by foreigners has produced another dialect in the English spoken to foreigners, a dialect satirized by Dickens in his description of Mrs Plornish's success as a speaker of Italian in *Little Dorrit*:

> Mrs Plornish was particularly ingenious in this art; and attained so much celebrity by saying "Me ope you leg well soon", that it was considered in the Yard but a very short remove indeed from speaking Italian. (Ch. 25).

We are so accustomed today to associating speech with the social standing of the speaker that we tend to forget that the two have not always been associated. The association in English seems to have begun, so far as can be deduced from the surviving evidence, during the sixteenth century. From that time onwards there are frequent references in literature which reveal the belief that certain forms of speech are proper for 'gentlemen' or 'the upper classes' and that certain others are not. It may be, of course, that such beliefs existed before the sixteenth century, but if they had been widespread they would probably have found more frequent literary expression.

One of the earliest references to English class dialect is in Book 5 of Sir Thomas Elyot's *Governour* (1531), where the author complains that the sons of gentlemen pick up slovenly pronunciations from their 'nourishes (i.e. nurses) and other foolish women'. It is mentioned by Shakespeare: Orlando, meeting Rosalind in the Forest of Arden, tells her that her accent is too good for a forester (*AYLI*, III, ii, 328), and Hotspur seems conscious of class differences when he complains that his wife swears 'like a comfit-maker's wife'. (1 *K. Hy. IV*, III, i, 249).

Swift, who had a keen interest in language, satirized the speech of one section of the upper classes of his day in his *Polite Conversations*. Some of the features that he satirized, such as the excessive use of slang and fashionable colloquialisms and the overworking of particular words and phrases, are just as prevalent today, though the words and phrases are different. Today Neverout would be saying 'Good show!' and Lady Smart would be using catch-phrases from some recent or not-so-recent television comedy series.

During the eighteenth and nineteenth centuries novelists showed a good deal of interest in one particular written class dialect. The badly misspelt letters of low-life characters are a common feature of eighteenth-century novels, and the tradition is continued in much of Thackeray's early work, notably in *The Yellowplush Papers.* The fashion spread to America and became a feature of the work of such authors as Josh Billings and Artemus Ward. The humour of these misspellings is today apt to seem rather tiresome, but they have the same sort of linguistic interest as the eccentric spellings in early diaries and letters: they provide valuable evidence of contemporary pronunciations, especially of those which were regarded as vulgarisms.

As one would expect, in view of the pre-occupation of the Victorians with class distinctions, references to speech as a measure of social standing are numerous in Victorian novels. Mrs General in *Little Dorrit* (Ch. 41) is an expert on the subject ('Father is rather vulgar, my dear').

In *Middlemarch* there is a particularly illuminating example. Rosamond Vincy objects to her mother's use of the phrase 'the pick of them', in reference to the young men of Middlemarch, on the grounds that it is 'rather a vulgar expression'. Her mother's correction to 'the most superior young men' arouses the scorn of Rosamond's brother Fred:

'Oh, there are so many superior teas and sugars now. Superior is getting to be shopkeepers' slang'.

'Are you beginning to dislike slang, then?' said Rosamond, with mild gravity.

'Only the wrong sort. All choice of words is slang. It marks a class'.

'There is correct English: that is not slang'.

'I beg your pardon: correct English is the slang of prigs who write history and essays. And the strongest slang of all is the slang of poets'. (Ch. 11).

With the substitution of the word 'dialect' for 'slang', this passage expresses an opinion that many people would endorse today.

Examples of the Victorian interest in class dialect could be
multiplied almost indefinitely. In *The Woman in White*, Lady
Glyde's maid, Fanny, uses expressions which Mr Fairlie quotes
with distaste and claims not to understand: *warming the pot*
(of tea) and *struck of a heap*.[1] Mr Fairlie refers to Fanny as the
Young Person, thus making use of his own class dialect.

Dickens made abundant use of dialect in the wider sense of
the term which includes social as well as regional variations.
Stephen Blackpool in *Hard Times* speaks what is clearly intended
to be a regional dialect, of which the following is a specimen:

> I ha' hed what's been spok'n o' me, and 'tis lickly that I
> shan't mend it.   But I'd liefer you'd hearn the truth concernin
> myseln fro my lips than fro onny other man's, though I never
> cud'n speak afore so monny, wi'out bein moydert and muddled.
> (Bk. 2, Ch. 4).

This speech may well include features from more than one
English regional dialect, and Professor William Matthews has
pointed out[2] that Dickens sometimes uses his 'Cockney' dialect
for the speech of country characters such as Peggotty.   Dickens's
skill in the use of dialect is to be seen chiefly in dialects which
have no regional significance. In *Bleak House*, for example,
there is a wide variety of different class dialects. The un-
grammatical lower-class speech of Jo and the clipped speech of
the debilitated cousin of Sir Leicester Dedlock represent two
extremes, but we also have the vulgarisms of Inspector Bucket
('Up!   Ain't it English?', Ch. 57), the pseudo-biblical prolixity
of Mr Chadband, and the mixture of levels in the speech of the
class-conscious Guppy.

In the present century the spate of allusions to class dialect
continues.   Hilaire Belloc was very much pre-occupied with
distinctions in vocabulary between different social classes.   Two
quotations from his novel *The Haunted House* (1927) will serve
to illustrate this pre-occupation: 'and there still survive gentle-
folk who say "napkin", side by side with those masters of the
modern world who say "serviette" ' (p. 84), and 'an advertisement

---

[1] *The Woman in White*, Frederick Fairlie's Narrative.
[2] *Cockney Past and Present* (Routledge, 1938), p. 157.

for that which the vulgar call ready-to-wear and the gentle ready-made' (p. 251).

George Bernard Shaw was keenly interested in both regional and class dialects, and his interest found frequent expression in his plays. He was much less willing than most dramatists to leave the interpretation of details of dialect to the discretion of the actor. Thus, the stage directions to *Captain Brassbound's Conversion* (1899) include a fairly detailed disquisition on the dialect of the Cockney character Drinkwater:

> His dialect, apart from its base nasal delivery, is not unlike that of smart London society in its tendency to replace diphthongs by vowels (sometimes rather prettily) and to shuffle all the traditional vowel pronunciations. He pronounces *ow* as *ah*, and *i* as *aw*, using the ordinary *ow* for *o*, *i* for *ā*, *ă* for *ŭ*, and *ĕ* for *ă*, with this reservation, that when any vowel is followed by an *r*, he signifies its presence, not by pronouncing the *r*, which he never does under these circumstances, but by prolonging and modifying the vowel, sometimes even to the extreme degree of pronouncing it properly. As to his *yol* for *l* (a compendious delivery of the provincial *eh-al*) and other metropolitan refinements, amazing to all but cockneys, they cannot be indicated, save in the above imperfect manner, without the aid of a phonetic alphabet.

Not content with this essay on Cockney pronunciation, Shaw distorts the spelling of all Drinkwater's speeches in order to represent the Cockney pronunciation. A typical example is:

> Naow! didger? Think o thet, gavner! Waw, sow aw did too. But it were a misunnerstendin, thet wors. Lef the court withaht a stine on maw kerrickter, aw did.

Compared with this, Shaw's representation of the speech of the Scottish missionary Rankin is restrained; he is content to suggest the Scottish pronunciation by occasional modified spellings such as *pairfection*, *espaecially*, and *verra*.

Both regional and class dialects play a prominent part in *Pygmalion* (1912). The panic which Eliza displays when she finds that her speech is being recorded is something of which most dialect field-workers have had experience, and Higgins shows remarkable skill in identifying dialects. After hearing only a few words, he is able to tell one bystander that he comes from Hoxton and another, Colonel Pickering, that he has come from Cheltenham, Harrow, Cambridge, and India. This sort of thing is too good to be true, as is Higgins's claim that, by listening to his speech, he can place any man within six miles, or, in London, within two miles and sometimes within two streets. The divisions between one English dialect and another today are as a rule not sufficiently clear-cut to make such precise identification possible.[1] The central theme of the play is the very doubtful contention that classes in speech-training can enable a Cockney flower-girl to be a brilliant social success. Some of the incidental features of the play are more convincing, as, for example, the pedantic correctness of pronunciation which is the first stage in Eliza's attempt to improve her speech, and the reversion to her former speech-habits which results from her sudden meeting with her father. In *Man and Superman* there is an illustration of one of the complications of class dialect. Tanner's chauffeur, Henry Straker, is introduced as a pair of legs saying 'Aw rawt nah', after which the author, perhaps rather unnecessarily, adds the stage direction that 'he does not at all affect the gentleman in his speech'. Shortly afterwards this dialogue occurs:

> *Tanner:* By the way, let me introduce you. Mr Octavius Robinson: Mr Enry Straker.
> *Straker:* Pleased to meet you, sir. Mr Tanner is gittin at you with is Enry Straker, you know. You call it Henery. But I don't mind, bless you!
> *Tanner:* You think it's simply bad taste in me to chaff him, Tavy. But youre wrong. This man takes more trouble to drop his aitches than ever his father did to pick them up. It's a mark of caste to him. I have never met anybody more swollen with the pride of class than Enry is'.

Inverted snobbery of this kind is not uncommon in matters of speech. It arises as a reaction against what seems to be an excessive pre-occupation with class indicators in speech.

---

[1] There may be occasional exceptions, especially when regional variations are reinforced by class differences. Humphry House says of Dickens: 'His ear for religious cliches was wonderfully quick. Mrs Pardiggle saying as early as 1853 that the Matins to which she took the children was "very prettily done", used a phrase which may be heard to-day in any of the streets between St Stephen's, Gloucester Road, and St Augustine's, Queen's Gate (*The Dickens World* (OUP, 1941), p. 118).

The representation of the pronunciation of spoken dialect in literature is at the best a set of rather sorry compromises. To those who are already familiar with the dialect in question, a few slight modifications of spelling are enough to serve as reminders, but to those who have no such familiarity dialect spellings in literary works are often regarded as a tedious nuisance. The pronunciation of dialect is best studied at first hand, not through the medium of literary works. The kind of dialect that is of most interest to the novelist and the dramatist and to those who enjoy their works is class dialect, and much can be gained from a careful examination of the use of class dialect in English novels and plays both of the past and the present. In such an examination the study of language and that of literature find common ground.

Select Bibliography

Many studies of special points are omitted from this bibliography, especially when they are written in foreign languages. Information about such monographs may be found in A. G. Kennedy, *A Bibliography of Writings on the English Language from the Beginning of Printing to the end of* 1922 (Cambridge, Mass., Harvard University Press 1927), in volume I of the *Cambridge Bibliography of English Literature* (CUP 1940), and in the *Supplement* to that work (CUP 1957). Many books dealing with the history of the English language contain references to dialects, but only the most important of these works are mentioned here. Many of the books and articles mentioned deal with the subject-matter of more than one chapter of the present volume. The classification of books under the various chapter-headings has been determined by what seems to be the most important aspect of the book in question. The date given is usually that of the latest edition containing important revision. The place of publication is London unless otherwise stated.

1. DIALECT AND LANGUAGE

Angus McIntosh, *An Introduction to a Survey of Scottish Dialects* (No. 1 of the University of Edinburgh Linguistic Survey of Scotland Monographs, Edinburgh, Nelson 1952, reprinted 1961) is a valuable introduction to dialect study. Much of the book deals with general principles which are just as applicable to the dialects of England as to those of Scotland. W. W. Skeat, *English Dialects from the Eighth Century to the Present Day* (CUP 1911) is a short, comprehensive work on the dialects of Old, Middle, and Modern English with illustrative extracts from dialectal texts. The best dictionary for the study of English dialect vocabulary from the earliest times until the present century is *The Oxford English Dictionary* (OUP 1933), which is a corrected re-issue, with a bibliography and supplement, of *A New English Dictionary on Historical Principles* edited by J. A. H. Murray, Henry Bradley, W. A. Craigie and C. T. Onions (OUP 1884–1928). Essays on various aspects of dialect in its relation to Standard English include Sir William Craigie, *Northern Words in Modern English* (SPE Tract No. 50, OUP 1937), R. W. Chapman, *Oxford English* (SPE Tract No. 37, OUP 1932) and G. N. Clark, 'The Bull's Bellow and the Ratton's Squeak' (in SPE Tract No. 33, OUP 1929). A. Lloyd James, *The Broadcast Word* (Kegan Paul 1935) contains essays on such subjects as 'Speech in the Modern World' and 'Standards in Speech'. J. Y. T. Greig's *Breaking Priscian's Head, or English as she will be Spoke and Wrote* (Kegan Paul n.d.), written in the 1920's, is a refreshingly hard-hitting defence of the use of various forms of dialectal English. Books on general linguistics often include chapters on linguistic geography which make clear the importance of dialect study to students of language. Of such a kind are Chapter 19 of Leonard Bloomfield's *Language* (George Allen and Unwin 1935), Chapter 7 of L. R. Palmer's *An Introduction to Modern Linguistics* (Macmillan 1936) and Chapter 6 of Simeon Potter's *Modern Linguistics* (Andre Deutsch 1957).

2. OLD ENGLISH

There is a good deal of information about Old English dialects in the standard grammars of Old English, of which the most important are *Altenglische Grammatik nach der angelsächsischen Grammatik von Eduard Sievers, neubearbeitet von Karl Brunner* (second edition, Halle, Max Niemeyer 1951) and A. Campbell, *Old English Grammar* (OUP 1959). Karl Luick's *Historische Grammatik der englischen Sprache* (Leipzig, Tauchnitz 1914–39) deals with both Old and Middle English. Alois Brandl's *Zur Geographie der altenglischen Dialekte* (Berlin, Königl. Akademie der Wissenschaften 1915) is less general in its scope. The chief Old English dialectal texts are edited by Henry Sweet in *The Oldest English Texts* (EETS No. 83, 1885), of which his *Second*

Anglo-Saxon Reader: Archaic and Dialectal (OUP 1887) is an abridgment with additional material from other sources. R. M. Wilson's 'The Provenance of the Vespasian Psalter Gloss: The Linguistic Evidence', in *The Anglo-Saxons: Studies in some Aspects of their History and Culture presented to Bruce Dickins*, edited by Peter Clemoes (Bowes & Bowes 1959), is a noteworthy study of a particular Old English dialect, and Johannes Hedberg, *The Syncope of the Old English Present Endings* (Lund Studies in English, xii, 1945) is a study of one particular dialect criterion. A new approach to Old English dialects is suggested by David De Camp, 'The Genesis of the Old English Dialects', *Language* xxxiv (1958), 232–244. P. H. Reaney's *The Origin of English Place-Names* (Routledge and Kegan Paul 1960) contains a short chapter on 'Dialect and Place-Names', which is chiefly concerned with Old and Middle English dialects. Similar information is contained in the introductions to the county volumes published by the English Place-Name Society.

3. MIDDLE ENGLISH

The problems presented by Middle English dialects are discussed by S. Moore, S. B. Meech and H. Whitehall in *Middle English Dialect Characteristics and Dialect Boundaries* (Michigan Essays and Studies xiii, 1935), a work which includes an important map showing the distribution of the chief dialectal features. Another map is to be found in J. P. Oakden, *Alliterative Poetry in Middle English: The Dialectal and Metrical Survey* (MUP 1930). The relations between the spoken and written dialects of Middle English are discussed by Angus McIntosh in 'The Analysis of Written Middle English', *TPS* 1956, pp. 26–55. Studies of special problems include H. C. Wyld, 'The Treatment of OE $\check{y}$ in the Midland and South Eastern Counties in Middle English' (*Englische Studien* xlvii (1913), 1–58), the same author's 'Old English $\check{y}$ in the Dialects of the South, and South Western Counties in Middle English' (*Englische Studien* xlvii (1913), 145–166), Mary S. Serjeantson, 'The Dialectal Distribution of certain Phonological Features in Middle English' (*English*

Studies iv (1922), 93–109, 191–198, 223–233), and R. Kaiser, *Zur Geographie des mittelenglischen Wortschatzes* (Palaestra 205, Leipzig, 1937). The West Midland dialects are studied by Mary S. Serjeantson in 'The Dialects of the West Midlands in Middle English' (*RES* iii (1927), 54–67, 186–203, and 319–331), and the London dialect is the subject of a monograph by Barbara Alida Mackenzie, *The Early London Dialect: Contributions to the History of the Dialect of London during the Middle English Period* (OUP 1928). Another study is R. E. Zachrisson 'Northern English or London English as the Standard Pronunciation (A Contribution to the History of Standard English)', *Anglia* xxxviii (1914), 405–432.

4. MODERN ENGLISH

A work of outstanding importance for the study of the vocabulary of Modern English dialects is Joseph Wright, *English Dialect Dictionary* (6 vols, OUP 1898–1905). *The English Dialect Grammar*, which forms part of the sixth volume of this work, was published separately in smaller format (OUP 1905). Most of the material contained in earlier dialect glossaries is incorporated in *EDD*, but there have been more recent glossaries of particular dialects, notably Alexander Warrack, *A Scots Dialect Dictionary* (Edinburgh, W. and R. Chambers 1911), George Watson, *The Roxburghshire Word-Book* (CUP 1923), Walter E. Haigh, *A New Glossary of the Dialect of the Huddersfield District* (OUP 1928), and Hugh Marwick, *The Orkney Norn* (OUP 1929). The first half of Elizabeth Mary Wright's *Rustic Speech and Folk-Lore* (OUP 1913) is a survey of Modern English dialects based upon the materials collected for *EDD*. Another readable miscellany is Richard Blakeborough's *Wit, Character, Folklore and Customs of the North Riding of Yorkshire* (OUP 1898). A vast amount of material, presented in a form that does not make for easy reading, is contained in Part V of Alexander J. Ellis's *On Early English Pronunciation*, under the title *The Existing Phonology of English Dialects Compared with that of West Saxon Speech* (EETS 1889). Ernst Leisi, *Das heutige Englisch* (Heidelberg, Carl Winter 1955) contains short sections on 'Die Hochsprache', 'Regionale Sprachformen', 'Slang' and 'Das Englische als Weltsprache', each with a bibliography. Margaret Schlauch's *The English Language in Modern Times* (Warsaw, distributed outside Poland by OUP 1959) has chapters on 'Modern English Dialects and their Literary Uses' and 'The English Language in the New World'. There are many monographs on the dialects of particular places or regions, of which the most important are: Börje Brilioth, *A Grammar of the Dialect of Lorton (Cumberland)*, (Philological Society 1913), Harold Orton, *The Phonology of a South Durham Dialect*, (Kegan Paul 1933), Sir James Wilson, *The Dialect of the New Forest in Hampshire (as spoken in the Village of Burley)*, (Philological Society 1913), *The Dialects of Central Scotland* (OUP 1926), and *The Dialect of Robert Burns as spoken in Central Ayrshire* (OUP 1923), William Matthews, *Cockney Past and Present: A Short History of the Dialect of London* (Routledge 1938), Eva Sivertsen, *Cockney Phonology* (Oslo University Press 1960), and G. H. Cowling, *The Dialect of Hackness* (CUP 1915). Among monographs on particular problems may be mentioned W. E. Jones, 'The Definite Article in Living Yorkshire Dialect' *LSE* vii–viii (1952), 81–91, Edward Kolb 'The Icicle in English Dialects', *English Studies* xl (1959), 283–288, and Harold Orton, 'The Isolative Treatment in Living North-Midland Dialects of OE *e* lengthened in open syllables in Middle English', *LSE* vii–viii (1952), 97–128. The language of schoolchildren is described by Iona and Peter Opie in *The Lore and Language of Schoolchildren* (OUP 1959).

5. ENGLISH OVERSEAS

There are chapters on English in Canada, South Africa, Australia, New Zealand and India, written by authors with knowledge of local conditions, in *British and American English since 1900* edited by Eric Partridge and J. W. Clark (Andrew Dakers 1951). The second volume of Karl Brunner, *Die englische Sprache, ihre geschichtliche Entwicklung* (Halle, 1951, revised 1962) contains a chapter dealing with 'Die englische Sprache ausserhalb Europas'. A good deal has been written on American English. There are studies by G. P. Krapp, *The English Language in America* (2 vols, New York, OUP 1925), and Hans Galinsky, *Die Sprache des Amerikaners* (2 vols, Heidelberg, F. H. Kerle 1951). H. L. Mencken's *The American Language* (fourth edition, Kegan Paul 1936), with its two supplementary volumes, *Supplement One* (New York, Alfred A. Knopf 1945) and *Supplement Two* (Alfred A. Knopf 1948) constitute a vast storehouse of material. Excellent short studies are Thomas Pyles, *Words and Ways of American English* (New York, 1952; London edition, Andrew Melrose 1954) and Albert H. Marckwardt, *American English* (New York, OUP 1958). The best dictionaries of American English are *A Dictionary of American English on Historical Principles* edited by W. A. Craigie and J. R. Hulbert (OUP 1938–44) and M. M. Matthews, *A Dictionary of Americanisms on Historical Principles* (2 vols, OUP 1951). On the dialects of American English Hans Kurath's *Linguistic Atlas of New England* (1939–43) and *Handbook of the Linguistic Geography of New England* (Washington, American Council of Learned Societies 1939) are of first importance. W. Nelson Francis, *The Structure of American English* (New York, The Ronald Press 1958) has a chapter on American English dialects by Raven I. McDavid, Jr, and Raven I. McDavid, Jr. and Virginia McDavid have written on 'The Study of American Dialects', *JLDS* viii (1959), 5–19. There is an article by E. Dieth, 'Linguistic Geography in New England' in *English Studies* xxix (1948), 65–79. H. W. Horwill has called attention to some of the differences between British and American English in *A Dictionary of Modern American Usage* (OUP 1935) and *American Variations* (SPE Tract No. 45, OUP 1936). Many special aspects of American English are discussed in the periodical *American Speech*. On the influence of American on British English see Brian Foster, 'Recent American Influence on Standard English' in *Anglia* lxxiii (1955), 328–360. F. G. Cassidy, *Jamaica Talk: Three Hundred Years of the English Language in Jamaica* (Macmillan 1961) shows a welcome extension of the range of

studies of overseas English. The best study of Irish English is
J. J. Hogan, *The English Language in Ireland* (Dublin, Educa-
tional Company of Ireland 1927). There is additional informa-
tion in J. J. Hogan, *An Outline of English Philology chiefly for
Irish Students* (Dublin, Educational Company of Ireland 1934).
An older book on the subject is P. W. Joyce, *English as We
Speak it in Ireland* (Longmans 1910). On Indian English see
R. C. Goffin, *Some Notes on Indian English* (SPE Tract No. 41,
OUP 1934). A readable account of Australian English, particu-
larly useful for its account of the vocabulary, is Sidney J. Baker.
The Australian Language (Sydney, Angus and Robertson 1945),
A. G. Mitchell, *The Pronunciation of English in Australia* (Sydney,
Angus and Robertson 1946) is an excellent survey with pre-
liminary chapters which serve as a corrective to emotional
comments on different varieties of English. A more recent
work by the same author is *Spoken English* (Macmillan 1957).
Australian pronunciation is considered historically by G. W.
Turner, 'On the Origin of Australian Vowel Sounds' in *AUMLA*,
*Journal of the Australasian Universities Language and Literature
Association*, xiii (1960), 33–45; another study is by G. R.
Cochrane, 'The Australian English Vowels as a Diasystem' in
Word, xv (1959), 69–88. There is a chapter on Australian
English in Eric Partridge's *A Charm of Words* (Hamish Hamilton
1960).

6. DIALECT RESEARCH

There is a good deal of information about Joseph Wright's
dialect researches in Elizabeth Mary Wright, *The Life of Joseph
Wright* (2 vols, OUP 1932). More recent work is described by
Eugen Dieth in 'A New Survey of English Dialects', *Essays
and Studies by Members of the English Association*, xxxii (OUP
1946), 74–104, and by A. H. Smith in 'English Dialects', *TPS*
1936, pp. 76–84. The work of the survey with its headquarters
at the University of Leeds is described by Harold Orton in 'A
New Survey of Dialectal English', *JLDS* ii (1952), 5–13, and
'An English Dialect Survey: Linguistic Atlas of England', *Orbis*,
ix (1960), 331–348. The questionnaire used by the Leeds field-

workers has been published: Eugen Dieth and Harold Orton, *A Questionnaire for a Linguistic Atlas of England* (Leeds Philosophical and Literary Society 1952), and the results of the survey are now in course of publication. The first parts to appear are the *Introduction* and *Basic Material for the Six Northern Counties and the Isle of Man* (Leeds, E. J. Arnold 1962–3). The work in progress at Edinburgh is described by Angus McIntosh in *An Introduction to a Survey of Scottish Dialects* (Edinburgh, Nelson 1952, reprinted 1961) and by J. C. Catford in 'The Linguistic Survey of Scotland', *Orbis*, vi (1957), 105–121. There is further information about Scottish dialects in John S. Woolley, 'The Linguistic Survey of Scotland and its Activities in Cumberland', *Journal of the Lakeland Dialect Society*, xvii (1955), 8–12, and J. C. Catford, 'Vowel-Systems of Scots Dialects', *TPS* 1957, pp. 107–117. Some of the problems which confront field-workers are discussed by Frederic G. Cassidy and Audrey R. Duckert, *A Method for Collecting Dialect* (*PADS* No. xx, Gainesville, Florida, 1953). There are many studies of the dialects of European languages other than English which throw light on the problems of dialect research, but very few of these are written in English. Sever Pop's *La Dialectologie* (2 vols, Louvain, published by the author 1950), is a massive survey of dialectal research all over the world, especially in the countries where Romance languages are spoken. The account of dialect research in Great Britain fills only four pages of more than 1300 pages in the whole work. R. E. Keller's *German Dialects* (MUP 1961) is an excellent account of German dialects, which includes studies of the phonology and morphology of eight dialects with selected texts.

7. CLASS AND OCCUPATIONAL DIALECTS

There is a discussion of English social classes with an extensive bibliography in T. H. Pear's *English Social Differences* (George Allen and Unwin 1955). An essay on class dialects that has been much discussed is Alan S. C. Ross's 'U and non-U: An Essay in Sociological Linguistics' in *Noblesse Oblige*, edited by

Nancy Mitford (Hamish Hamilton 1956). Varieties of Modern English that can be regarded as dialects are discussed by Randolph Quirk in ' "Dialects" within Standard English', *TYDS* lviii (1958), 29–42. The occupational dialect of civil servants is discussed by Sir Ernest Gowers in *Plain Words* (1948) and *ABC of Plain Words* (1951), originally published by H.M. Stationery Office and later reprinted in Penguin Books. The best studies of English slang are Eric Partridge, *Slang Today and Yesterday* (third edition, Routledge 1950), *A Dictionary of Slang and Unconventional English from the Fifteenth Century to the Present Day* (fifth edition, Routledge 1961) and *A Dictionary of the Underworld, British and American* (second edition, Routledge 1961). The same author's *A Charm of Words* (Hamish Hamilton 1960) contains essays on business English and the language of advertising. R. W. Chapman's *Names, Designations and Appellations*, (SPE Tract No. 47, OUP 1936) is a study of one aspect of Modern English usage which has a bearing on class dialect. Heinrich Straumann, *Newspaper Headlines: A Study in Linguistic Method* (George Allen and Unwin 1935) deals with one aspect of the language of newspapers.

8. DIALECT AND LITERATURE

The best bibliography of literature written in English dialects is still the very full one, classified by counties, included in Volume VI of *EDD*. The northern counties have been most productive of anthologies of dialect verse and prose. Among the best are F. W. Moorman, *Yorkshire Dialect Poems (1673–1915) and Traditional Poems* (second edition, Sidgwick and Jackson for the Yorkshire Dialect Society 1917), W. J. Halliday and A. S. Umpleby, *The White Rose Garland of Yorkshire Dialect Verse and Local Folk-lore Rhymes* (Dent 1949), and May Yates, *A Lancashire Anthology* (Hodder and Stoughton for the University Press of Liverpool 1923). Among studies of the work of particular authors or regions may be mentioned Ernst Bussmann, *Tennysons Dialektdichtungen* (Weimar, 1917), Karl Brunner, *Die Dialektliteratur von Lancashire* (Vienna, 1920), and

Giles Dugdale, *William Barnes of Dorset* (Cassell 1953). Sir William Craigie discusses some of the problems presented by the use of dialect in literature in 'Dialect in Literature', *Essays by Divers Hands*, xvii (1938), 69–91. Chaucer's use of dialect in the *Reeves Tale* is discussed by J. R. R. Tolkien in 'Chaucer as a Philologist', *TPS*, 1934, pp. 1–70. There are several studies of the use of dialect by the early dramatists. These include Adolf Weiss, *Die Mundart im Englischen Drama von 1642–1800* (Giessen, 1924), Wilson O. Clough 'The Broken English of Foreign Characters of the Elizabethan Stage' in *Philological Quarterly*, xii (1933), 255–268 and J. O. Bartley and D. L. Sims, 'Pre-Nineteenth Century Stage Irish and Welsh Pronunciation', *Proceedings of the American Philosophical Society* xliii (1949), 439–447. Dickens's use of regional and class dialects is discussed by W. Franz in 'Die Dialektsprache bei Ch. Dickens', *Englische Studien* xii (1889), 197–244, Ernest Weekley in 'Mrs. Gamp and the King's English' in *Adjectives and Other Words* (John Murray 1930), and Randolph Quirk in *Charles Dickens and Appropriate Language* (University of Durham 1959) and 'Some Observations on the Language of Dickens', *Review of English Literature*, July 1961, pp. 19–28.

Subject Index

No references are given to entries in the
Select Bibliography

Word Index

Foreign words and Old and Middle English forms are not included in this index. Place-names are included when the interest lies in the form.

225

227

meaverly, 30
meet, 122
mense, 84
mental, 169
merle, 91
messenger, 98
miching, 186
mimeographed, 115
mint, 185
missile, 118
mob, 120, 169
mobled, 187
moccasin, 114
moider, moither, 31
moil, 88
momenty-morries, 86
mongrel, 94
moor, 134
moose, 114
more, 103–4
mort, 85
mouses, 103
movie, 120
muckment, 99
mudguard, 116
mullen, 185
mullock, 130
mun, 84
mustang, 114

nadder, 101
nangnail, 101
nanny, 86
napper, 86
napron, 101
naunt, 101
nay, 92
nayword, 187
neam, 101
neist, 102
neither, 122
nesh, 31
never-sweat, 99
news, 119
newt, 81–2, 101
Ngaio, 134
nightingale, 98
no, 92
noil, 131
nominy, 86
non-plush, 86
nook-shotten, 186
nous, 85
nowt, 84
noy, 85

nuncle, 101
nurchin, 101

Oake, 60
odious, 169
offsider, 130
often, 118
oilins-boilins, 86
old, 41
once, 97
one, 36, 97
only, 36
oonts, 79
oonty-toomps, 79
opossum, 114
ort, 187
oss, 31
ought, 109
ourn, 105
ousel, 91
outback, 130
outspan, 129
overfaced, 81
owe, 187
own, 90

paddock, 131
painful, 91
papoose, 114
paraffin, 161
pardon, 171
parleys, 87
passenger, 98
pawky, 81
pax, 86
pea, 120
pearls, 87
peas, 87
persimmon, 114
petrol, 116
Petworth, 60
picayune, 114
pickaninny, 114
pick-thank, 187
pig(gy), 89, 117
pig-pen, 123
pig-sty, 123
point-vice, 91
poison ivy, 123
poison vine, 123
polarity, 180
potato, 114
prairie, 114
pram, 128
primrosen, 102

231

WORD INDEX

wick, 91
wicked days, 100
wigwam, 114
will, 121–2
wilt, 116
Wilton, 42
Windhill, 60
wintredge, 38
wisty, 185
witchert, 30, 186
Wolds, 42
wood, 131
Woolcombe, 42
wopse, 98
work, 102
worser, 104
wowser, 130
wrought, 106

yahrs, 109
Yalland, 42
Yankee, 114
yat, 101
Yeo, 42
yes, 92
yesterday, 168
yon(d), 105
yonder, 105
yonderish, 99
yonderly, 99
you-all, 125
yourn, 105

Zeaston, 61
zwaggered, 202